AF574321

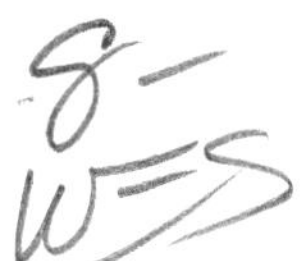

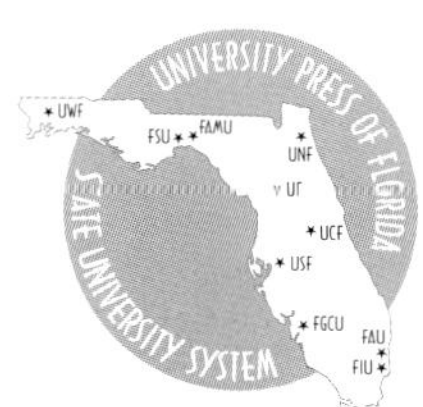

Florida A&M University, Tallahassee
Florida Atlantic University, Boca Raton
Florida Gulf Coast University, Ft. Myers
Florida International University, Miami
Florida State University, Tallahassee
University of Central Florida, Orlando
University of Florida, Gainesville
University of North Florida, Jacksonville
University of South Florida, Tampa
University of West Florida, Pensacola

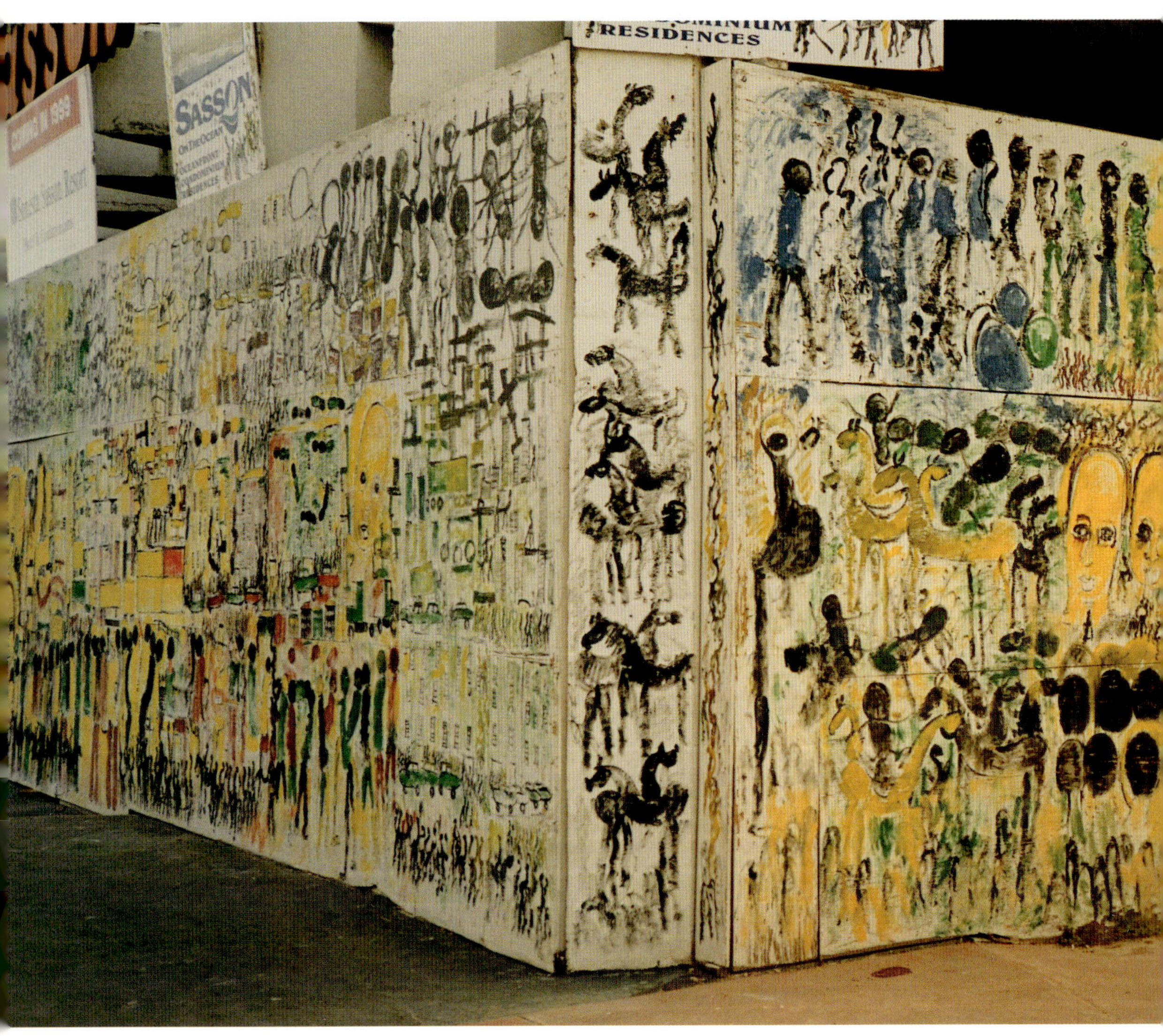

University Press of Florida
Gainesville Tallahassee Tampa Boca Raton Pensacola Orlando Miami Jacksonville Ft. Myers

Text and photo portraits by Gary Monroe

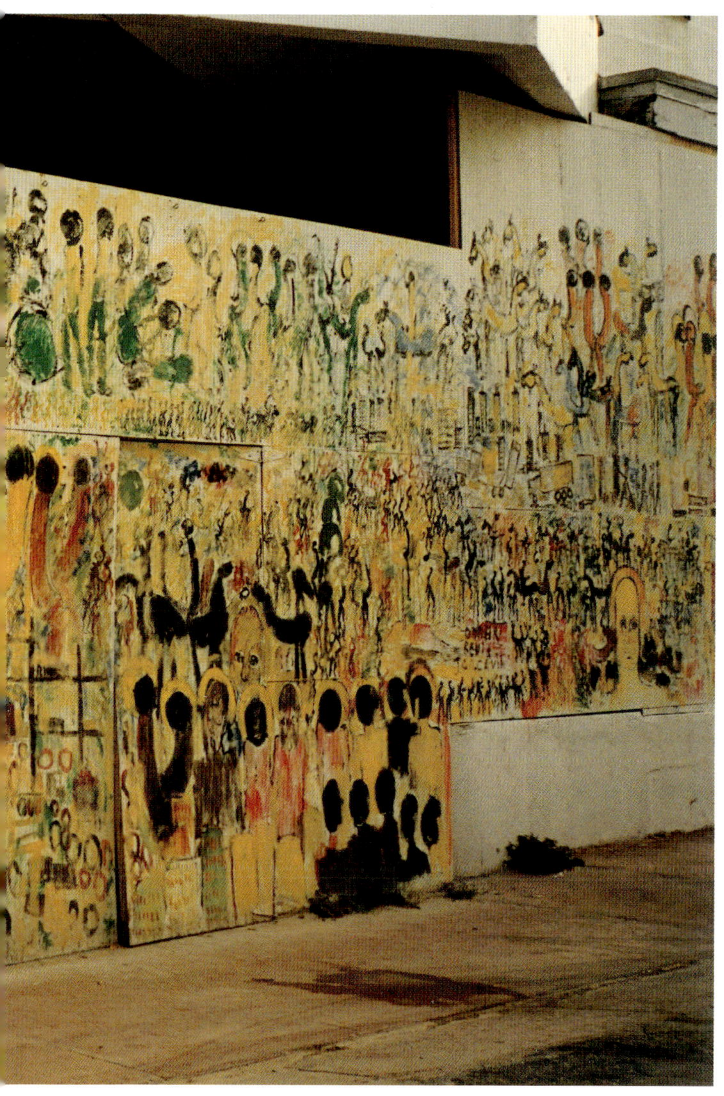

EXTRAORDINARY INTERPRETATIONS.

FLORIDA'S SELF-TAUGHT ARTISTS

Printed in China on acid-free paper

08 07 06 05 04 03 6 5 4 3 2 1

Library of Congress Cataloging-in-Publication Data
Monroe, Gary.
Extraordinary interpretations: Florida's self-taught artists / text and portraits by Gary Monroe.
p. cm.
ISBN 0-8130-2670-9 (cloth: alk. paper)
1. Outsider art—Florida—History—20th century. 2. Folk artists—Florida—Biography—History and criticism. I. Title.
N6530.F6M66 2003
709'.759'09045—dc21 2003048425

The University Press of Florida is the scholarly publishing agency for the State University System of Florida, comprising Florida A&M University, Florida Atlantic University, Florida Gulf Coast University, Florida International University, Florida State University, University of Central Florida, University of Florida, University of North Florida, University of South Florida, and University of West Florida.

University Press of Florida
15 Northwest 15th Street
Gainesville, FL 32611-2079
http://www.upf.com

To the memory of Jorko "George" Voronovsky

folk artist extraordinaire

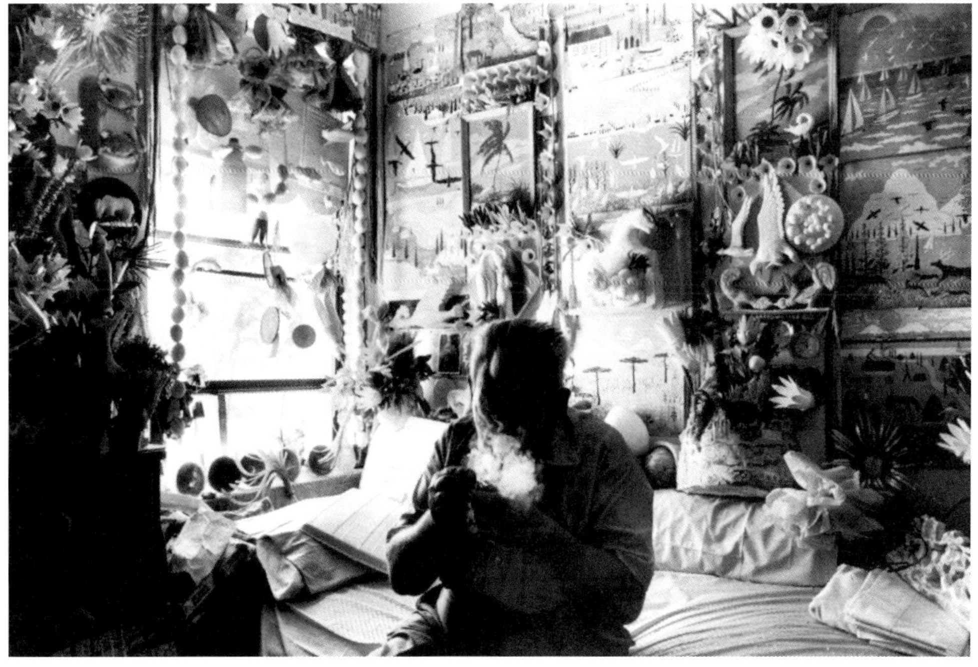

There are no wrong notes.
—Thelonious Monk

Man's extraordinary success as a species springs from his discontent, which compels him to employ his imagination.
—Anthony Storr, *Solitude: A Return to the Self*

CONTENTS

PREFACE

Growing up in kitsch-infused Miami Beach in the fifties and sixties no doubt affected my sensibilities. Tourist culture, tropical exotica, and the city's opulence contrasted with the "blighted" South Beach community, awakening in me a curiosity about different lifestyles and values. Solitude fuels creativity, and my being something of a loner opened me up, I believe, to a certain consciousness. Later, the camera became my confidant.

Upon returning home to Miami Beach after completing graduate school, I possessed the necessary naïveté to want to photograph—daily for ten years—the Old World Jewish community that then existed in South Beach. Now, of course, the few square miles that contained that community have become the very trendy art deco district, but until the mid-eighties, the area remained a modern-day *shtetl.*

One morning, walking from my family home to the beach, two colorful windows on the top floor of the Colony Hotel caught my eye. Decorations floating in the breeze seemed a revelation amidst the whitewashed concrete hotel facades along Ocean Drive. I had once photographed a woman in a room adjacent to the one whose bright windows captured my attention, and I asked her about the occupant of the neighboring room. She laughed as she knocked on his door and said, "George."

A man with the stoop and stature of Santa Claus answered the door. George bowed his head slightly, smiling, and invited me in. I walked into a dream world. As he beckoned me farther inside, George walked backward, somehow not stumbling into any one of the hundreds of sculptures and decorations that transformed the small space into a virtual paradise. He offered me soup, fish heads simmering on the burner. I entered in wonder, a wonder that stayed with me until George Voronovsky died five years later. The effect that he would have on my wife, Teresa Gurucharri, and on me was unimaginable, and the time we all spent together amazes us still.

George was the embodiment of a self-taught artist: disenfranchised, passionate, and fueled by his longings and dreams. He was not a modern-day fauve but rather a memory painter. Thumbtacked to the walls of his tiny room were a few dozen watercolor paintings reminiscent of his youth in the Ukraine. He had painted them to add color to his life; he told me that white walls bothered him because they seemed to invite unpleasant memories. On every surface and suspended from the ceiling were tin stars cut from soda cans and flowers fashioned from candy wrappers. Carved animals made from discarded Styrofoam were scattered about. The visual cacophony went on and on, covering his chair, bed, kitchenette, and the floor. His radio—its dial frozen to the classical music station—was always on, while the sea air and its radiant light washed his room.

Although I expressed my attraction to different cultures through photography, my curiosity about contemporary folk art seemed a more intellectual response. The self-taught artist's unbridled and vivid imagery is privately constructed. I took from writer Anthony Storr the idea that discontentment is the source of creativity. I know that that was true for George Voronovsky.

A shaping premise of this book is that understanding the origins of someone's art is crucial to experiencing that person's imagery. This notion challenges the modernists' view of the artist as a conduit through which art and meaning mysteriously flow. Art does not speak for itself. I doubt that it exists beyond the sensibilities of the viewer. By knowing about the artists and understanding the formal modes they use to articulate their ideas, viewers may "learn the language" and demystify the "aura" that surrounds the imagery.

In exploring the work of self-taught artists, it is too easy to focus on the stereotype of what was once called the "outsider artist": the poor old black rural southerner driven by religious fervor and/or emotional strife, an artist whose artistic sources are unknowable, who must create for unknown reasons, and who seems guided by grace. Although religion, alienation, and trauma fairly characterize the beginnings of many artists who work outside of the mainstream, others are driven by different forces to create their artwork. (Not every artist's brush strokes need be a primal scream.) This book offers a look at sixty-two self-taught artists who have made Florida their home. Their personalities and their art are as diverse as the Sunshine State. Rather than engage in exclusionary politics or cubbyholing, I tended to be inclusive in selecting the artists. Time will tell which artists' works maintain a connection to society.

Aesthetics is concerned with the nature and philosophy of beauty; consequently, it reflects our changing tastes and understandings. As we have gotten beyond representation as a measure of artistic success, beyond the rationalization of art-for-art's-sake, and beyond abstraction as ersatz expression, it is possible and fulfilling for us to imagine along with these artists, to recognize—through their labor and passion—things essentially human.

I hope that my reflections about the artists and their works shed light on the creative process—how some people explore/express themselves in ways that are unabashedly content driven, while letting the forms sort themselves out—but not in theoretical or self-referential ways. These artists create in ways that are relevant to what it means to be alive. They are survivalists of the material world.

Acknowledgments

My appreciation to my wife, Teresa, and our children, Mathew and Jessica, could never be overstated or undervalued. I traveled more while writing than imaginable; never relying on phone interviews, I visited many of the artists repeatedly. Thank you for allowing me peace of mind. It was much more than my Jewish guilt that brought me hurrying home.

Book production is collaborative, and I approached writing this way. I gladly worked with the artists, sharing drafts with many of them. The artists and their families let me close, at times, to the flames of their lives. Never was I asked to compromise, nor did I bend to become their publicist—although I do think that writing appreciatively about art is more difficult than writing indulgent criticism. I strove for an inside look at the artists' motivations, and I am thankful for their trust.

I'm grateful to Meredith Morris-Babb, editor-in-chief at the University Press of Florida and also my editor-and-conscience. She stuck with me when it would have been easier not to do so, saying "yes" when she could have easily said "no." It is her style to choose the more challenging path. I also value my collaboration with others at UPF—Lynn Werts, Larry Leshan, Deidre Bryan, and Gillian Hillis—and freelance copy editor Susan Brady, who edited this manuscript with grace and insight. It's great to work with people who share your passion. This is our book.

John Knaub, art, publication, and production supervisor with Academic Technology at the University of Florida, photographed almost all of the artwork for reproduction. Randall Smith; Randy Batista/Media Images Photography; Gallery on the Greene; and the studio of Howard Austin Feld made some of the transparencies.

The Florida Humanities Council has long supported my endeavors. This has been especially gratifying because "artist-photographer" falls outside of their purview. After I had completed a few FHC scholar-humanist fellowships, they kindly no longer required that I have an "academic" looking over my shoulder. Thank you, Fran Cary, Susan Lockwood, and Janine Farver for your enthusiastic support and your unwavering stewardship to all Floridians. Joan Bragginton, David Reddy, Rene Reno, Ann Schoenacher, and Laurie Berlin have been especially helpful over the years. I appreciate being appointed to the FHC's Speaker Bureau.

Being miserly with words is an art that I wanted to practice with this book especially. It is very difficult to reflect meaningfully on a person's life and art in a few paragraphs. I could not have done it without the assistance of scholar Mallory O'Connor. Her editorial skill helped to keep my active mind on course and my verbose tendencies in check.

I'd like to thank Dr. Kent Sharples, the president of Daytona Beach Community College, where I teach, for his "life-is-relationships" managerial style. His staff has shown me consistent courtesies, both professional and personal. I am enriched by knowing and working with Brian Babb and Nancee Bailey. My colleagues Dan Biferie, Patrick Van Dusen, and Eric Brietenbach have become my friends.

Many people have given to ensure that I make this book a thorough and thoughtful survey. Chief among them are art dealers Jeanne Kronsnoble of Main Street Gallery in Clayton, Georgia, and Ty and Jean Tyson of Tyson Trading Company in Micanopy, Florida. Art collectors and patrons Michael and Marilyn Mennello's support has benefited those of us who care about contemporary folk art; the Orlando museum that bears their name is a boon whose value will increase with time. Their pieces by Aaron, Cunningham, Dickerson, Gerdes, Latour, Richardson, and the Sculls constitute a major contribution to this book. I appreciate their interest in my work and ideas.

At the start I had to establish parameters in response to the polemics about what constitutes a folk artist today. I dreaded spending time with the "who's in, who's out" positioning. Margit Rowell, chief curator of the Department of Drawings at the Museum of Modern Art, responded to my inquiry about her including Bill Traylor in an exhibition with recognized "academic" masters by saying, "good art is good art." This was liberating, and it informed my selection of artists for this work.

Others' ideas about specific artists served me well. I appreciate the information given to me and hospitality shown to me by Jim and Alexia Roche, Bob and Jill Sindelir, Lennie Kesl, Claudia Sabin, Amy Dickerson, Carolyn West, Lee Lewis, Jane Simpson, Nance Frank, Carolyn Seiler, Frank Holt, Kenn Piotrowski, Robert McIntosh, Marcia Weber, Judy Hoffman, Donald and Sandra Talarico, Suzy and Fred Peace, Bev and Daniele Hurlick, Jeffrey and Dina Knapp, Jane and Jim Backstrom, Isabel and Jorge Hernandez, Don Cavanaugh and Ed Blue, Debra Sickler-Voigt, Sara Van Arsdel, Barbara Wolfson, and Marice Cohn Band. Noted author Carol Crown's support was especially meaningful.

Many of the artists have lent their artworks for reproduction in this book, as have others, including the Mennello Museum of American Folk Art; the City of Orlando; Tyson Trading Company; Don Cavanaugh and Ed Blue; Mark Newman; Josh Feldstein; Oshun Bunmi Olafemi; and Sally Steele. Thank you.

—G.M.

Some Principles

The artists in this book work on the fringes of art and life with little, if any, support. No institutions have given any of them a stamp of approval, and they generally don't care to be certified anyway. Since the self-taught are not part of any school or movement, they have no tradition to work their way out of or into. Irreverent toward material, plastic values and the concerns of academic art, self-taught artists generally remain elemental in their style of representation, comfortable in not knowing how to draw the proverbial straight line. Composition may be a foreign concept and color more a function of fun than theory. The point is not technical rendering. They are interested in creating a world in which they want to live, examining the one in which they have lived, or exploring the one in which they do live. Idiosyncrasies, if not personal turmoil, typically inform their imagery, and without rules they are far removed from the conceits of the fine art world.

Applying a label to these artists is problematic. For example, *folk art* was once limited to craft-oriented traditions, to utilitarian objects including quilts, baskets, kitchenware, weather vanes, and signs. Today, though, the untrained artists who have caught our attention work outside of the established ways. A self-taught artist is not necessarily a folk artist—not as long as one defines a folk artist as a trained artisan making things within a community. Likewise, the referent *naive* is misleading because an artist who is inexperienced in the ways of established art techniques isn't necessarily unsophisticated otherwise. The moniker *visionary* seems too exalted. Some of the self-taught artists, especially those who were once considered "outsider" artists, have indeed entered uncharted territory, but the term *outsider* engenders further marginalization.

Self-taught has become the accepted term for those artists who arrived at their art on their own, outside of the academy. The roots of the term *outsider art* extend back to Jean Dubuffet's *l'art brut* (raw art), a term he coined in the mid-1940s to describe art made mostly by people in insane asylums. When such work became recognized in America, championed by English scholar Roger Cardinal, it was called *outsider art.* The modernists' good-bad paradigm for assessing its imagery hardly applied; it was not a part of the western tradition of aesthetic thought.

Such criticism is not appropriate for much of the expressive imagery by self-taught artists either. Their work can stand alongside examples of "high" art, but their creations beg for information about the maker. Art-for-art's-sake is not the modus operandi for these people; self-exploration and its unbridled expression is more likely the point. Although exploring the work of Dubuffet's institutionalized psychotics proved critical for integrating fresh ideas into art theory, the notion that self-taught artists are unable to be socially adept or productive is inaccurate today and certainly incomplete.

Curator Karen Valdes's 1987 exhibition *A Separate Reality: Florida Eccentrics* at the Fort Lauderdale Museum of Art took her (inevitably) off the beaten art path to find sixteen self-taught artists for a landmark exhibition. In 1995, Claudia Sabin curated another important exhibition, *The Passionate Eye: Florida Self-Taught,* for the Terrace Gallery at Orlando's city hall. Of the seventeen artists she chose, only three had been represented in the Fort Lauderdale exhibition, and two of them had been represented there posthumously. Both exhibitions brought imagery by untrained artists into focus by breaking the modernists' paradigm in favor of engaging the viewer to respond to the artists' raw emotions, which were displayed without regard for artistic tradition.

Jeanne Kronsnoble, a noted folk art dealer, points out that the self-taught are uninfluenced by others and proceed by inner inspiration. "Their work," she states, "is theirs alone," adding that the style of self-taught artists "seems to hatch already fully grown and tends not to evolve much over the course of their lives. Most have no interest in experimenting, borrowing ideas from others, or refining their techniques. The artists use intensely personal ingredients to make their art,

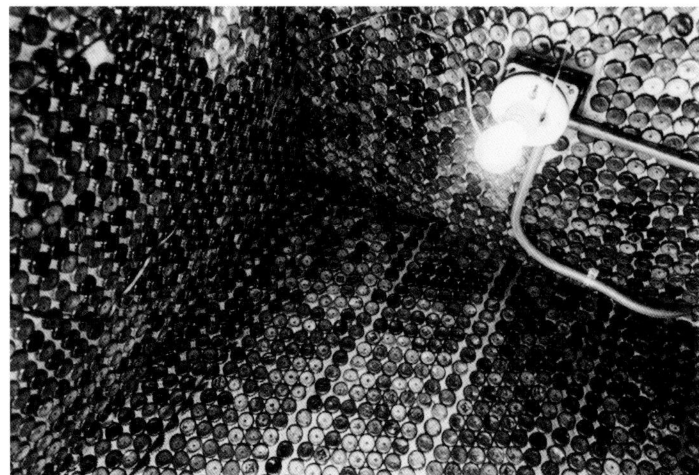
Bottle Cap Inn

and they remain steady in their resolve." Unencumbered by theory or convention, they often are uncompromising. Bill Swislow, in *Intuit* magazine, points out that isolation "from the art market, from formal artistic traditions, from other artists, from culture itself" is key to the definition of an artist working outside of the mainstream. "But if isolation makes for nice clarity," Swislow writes, "it is more easily honored in the breach than in the biography."

Some Places

Many artists create to stave off "the blues" instead of vainly trying to know its sources. Catharsis seems more available than answers and is perhaps more satisfying. Personally constructed spaces offer testament to the independent spirit. Environments—more emotional refuges than artistic statements—play significant roles in the lives of many of these people who, incidentally, generally do not consider themselves artists. Florida offers some prime examples of such artists.

Bottle-cap art became popular as soon as Coca-Cola began bottling the soft drink at the turn of the twentieth century. The ever-present caps were transformed into people, umbrella stands, trays, vases, picture frames, bowls, and more. In Miami, disabled World War I veteran Joe Wiser washed, varnished, and nailed three hundred thousand to one million caps (depending on sources) to cover walls, ceiling, doors, tables, stools, and the bar of his Bottle Cap Inn. Fixtures—including a piano—were also transformed by bottle caps to fully divorce a patron from his or her daily woes, creating a fitting motif for a lounge.

The tavern, on a hot dingy thoroughfare in North Miami, was once a place where the neighborhood's blue-collar patrons came to relax. A dark, misty, timeless chill invited another beer and made the world seem less and less important. In the mid-1990s, a Haitian congregation bought the building to use as their church. Their first order of business was to trash all of the Inn's accoutrements.

Contrasting with that lyrical environment is the Coral Castle in Homestead. There Edward Leedskalnin's (1887–1951) *Sweet Sixteen* edifice rose as a homage to the young woman who broke his heart. His epic accomplishment is as carefully calculated as it is romantic. No one saw him laboring or knows how he quarried, carved, and lifted into position the eleven hundred tons of native oolitic limestone by himself using only handmade tools. Cosmic laws and ancient truths, he claimed, aided his knowledge of science, astronomy, and Egyptology. So precise is his work that a child easily can push open a nine-ton gate.

People were long delighted by the wispy treelike structures intended to heighten travelers' anticipation as they approached the Cypress Knee Museum. These sixty signs guided travelers with their cryptic and not-so-cryptic messages through a twilight zone to Tom Gaskins's (1909–1998) reality. His museum sits like an oasis along a stretch of Highway 27 in Palmdale. Gaskins constructed the small, open-air cinder-block building in 1937 to showcase the finest specimens of cypress

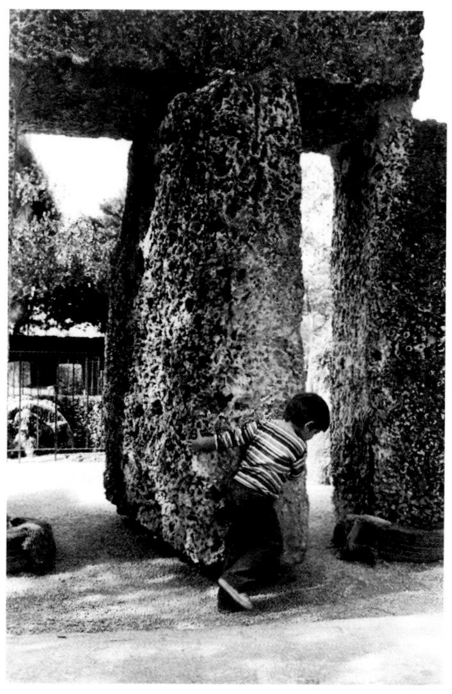

Coral Castle

knees that he could find—beginning a true love affair. For decades, when it was common for vacationing families and busloads of tourists to drive the state's never-ending two-lane roads, these visitors stopped to see and delight in the suggestive natural sculptures.

The signs became landmarks and an unintended environmental artwork. Imagine driving mindlessly in desolate cattle country with few other cars in sight and coming upon one of Tom Gaskins's "trees" set against grasslands and big skies, transforming the landscape into an existential field. For twenty miles to the north and to the south of the Cypress Knee Museum, messages displayed like commandments would proclaim things such as, "OVER 50 YRS. WITHOUT YOU? TSH TSH." His thoughts found their poetry as the elongated words were laid out on lines, or more aptly, on branches. Another begins, "LADY IF HE WON'T," continues on the next line with, "STOP. HIT," and then below reads, "HIM ON THE HEAD WITH A." The bottom branch carries the word "SHOE."

One sign begins, "LOVELY DAY," and on the other branch questions, "ISN'T IT?" But the most outstanding tree contains four words: "BEAUTY HUMOR NATURE KNOWLEDGE." The "Knowledge" sign now pathetically hangs like a limp more than a limb. This sign, like most of the others over the years, has fallen apart. Gaskins's son mends them, but it isn't the same. At one time the "Beauty Humor Nature Knowledge" of Gaskins's artwork blossomed, but letters have fallen like leaves, and the winds have twisted phrases. In 1994, the corporation that owns much of the land in the region forced the Gaskins family to remove the signs. Now the forty-five remaining trees are planted in a cluster behind the museum building, forming a kind of elephant's graveyard. It may have been just as well that Gaskins was in a nursing home by the time the trees were moved.

Disney World, an environment seamless in its grand illusions, is paramount in recognizing that giving people what they have been convinced that they need may lead to a predictable, homogenized, and insipid surrogate for natural experience. This results in what

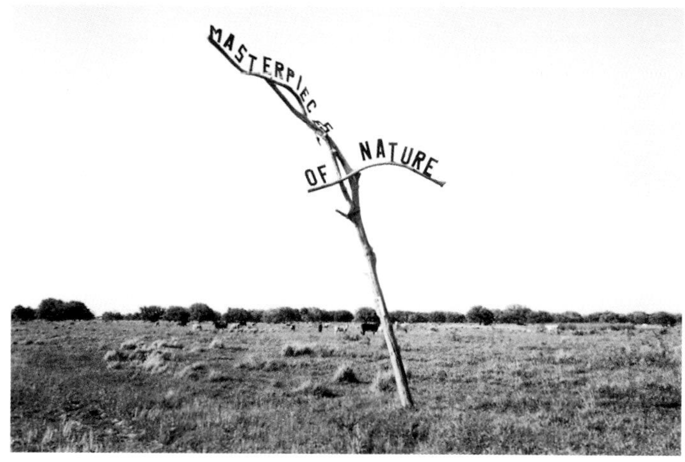

Sign on the road to the Cypress Knee Museum

New York Times Magazine writer Michiko Kakutani describes as "the democratization of creativity," which exemplifies "our eagerness to substitute public opinion for personal belief, market demands for authentic artistic and political vision." It's understandable that Tom Gaskins planted one of his trees with a sign that read, "FORGET DISNEY."

Visual art is not necessarily a means for communicating things literal. Nor is it any longer in the service of the church or state. Television, movies, and the Internet do a much better job of reaching the masses. Advertisements deftly promise that by merely wearing brand-name sneakers or drinking a certain soft drink, one will catapult to stardom after making a flying slam-dunk shot. It might be that the nonconforming self-taught artists—positioned far from the center of the culture—are primed to see and codify their relationship to society most clearly. Maybe their images are an antidote for the impossible dreams that are so well marketed by the mass media.

Some People

In *One Writer's Beginnings,* Eudora Welty writes: "Children, like animals, use all their senses to discover the world. Then artists come along and discover it the same way, all over again. Here and there, it's the same world. Or now and then we'll hear from an artist who's never lost it." It is difficult not to lose "it" in the material world, but these artists may come closest to retaining that original vision. Perhaps they are the ones who lost it most profoundly and who are reclaiming their sense of self with more of a vengeance than their trained counterparts. To those who have given up, self-taught artists may be a source, and their art, a wellspring. The most interesting artists seem to say that anyone can be an artist by going deeply enough into one's own psyche to mine what lies dormant. Florida's ever-changing art scene has created a pantheon of self-taught artists.

Jesse Aaron (1887–1979) began sculpting when he was eighty-one years old because, he said, the Lord directed him to carve. He lived in Gainesville and worked with a chain saw, chisels, and other woodworking tools. "I can see faces on anything," he once remarked. His sculptures reveal the personas that were suggested by the cypress and cedar branches and roots he had claimed. Occasionally he burned the sculptures to add texture or alter their color; he often set nails in resin using egg cartons as forms to create eyes. His completed pieces maintain their rough forms that acknowledge the artist's conviction that God predetermined the content and that he only served to show what was already there.

Earl Cunningham (1893–1977) kept to himself in St. Augustine while painting scenes

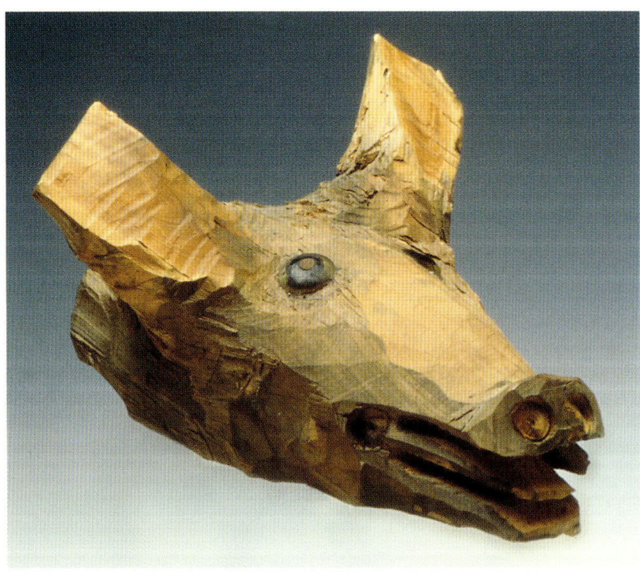

Jesse Aaron. Untitled

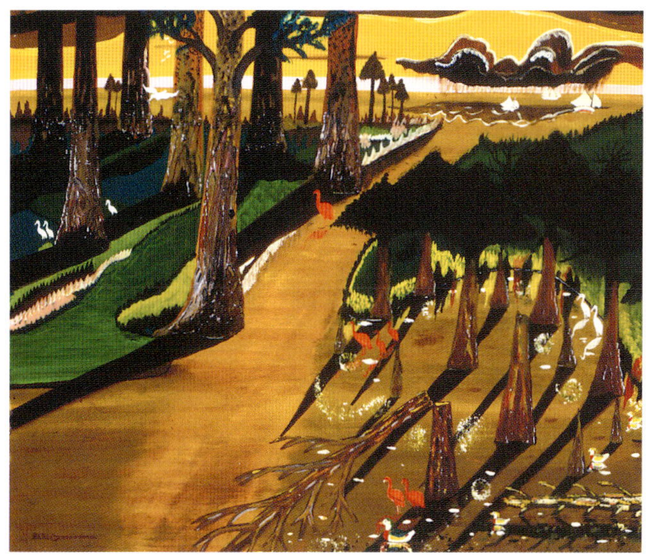

Earl Cunningham. *Old Thundercloud.*

of abundant life around waterfronts, mostly on the coasts of Maine and Florida. Although he built a gallery to display his memory-influenced paintings, they weren't for sale in his antiques and curio shop on St. George Street. Selling them, he claimed, would be like separating siblings. His oeuvre reveals an exotic world, imagined after his itinerant youth and adventuresome seamanship. His hillside views differ from the cold abstractions of bird's-eye views; Cunningham's attitude is that of an overseer caring for the land. He mixes schooners, Viking ships, and Seminole Indians in untamed tropical settings with audacious color—his work is more about freedom (for which his ever-present seas serve as metaphors) than mere recollections. His color sensibility questions whether life is a function of what has happened or of what one dreams.

Sybil Gibson (1908–1995) became an artist as a result of her fascination with a piece of gift wrapping paper she saw in a Miami department store. She showed her first paintings to her family at their Thanksgiving dinner in 1963. She was fifty-four years old when she began to paint pictures of flowers and children on brown grocery bags. She would soak the bags to dissolve the glue and unfold the paper, then paint on the still-damp paper. The tempera paints ran slightly, blending to yield a soft, dreamy effect. Faces dominate Gibson's later work, sadness belying her lyrical style. Many are haunting, seemingly with alter egos. She lived a vagrant's life until surfacing in Alabama, blind and diabetic but painting. Her daughter, Theresa Buchanan, explains that by penciling her name largely and boldly, Gibson "showed her importance with her signature."

Edward Mumma (1908–1986), who called himself Mr. Eddy, was a "hobo" for part of his youth; later he farmed and was a junk dealer. He moved to Gainesville in 1966, after his wife died, to be close to his daughter.

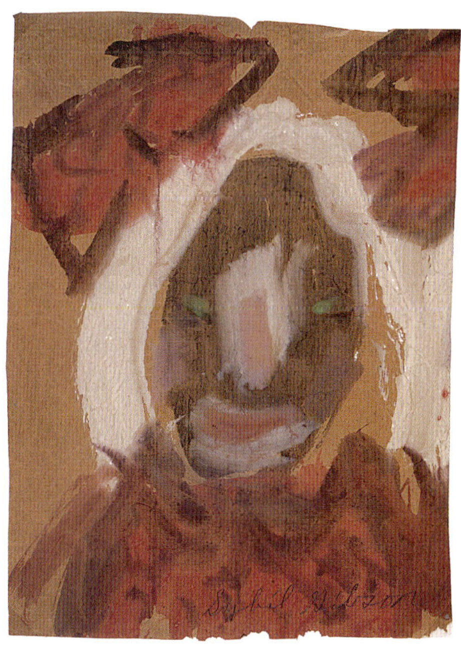

Sybil Gibson. Untitled.

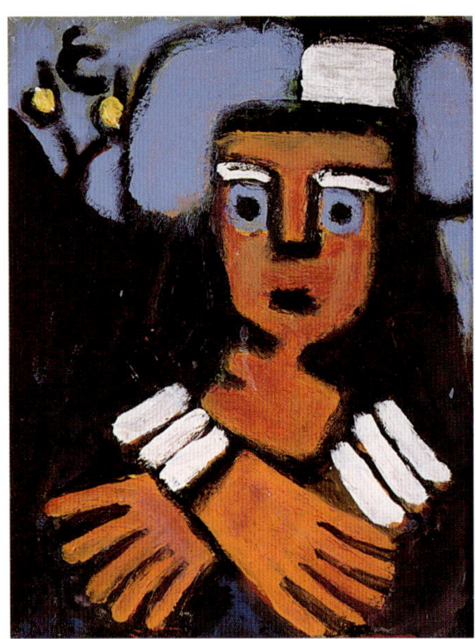

Edward Mumma. Untitled

With her encouragement, he enrolled in a painting class. The instructor criticized his work for being sloppy, so Mr. Eddy never returned. He was unemployed due to alcoholism and ill health—diabetes would necessitate the amputation of both of his legs. Homebound, he tried to paint a picture a day, creating many variations of a figure with the "same" face and hands-on-chest pose. The images were zealously realized and sometimes painted on both sides of the boards. With bold lines and painterly brush strokes, his freewheeling use of color made each one a distinct portrait. "A magician in color," Mumma's friend, the artist Lennie Kesl, said about him. It is estimated that Mr. Eddy made five hundred such pictures. At the time of his death, they covered the walls and floor of his small home.

Rene Latour (b. 1906) was an "occupational folk artist," a term coined by folklorists to describe craftsmen who take their work home with them, so to speak. The vocation gets in their blood, defining the person. Latour labored as a sheet metal worker around Daytona Beach most of his adult life. In 1959, he opened Ormond Sheet Metal and Roofing, and two years later, he constructed his first tin man to advertise his shop. His was the time before plastics sucked the skill and pride away from the tough tradesmen. In Latour's day, tin men were often seen in front of sheet metal shops and functioned as trade signs, showing the public that the proprietor could design and weld adeptly. Tin men display every conceivable skill and trick of the trade; the material is the message. Fascinated by Buckminster Fuller's geodesic dome, Latour based the faces of his creations on this form. He used himself as the model. "It's very natural. That's why my work is so outstanding," he said of his cast of characters.

Mario Sanchez (b. 1908) spent many of his active years at "Mario's Studio under the Trees" in Key West, where he lived and drew inspiration. He made charming bas-relief pictures of life in the onetime village, portraying street scenes, public buildings, and neighborhood activities with accuracy of place and feeling. He began with pencil sketches on paper, which he transferred onto wood by using carbon paper. Then, with chisels and mallet, a piece of glass, a razor blade, and cheap brushes, he would craft the scenes to life—images not of Margaritaville but of the old Conch Town flavored with its Cuban heritage.

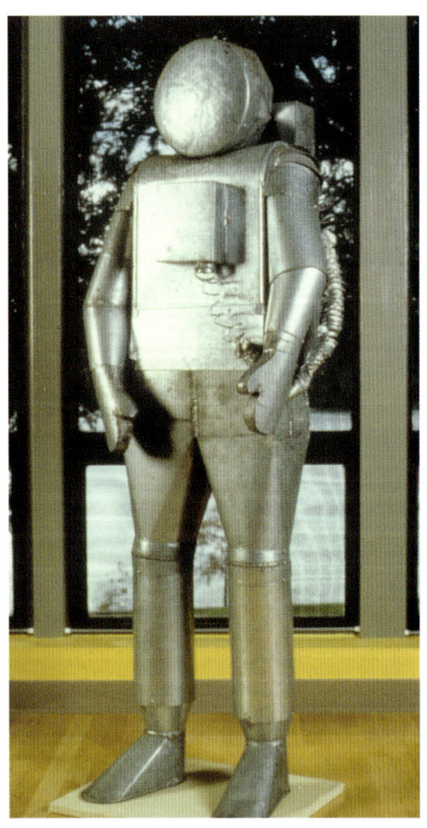

Rene Latour. *Moonwalker.*

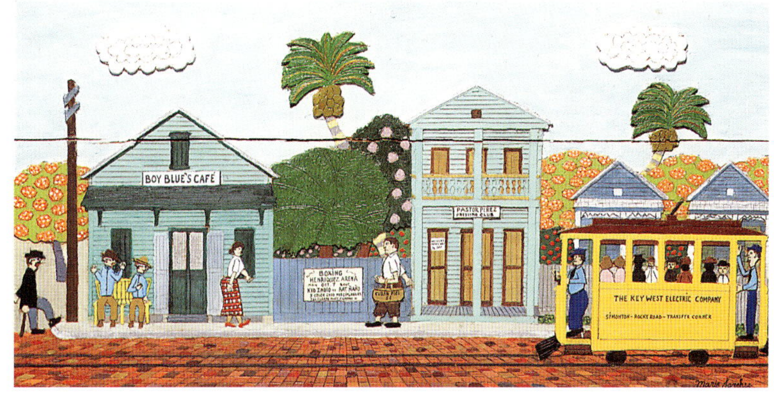

Mario Sanchez. *Blind Sharks.*

George Voronovsky (1903–1982) lived the last decade of his life on a railroad pension in one room in South Beach's Colony Hotel. His was the top-floor room visible in the chic print ads and television commercials shot along trendy Ocean Drive. But when he died, South Beach was still just a strip of white-washed hotels, and Voronovsky had been a solitary figure, alone among a sea of elderly retirees. No one saw the work that was tacked up throughout his room, painted with cheap watercolors and brushes on pizza boxes that he found in alleys. His visual recollections of his charmed youth in the Ukraine along with a myriad of decorations he fashioned out of refuse (stars from aluminum cans, flowers from paper, and so on) covered his walls and ceiling. It never occurred to him to sell his paintings. Voronovsky's work reflected an idealized past that he preferred to the real one. He used his art to direct his mind's wanderings, because the room's white walls allowed his thoughts to meander in painful directions.

As was true of their predecessors, an independent spirit and a need to create bind contemporary self-taught artists. Admirers of their art are not awed by skills and techniques but rather by the artists' experience—the artists' voices and their own responses to something essential about being human that is expressed in the work. The work of self-taught artists is ripe with fresh ideas and deep emotions. These artists have changed the curator's job from being a gatekeeper to becoming an explorer, and many people are seeking out self-taught artists on their own rather than waiting for them to receive official recognition. Florida is fertile territory for discovering self-taught artists. It is not unusual to see a car with an out-of-state license plate at a Florida roadside produce stand, the sojourner appraising paintings instead of peaches or tomatoes.

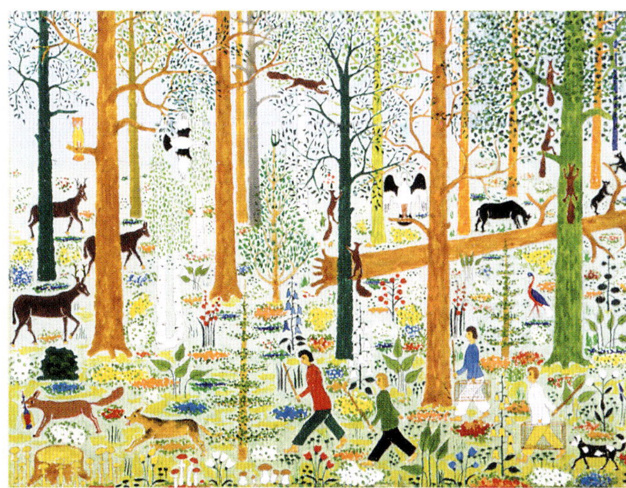

George Voronovsky. Untitled.

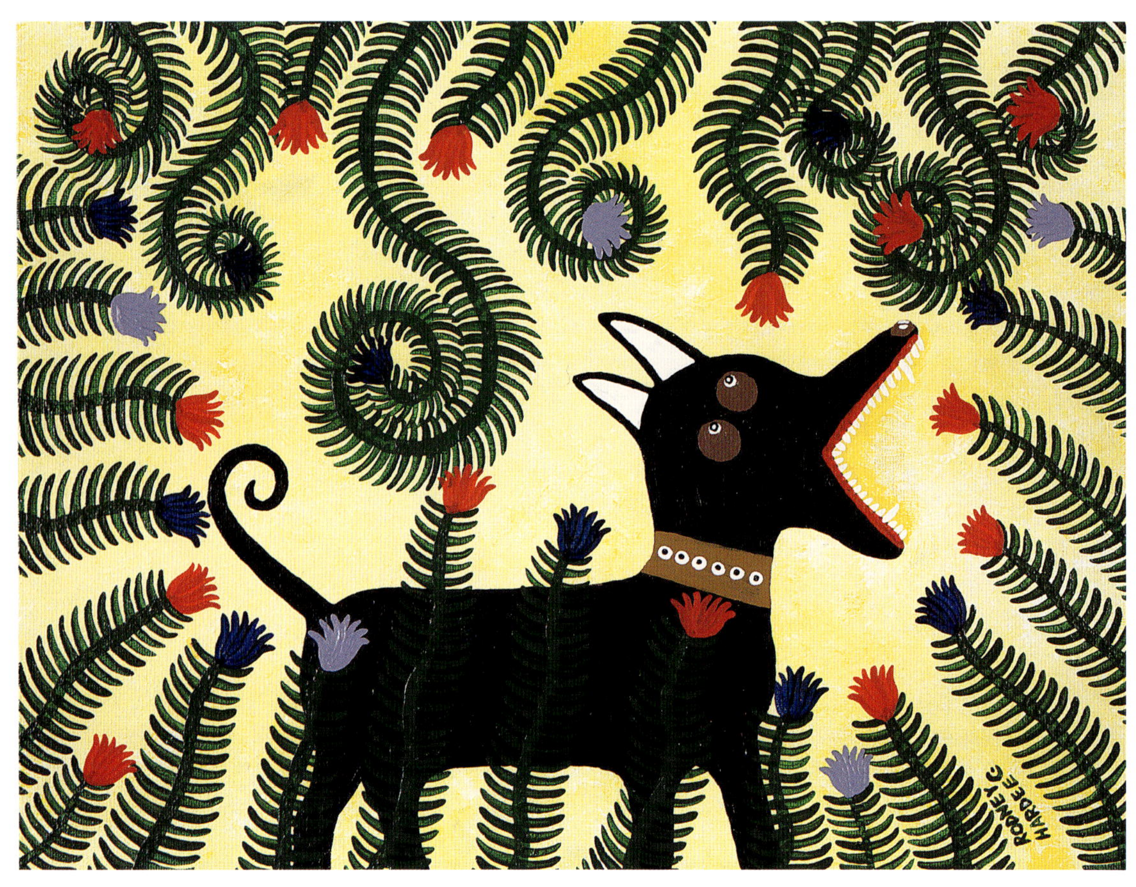

Rodney Hardee. *The Barking Dog in the Garden.* 2002. 12" x 16".

RODNEY HARDEE

b. 1954

Years ago, as Rodney Hardee was driving along a deserted stretch of Highway 60, a series of marketing signs led him to an unusual produce stand owned by Ruby Williams. He befriended "Miss Ruby," who lives there and paints pictures beneath a wooden lean-to from which she can oversee the sale of the fruits and vegetables that she grows. His efforts to get Williams to express herself through painting were successful, and her painting style has evolved from the functional signage she once placed along the road to whet the appetites of hungry travelers. Like many painters, she is indebted to Hardee. Indeed, he seems more concerned with stimulating the creativity of others than in extolling his own: in the process of seeking out raw talent he has created an atelier without walls.

Hardee gives freely of his time, his insights, and his limited resources in order to encourage and benefit artists in the Lakeland area. He possesses an egalitarian belief that talent is the result of effort, and that everyone is—at least potentially—an artist. Each individual, he feels, has something special to offer and can create earnest imagery by going deeply into his or her own psyche.

Rodney Hardee's own paintings of cat faces and Madonnas convey his affability. He paints fewer than twelve pictures a year and numbers each one—at the millennium he had made 230 paintings. On the back of his paintings are journal-like entries that read like his part of a casual phone conversation; he discusses the current affairs of his painter friends or describes the doings of his wife and children. Each piece also carries the message "Jesus Loves You."

Like many contemporary folk artists, Hardee's paintings lack the illusion of depth, and the colors are applied without gradation. But his paintings—whether they depict Adam and Eve or a barking dog—are pleasing and usually accented with gracefully climbing vines. Rodney Hardee seems happy to leave angst-ridden imagery to other, more tortured souls.

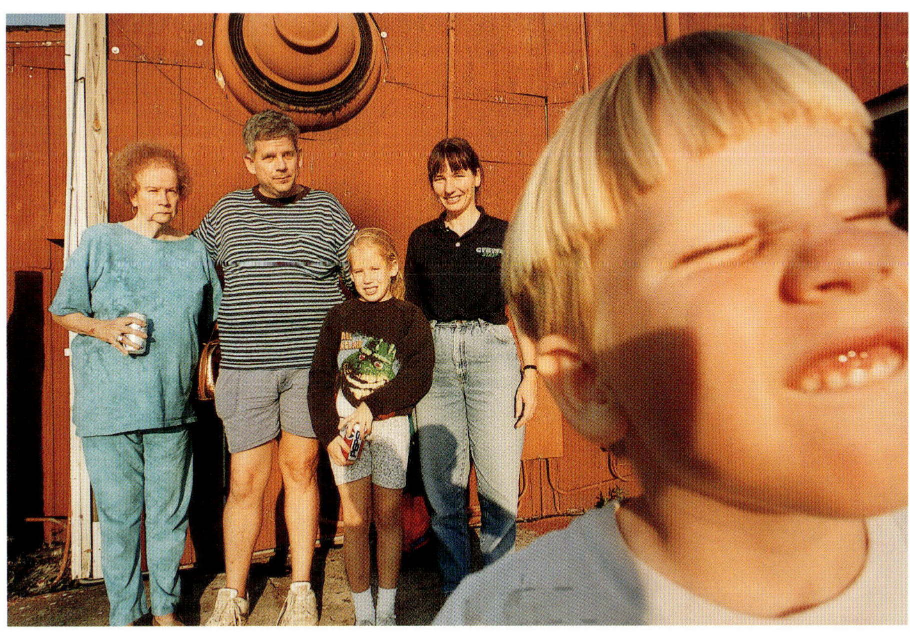

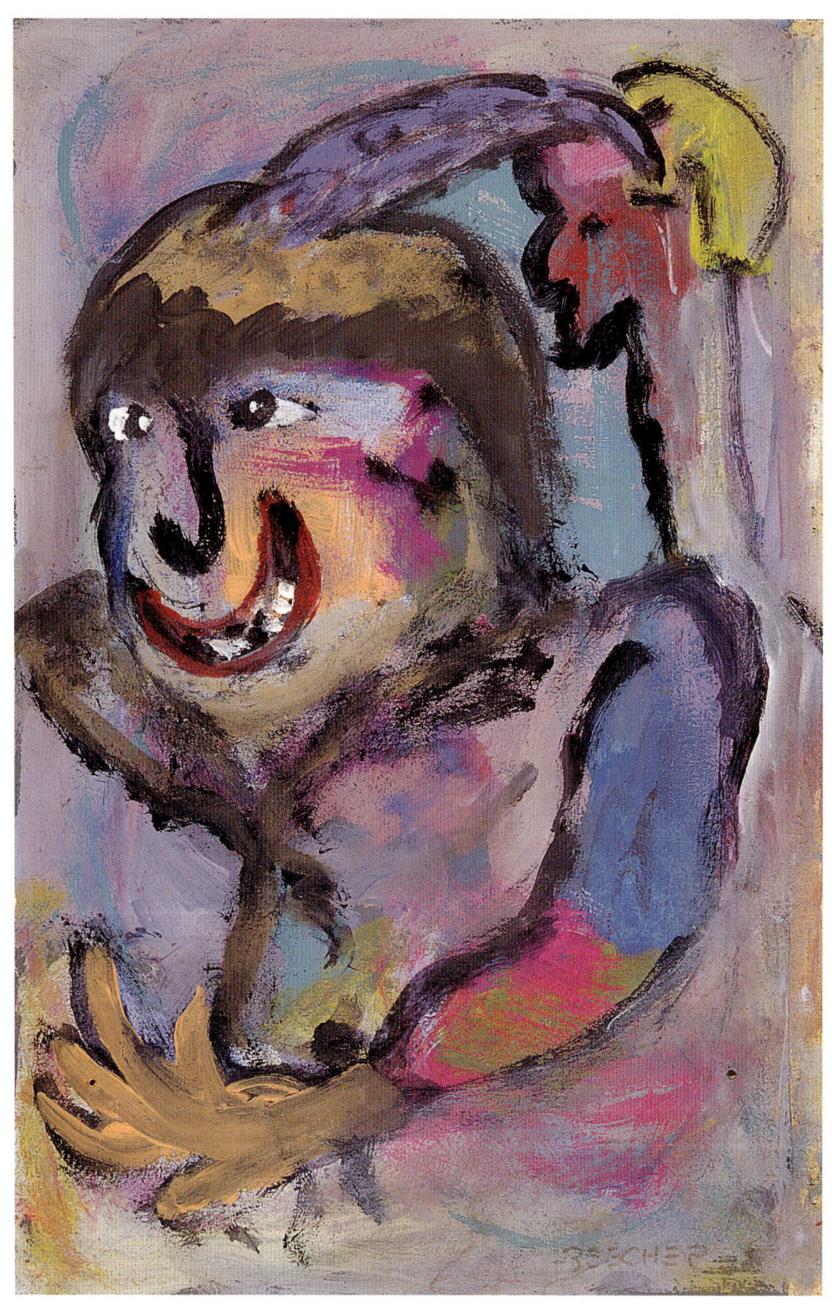

Eugene Beecher. *Stepping Out.* 1995. 17" x 11".

EUGENE BEECHER

1909–2002

Gene Beecher's paintings are enigmatic. Beginning with broad, intuitive gestures and abstract color fields, he creates his "unseen friends." Their twisted bodies and distorted faces—many in somber but glowing, almost ghoulish colors—come alive and appear to be caught at an emotionally charged moment. Loose, vigorous brush strokes heighten a feeling of turmoil. Color and image assault and disturb the viewer.

However, his paintings are also amusing, or at least Beecher found them so. He smiled like a prankster, and in a quiet voice reluctantly admitted that, yes, he sometimes did see his images as "atrocious." They reminded him of his dreams—night terrors that have startled him awake throughout his life, nightmares he only escaped by "leaving a light on."

Perhaps his images have roots in his experience of arriving stillborn and being "put outside in a slop jar." Only through the persistence of a rural Texas midwife who bathed him alternately in hot and cold pans of water was he brought to life. Or maybe the terrifying childhood experience of falling down an outhouse hole one dark night informed his images.

Whatever their origin, Beecher began to paint in 1982, when for health reasons at the age of seventy-three, he moved from Ohio to Florida. Almost immediately, his dormant appreciation of color bloomed in the Florida sunlight. He painted almost every day of his life thereafter until one night in the summer of 2002, when the ninety-three-year-old artist was found bewildered, wandering the halls of his Lakeland retirement home: he had spray-painted himself with Day-Glo paint and sprinkled himself with silver glitter. He never painted again.

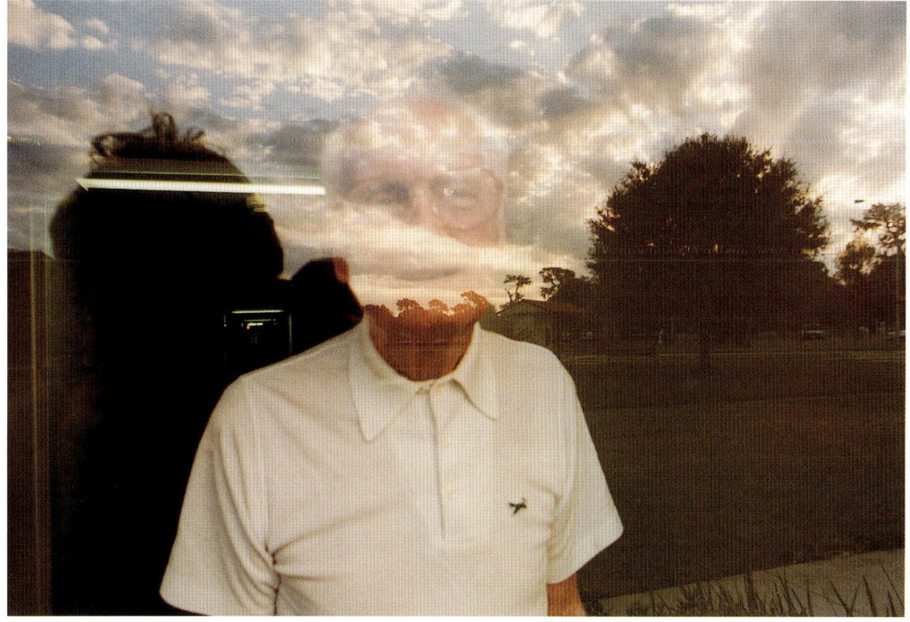

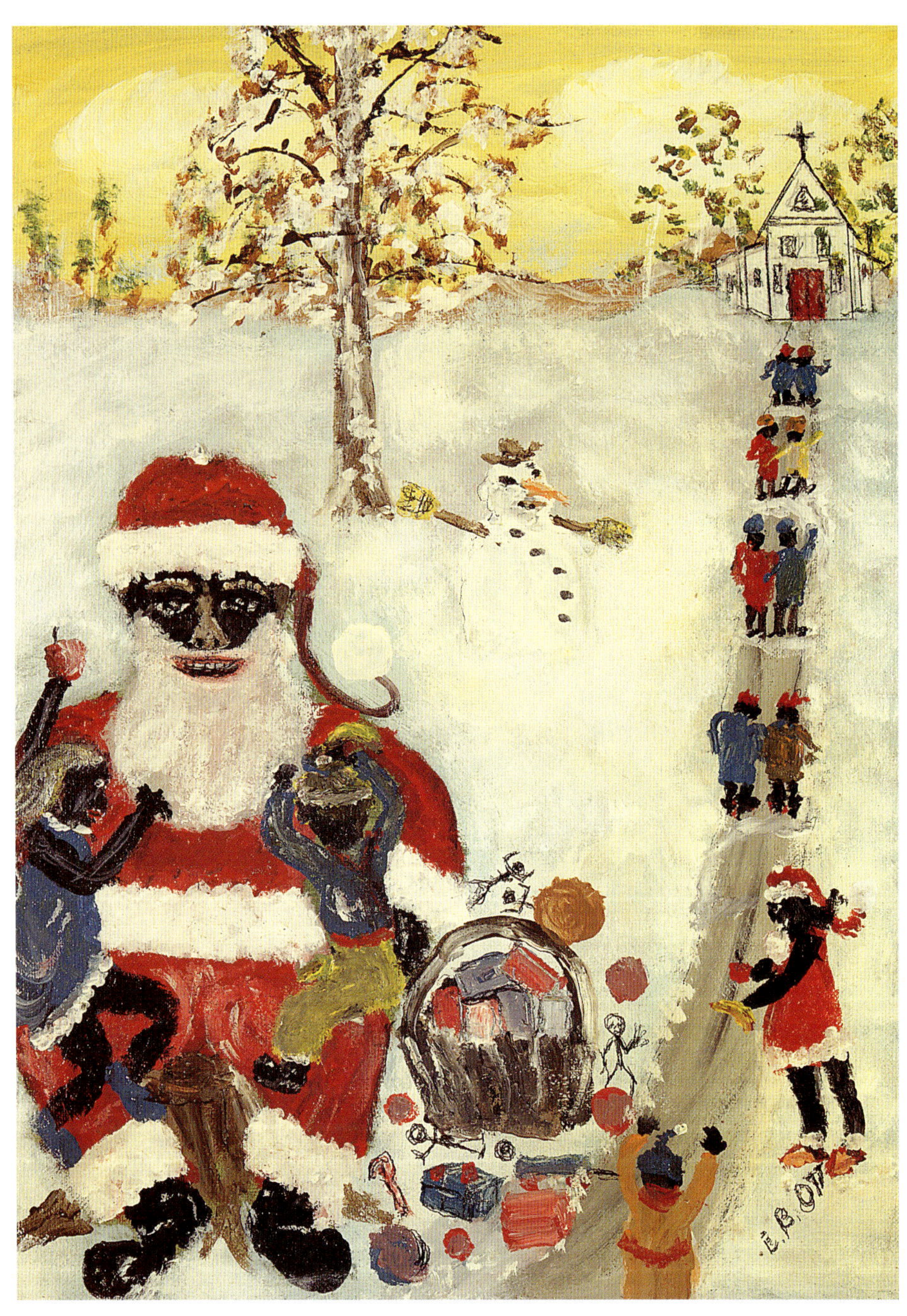

Edward Ott. Untitled. 15.5" x 11.5".

EDWARD OTT

1914–1997

Just months before his death, Edward Ott finished converting a long trailer in his yard in Lakeland into a gallery to display his own paintings. There he proudly pointed out his artistic skills and accomplishments: "Not everyone can paint smoke like that," he would say. Or he would show off the detail in any one of the many objects he had included in a room or beside a barn in his pastoral scenes. Sometime during his ten-year artistic foray that began as a way to recuperate from a car accident, Ott began painting black Santa Clauses. Creating these both excited and contented him. He didn't see any "soul in the eyes" of his white Santas.

Although Ott's paintings are basic in concept and execution—or perhaps because of a reciprocal relationship with this naïveté—he was confident and proud of his work. Or maybe his advanced age elevated him above the concerns of younger people who are still climbing the mountain or standing on a plateau wondering about meaning.

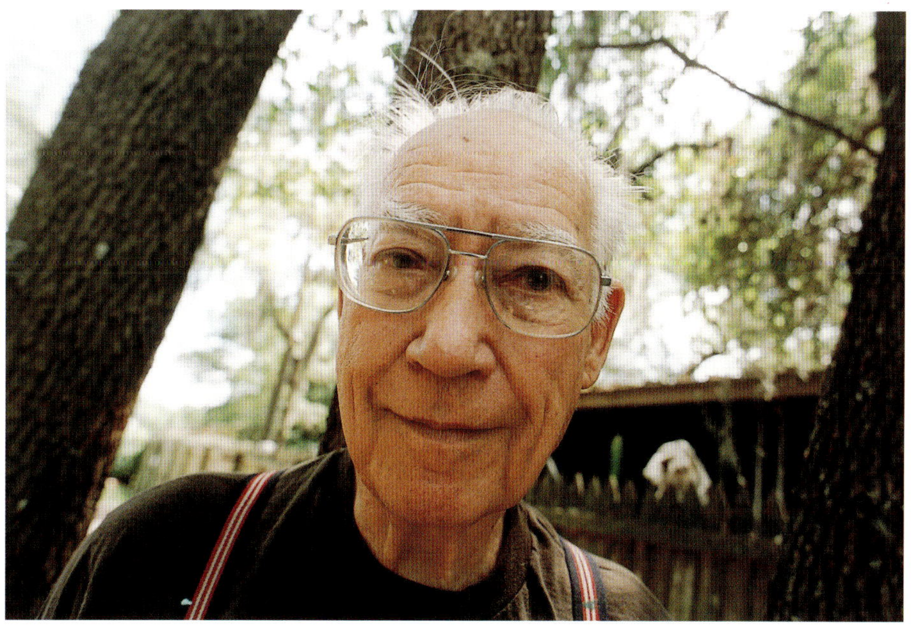

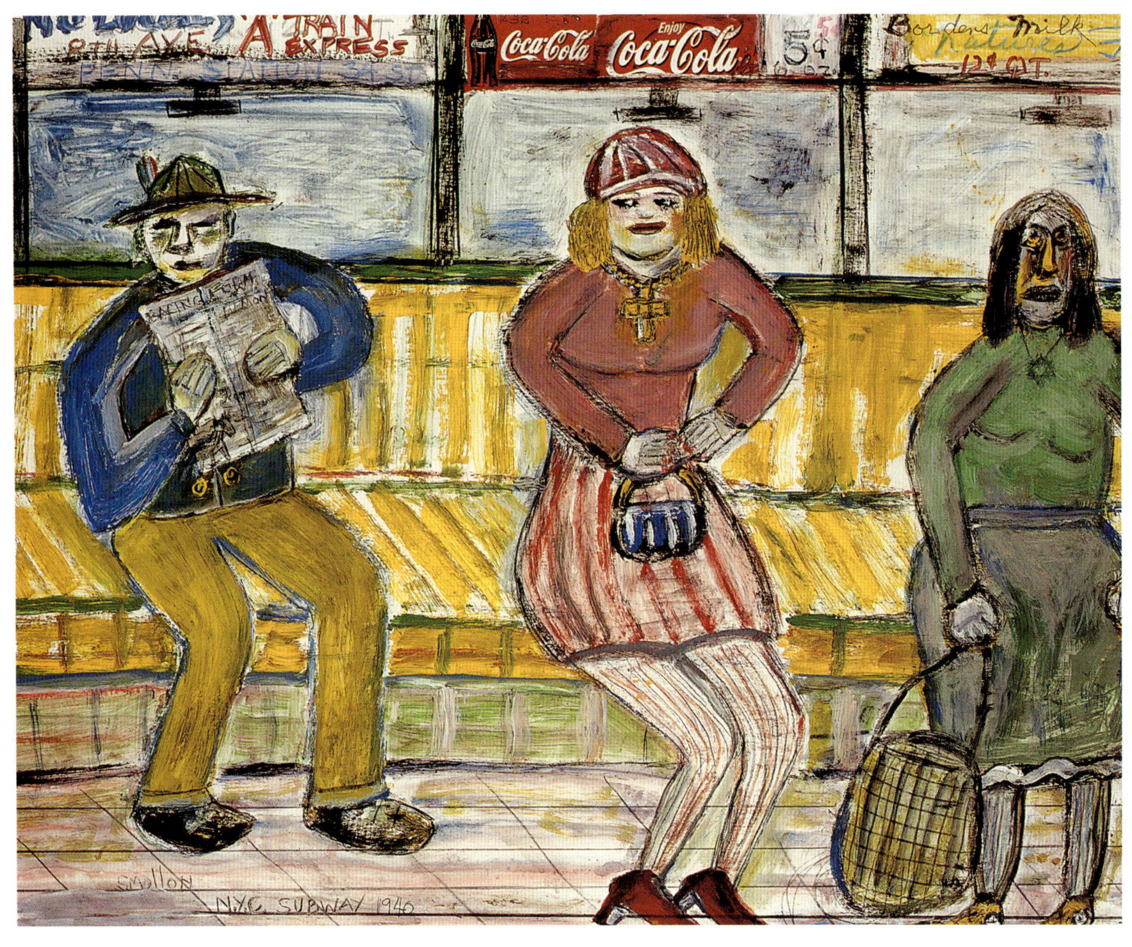

Joey Smollen. *New York City Subway.* 1940. 15.5" x 19.5".

JOEY SMOLLEN

1927–2001

Joey Smollen claimed to have signed his paintings "Smollon" to reflect his Irish ancestry; his son said he did it to avoid the tax collector! Smollen was reared in New York City's mean streets, where a lesson meant a bloodied nose. As a youngster, his mother instilled in him a love of learning. He credited his voracious image making to his being an avid reader, street smart, and a world traveler. He was a storyteller, and by bearing witness, painting allowed him to "rise above it all" in spite of a rough upbringing, tough life, and living in near-poverty during his latter years. Smollen said: "I did it my way. . . . The only difference between Sinatra and me is that Sinatra went to Hollywood and I went to war." Smollen had a way with words, and it seems that he knew what he was talking about.

Rodney Hardee points out that Joey Smollen "lived all the stuff he's painted." Coming to terms with his experiences distinguishes his imagery. As a merchant marine, Smollen had "been around the world a few times" by his twenty-first birthday. Soon afterward he married and stumbled into a job at a car lot. He made enough money to "indulge" his wife and their five children, but drinking, gambling, and "a sailor's spirit" led to divorce. He married four more times "for something to do." Eventually, while driving from Philadelphia to tour Florida, his car broke down in Lakeland. He settled there after years of moving around the country from one car dealership to another.

At the heart of Joey Smollen's crude renditions of past remembrances is his attitude that "I never added anyone up; they add themselves up." And in his paintings the sums are greater than their parts. Perhaps pathos comes from the way he freezes a moment, with insightful nuance and gestures, making one wonder about the hopeless faces that populate his pedestrian scenes.

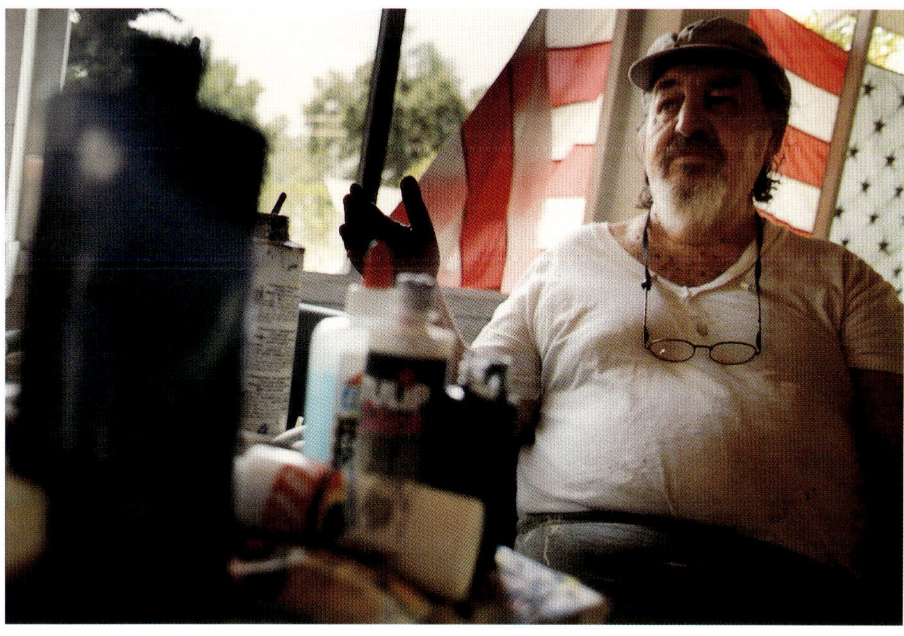

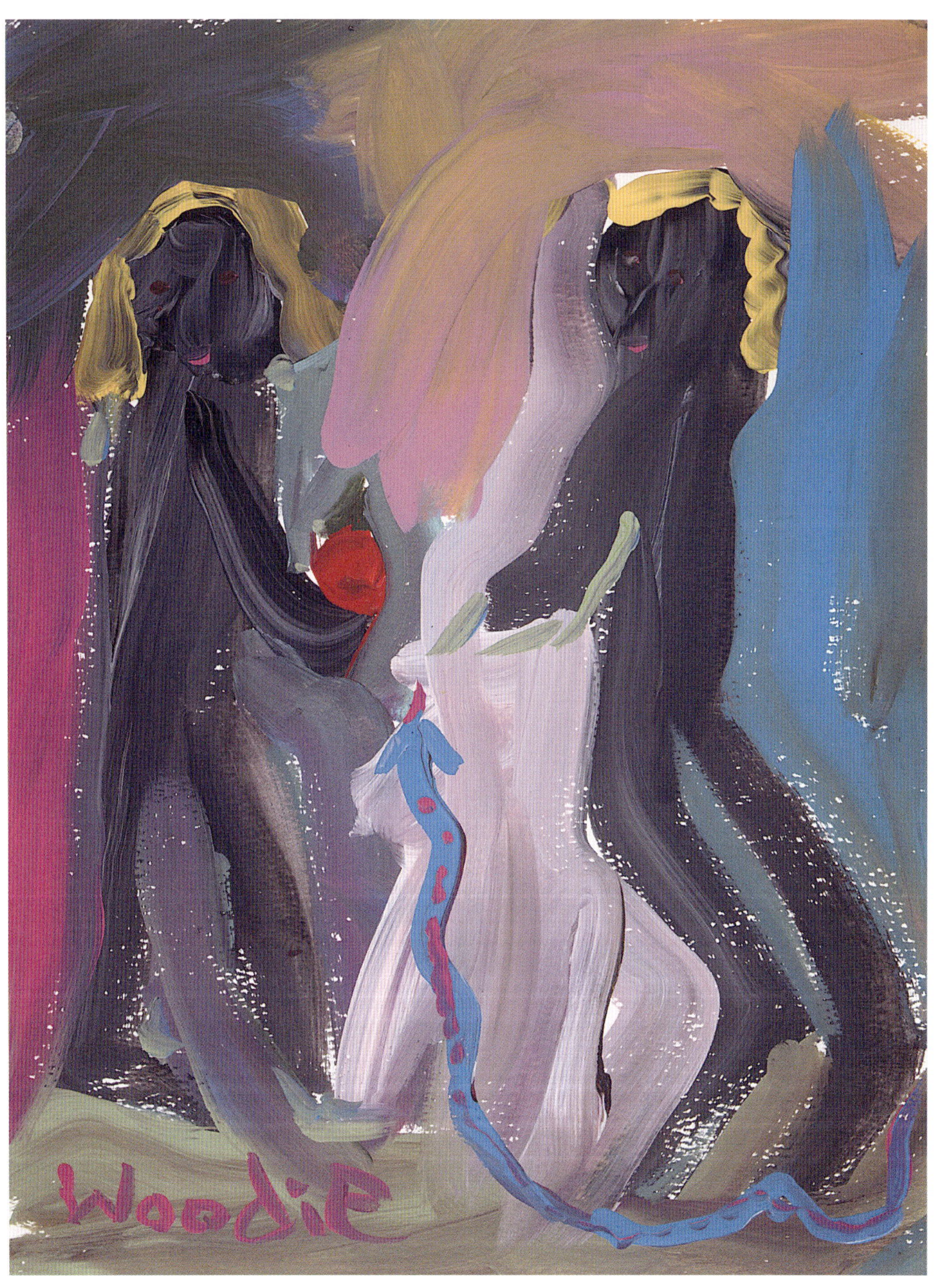

Woodie Long. *Adam and Eve.* 2000. 12" x 9".

WOODIE LONG

b. 1942

Woodie Long, one of twelve siblings, is a sharecropper's son. "Daddy had us for a reason, that was to be field hands," he says. Kept out of school to harvest crops, he learned math by rearranging the boxes of fruit he peddled to create an extra box to sell. When he was thirteen, his parents moved the family to a housing project in Tampa; two years later, his father abandoned them.

As a young man, Long set tile on ships, and at the boat yard, he spray painted scenes of people fishing and animals cavorting on the ships' gunnels. These were carefree images, for he knew that they would be sandblasted away the following day. Years later, he went to Saudi Arabia, where he wound up painting palaces and a king's mosque and meeting his future wife, Dot. In 1988, using Dot's brushes and maintaining his loose approach, he began the gestural painting that has remained his personal style. The couple settled in Santa Rosa Beach and opened a gallery to sell his paintings. Long estimates that by the start of the new millennium, he had made nearly fourteen thousand paintings.

Sharecroppers and flowers are among the subjects that hold special meaning for Long. He is miffed even today when remembering that "we couldn't drink out of the same water fountains [as blacks] but drank from the same water buckets in the fields." His *Momma's Flowers* series is a homage to her memory. "She deserves them," he says. He also paints angels, chicken fights ("I tell people they're just kissing."), children jumping rope and flying kites, women quilting, and men gambling. He returned from New Orleans to paint musicians and from New York City to take on Manhattan's skyline as a favored scene. But the tenor of his work is defined less by subject than by his elongated, expressive figures. His bright palette adds further whimsy to the abstracted portrayals of his recollections.

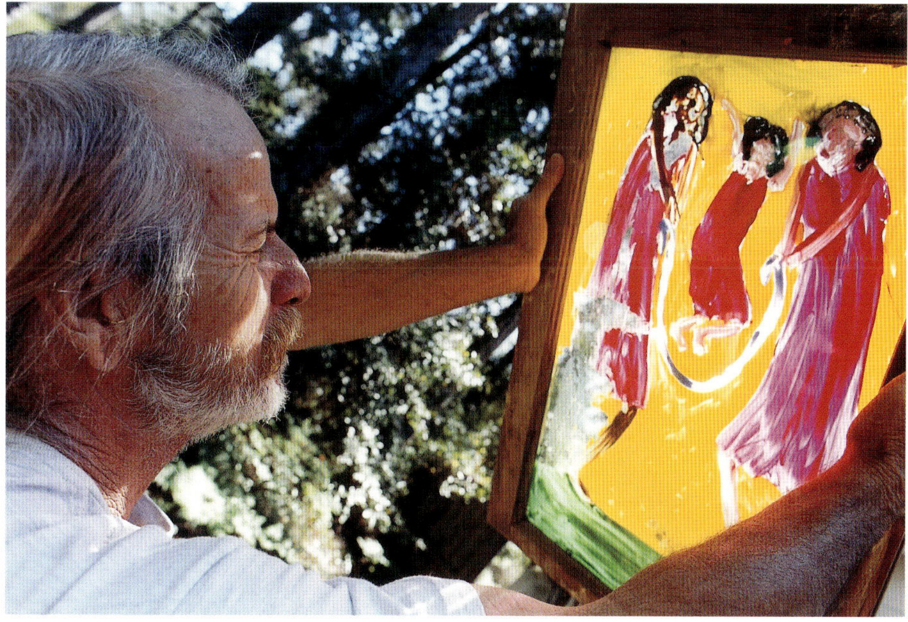

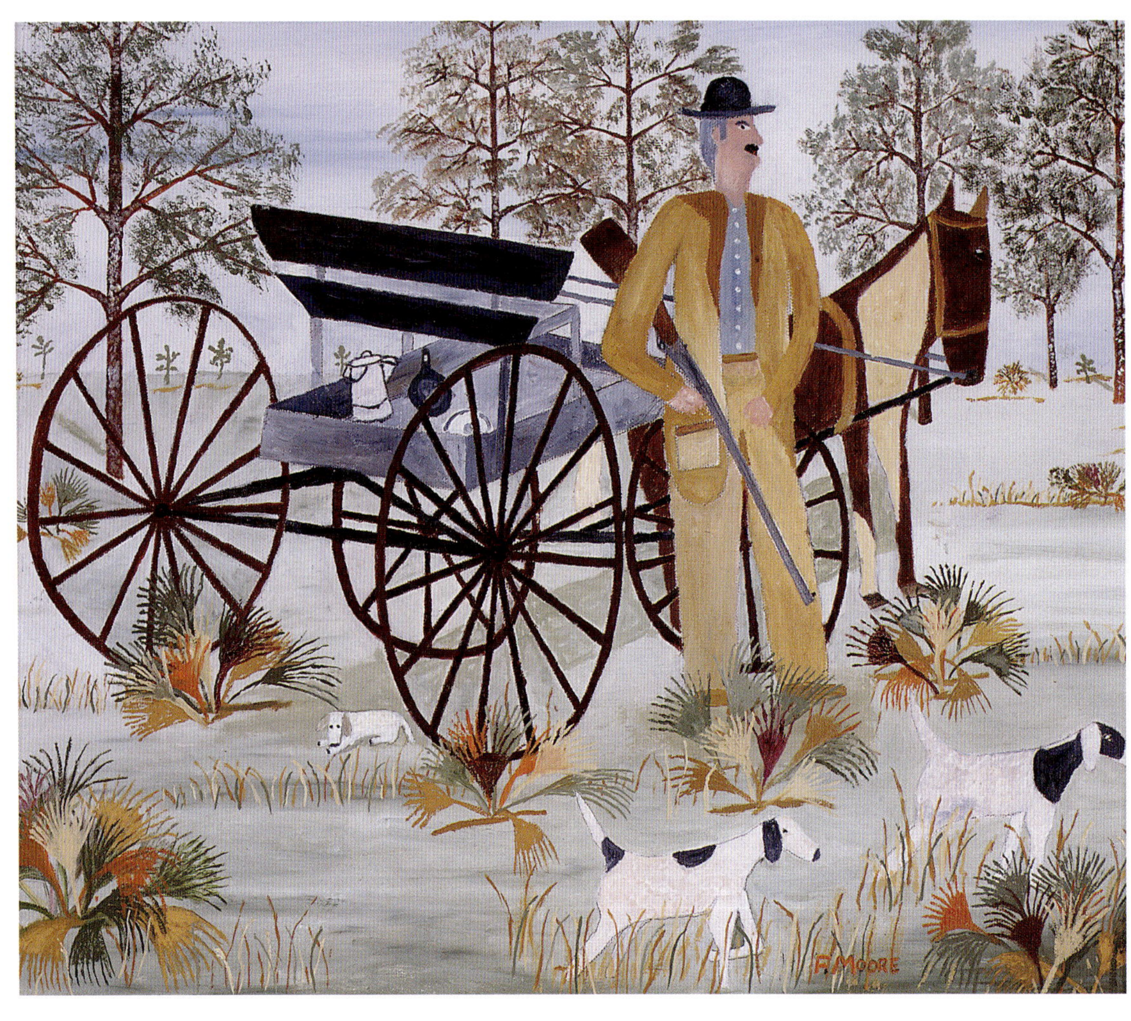

Francis Moore. *Quail Hunting*. 1985. 15.25" x 19.5".

FRANCIS MOORE

b. 1917

In 1975, well into his retirement, Francis Moore grudgingly took an art class. Ten people were needed to form the class, but since only nine had registered, Mrs. Moore enrolled her husband. He said, "I'm not going to do that." She said, "You have to because I paid for it!" The rest is—as they say—history.

Moore had no interest in painting still lifes in watercolor. The only thing that made sense to him was to paint scenes of his rural hometown—Hawthorne. For twenty years, until declining health forced him to stop, that's exactly what he did. He has created an archive of storybook interpretations of his time and place.

Moore tells schoolchildren for whom he demonstrates his "primitive painting" that "the dog [in the pictures] used to be my dog, but it died and now comes back as a ghost." The paintings are like ghosts too; only a shadow remains of the places they depict. Moore's Hotel was converted in 1964 to the Hawthorne Apartments, and the old library is also a thing of the past. "They tore down his old red brick schoolhouse and built something that looks like a motel," laments the artist's wife, Mary.

The Moores still live in the house where Francis was born. His father was born in Moore's Hotel, which his grandfather had built. Although some changes have taken place in Hawthorne over the years, Francis Moore has remained true to his valued past and cherished memories.

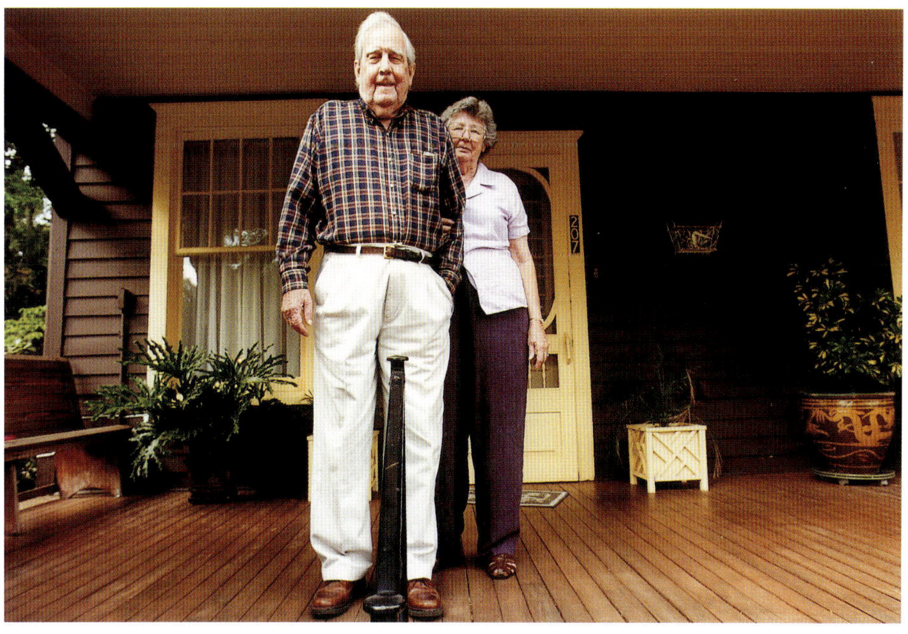

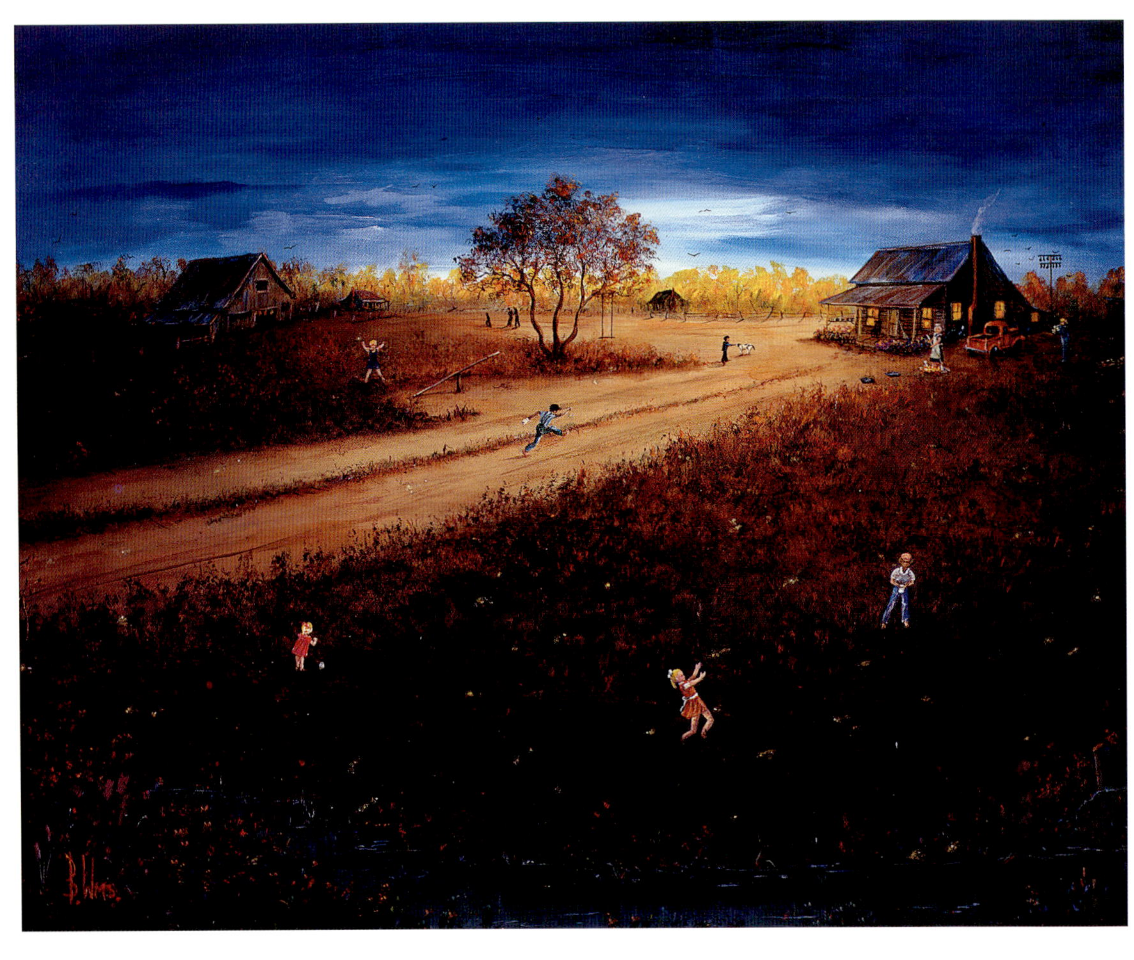

Bettye Williams. *Summer Night's Awesome Lights.* 2000. 28.5" x 34.5".

BETTYE WILLIAMS

b. 1935

What William Ivers called "the remembered reality" is at the core of memory painter Bettye Williams's work. Her carefully executed visual reminiscences of rustic settings and placid scenes tap into our longings for an idealized past—for a place where the water is clear, the groves are full of oranges, the general store is well stocked, and repairing a broken car is considered family fun. Nobody locks his or her door in Williams's Florida.

Williams has fond memories of growing up in Monticello, a small town in the Florida Panhandle near the Georgia border. She recalls that in the family's "cracker" home, "Mama cooked on the fireplace for a while using green wood from pecan trees—it smoked more than it flamed. Boards were missing from the floor next to the fireplace, and you could see the hogs that belonged to the owner walking around underneath. Still, we had a home of our own."

These days, Williams lives in Bartow, and the Florida that she knew lives only in her memories. But in her home, the fresh turnip greens seasoned with salt pork, the fried pork chops and skillet corn bread, the sliced Vidalia onions and crystal pickles (which require three weeks to prepare), the boiled green peanuts, and the twice-sweetened, fresh-brewed iced tea and vanilla ice cream—all presented with southern hospitality—lend authenticity to her southern tales, both spoken and painted.

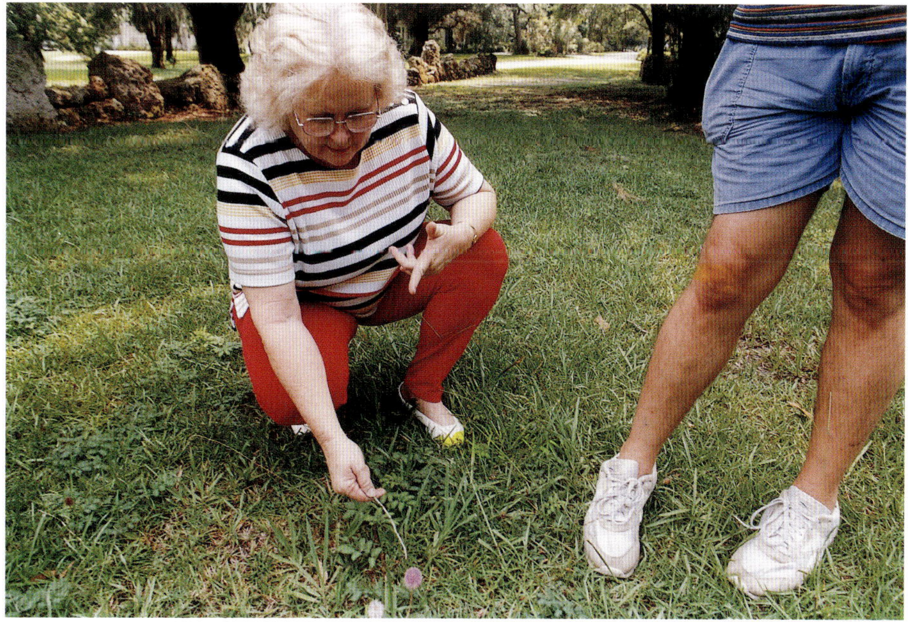

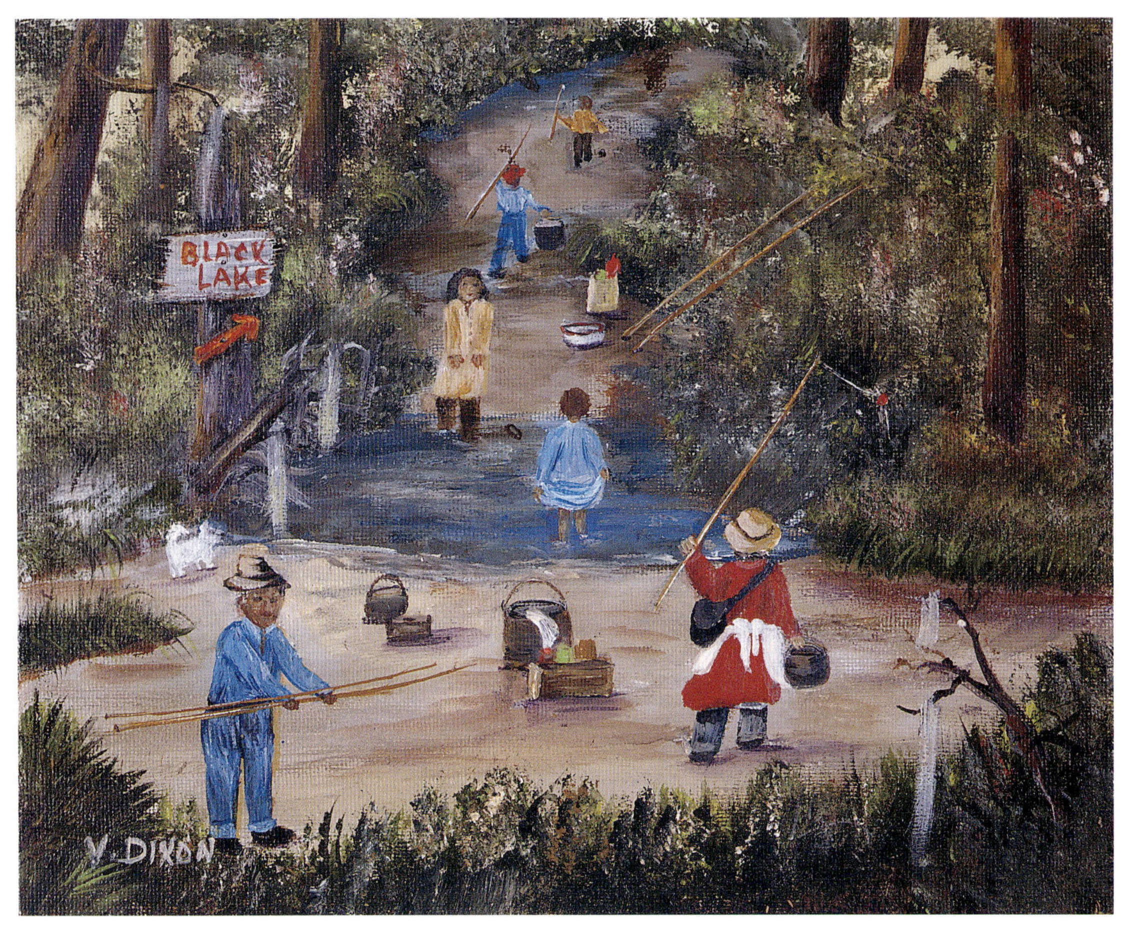

Virginia Dixon Shealey. *Black Lake.* 8" x 10".

VIRGINIA DIXON SHEALEY

b. 1933

In 1980, Bettye Williams's sister, Virginia Dixon Shealey, was encouraged to paint by her daughter, Terrye Wheeler. Terrye told her mom, "If Aunt Bettye can do it, Mama, you can do it too." Shealey accepted the challenge to appease her daughter. In those days, Shealey would rather have fished than painted. She enjoyed painting, though, and as the years passed, she painted more and fished less. Shealey painted her fond memories of life during the Great Depression.

Williams says that her sister's paintings are "so basic, so simple, so honest . . . about the localities where things took place; mine are more about conversations that took place." Whereas Shealey painted recreational imagery, Williams zeroed in on labor and survival. Williams, for example, painted their grandmother gathering debris to make a small fire so its smoke would keep the mosquitoes away, and "the family could be able to spend some time on the porch, giving the house time to cool down enough to be able to sleep." Virginia Dixon Shealey enjoyed the country and liked to express the leisureliness with which folks enjoyed themselves during those bleak days, often portraying wooded scenes with ponds where people fished or clearings where they picnicked. She left crop harvesting to her sister, preferring to tend the garden.

In 1985, at age thirty, "Terrye was called home to the Lord." A week before passing, she asked her mother to promise to keep painting. "I told her I would," said Shealey. But in 2001, Shealey was put on dialysis and her husband was diagnosed with terminal lung cancer, so she doesn't have the strength to paint. The scenes are still in her imagination, though. "I miss it [painting] a whole lot," she says from her Lake Wales home. Indeed, Virginia Dixon Shealey's views of family togetherness in the face of adversity were prophetic: the best things in life *are* free. Her hardships proved her values.

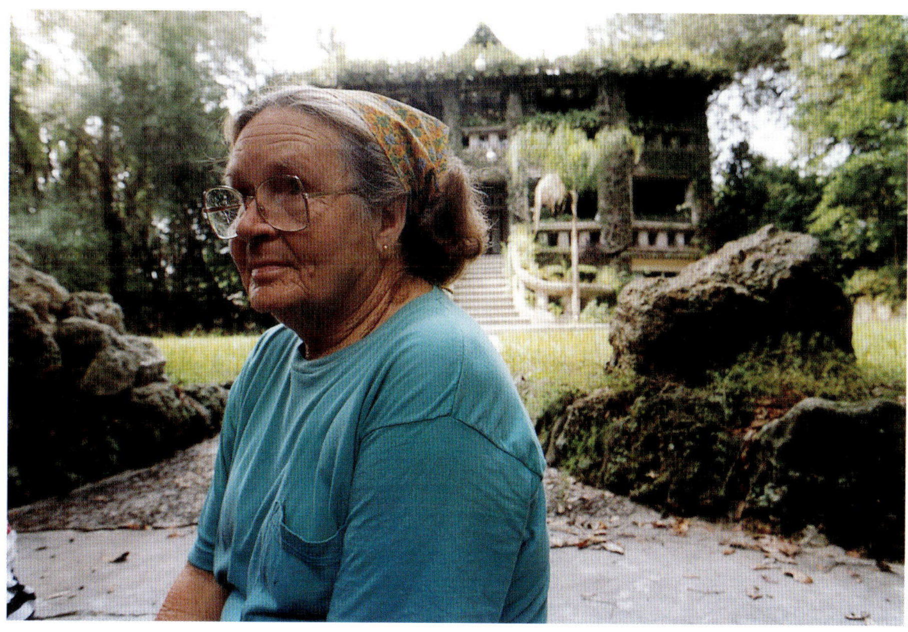

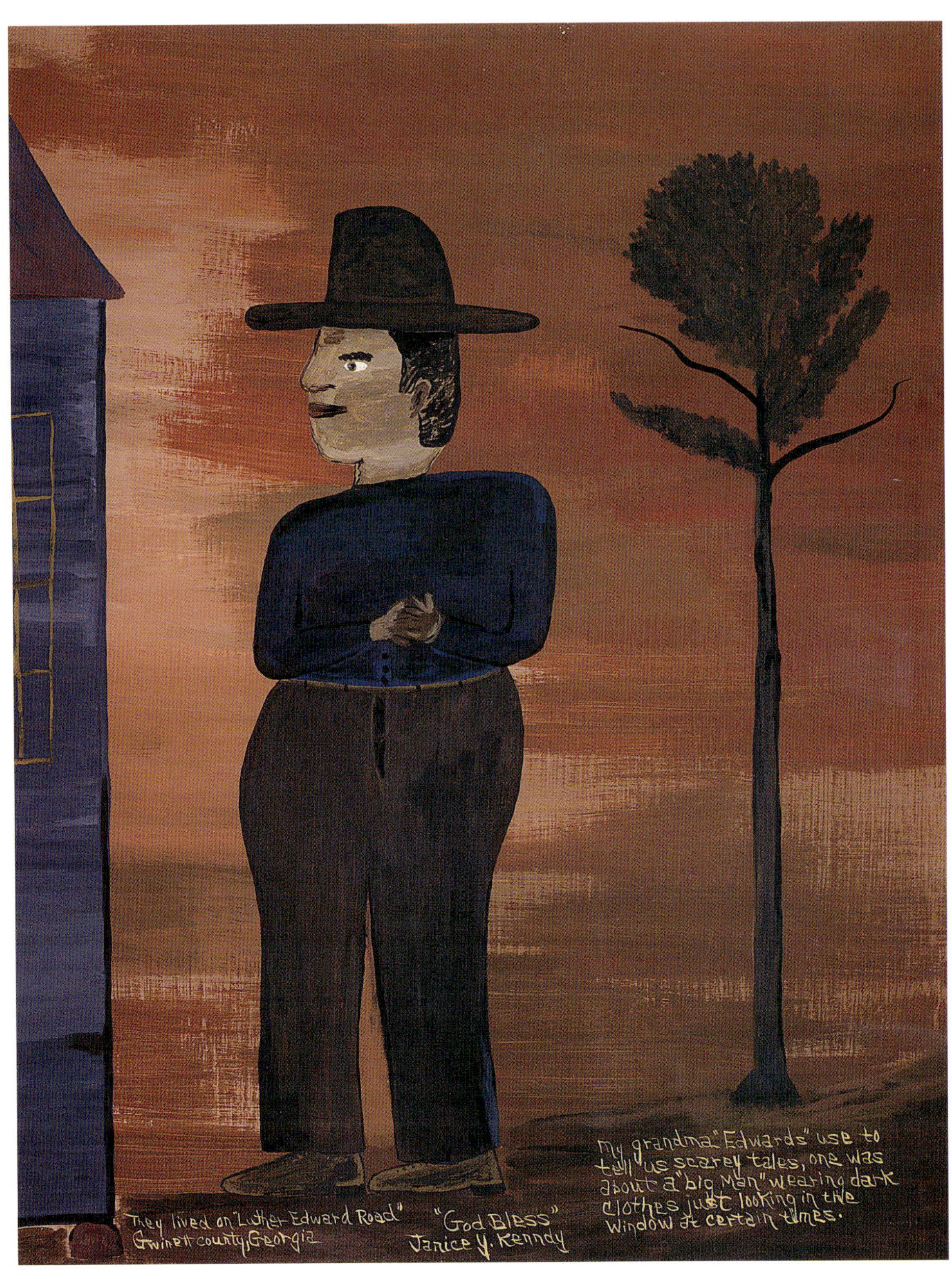

Janice Kennedy. *A Big Man Wearing Dark Clothes.* 19.5" x 15.5".

JANICE KENNEDY

b. 1941

Janice Kennedy always liked art, but it wasn't part of the lives of her Georgia sharecropper family. She longed to escape to a better, fuller life—one that would exclude her father, who was "a horrible man, possessed by the devil." In a perverse way, however, her father may be the source of her creativity; for if she had not suffered abuse, Kennedy might not have had the impetus to paint the soul-searching images through which she has tried to come to terms with her past. She tells how her father kept her from attending school so that he would have her to labor in the fields and how he hired her out to other sharecroppers after she had pulled his cotton.

The figure in her painting that includes the text "My Grandma Edwards used to tell us scary tales, and one was about a 'big man' wearing dark clothes just looking into the window at certain times" is cast from a low vantage point and positioned beside a two-story farmhouse near a thin-trunked tree. Leafless branches suggest doom. The man's body is the size of the building, and he gazes ominously toward the structure. A rusty sky—its apocalyptic tenor heightened by an eerie muted orange glow—is more a backdrop than a background. Only the white of the man's eye is bright. Kennedy is aware that the man never really existed, but she is still haunted by his presence.

This painting is not typical of the artist's body of work. It is, however, evocative of her psychological history. It took a nervous breakdown for Kennedy to begin to get over her past. After suffering the breakdown, Kennedy "found Jesus, was born again, and began painting." That's when she "buried" her deceased father. She says that now "the Lord guides my thoughts and my hand."

With morning light filtering through the blinds in the Kennedys' Citrus Park trailer, she prays and lets the past manifest in the present. Kennedy sees her harsh past as part of history. As she describes southern environs, she reclaims her youth. So she freely changes "the gray skies to sunshine," tampering with history to express her hope that others will know but never experience the hardships that she did. Meanwhile, her husband, Richard, dutifully and proudly refinishes old frames to show off the images that celebrate his wife's rebirth.

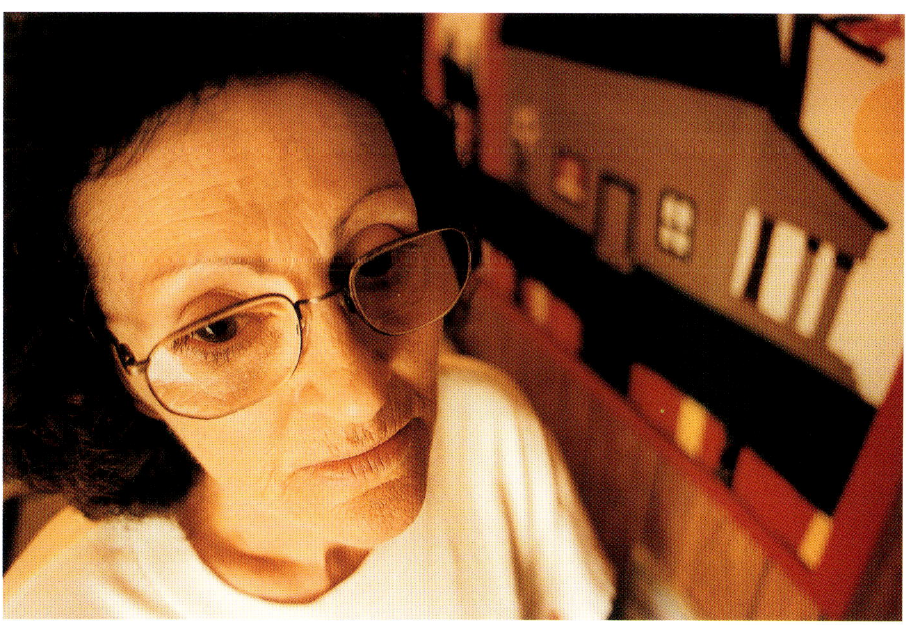

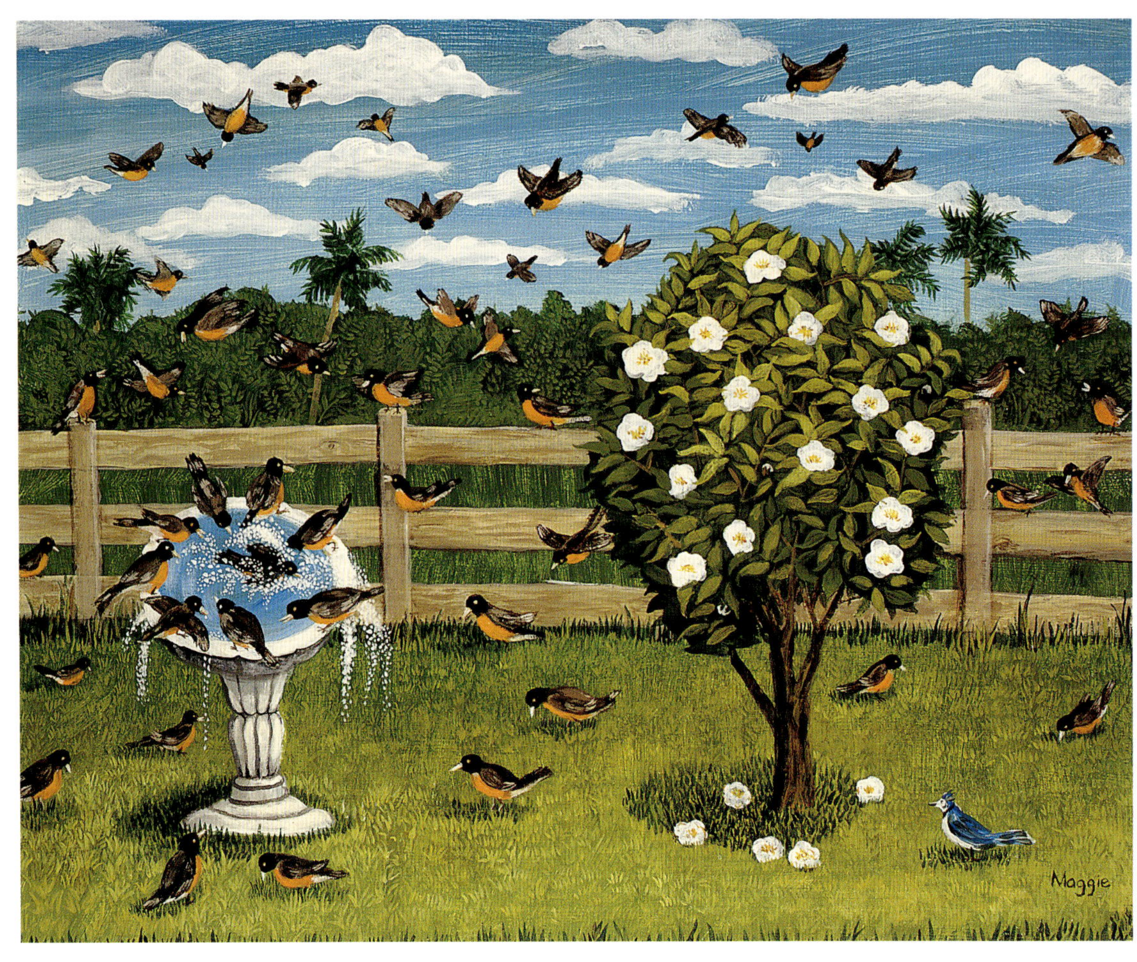

Margot Warren. *51 Robins.* 1983. 13.5" x 17.25".

MARGOT WARREN

b. 1929

Margot Warren studied textile design and worked in the industry until marrying and having children. After a twenty-year hiatus from the arts, including relocating from Philadelphia to Winter Haven in 1969, the glowing quality of winter light inspired her to pick up her brushes once again. Then she began painting everyday scenes in the tradition of American nationalism.

Her subject matter consists of the things that impress her about Florida living. Warren builds upon these perceptions—her husband watering the plants, cows grazing, migrants picking fruit, her grandchildren swimming in the community pool—by showing multiple activities in a single painting. She "tilts the land"; less than gaining a bird's-eye view, this shows perspective (via height on the picture plane), but more important, it allows her to integrate her training in the design arts. The backgrounds contain primary forms that repeat themselves; within these shapes, patterns bring the images to life. Her style yields a sense of the events happening over time.

Her work *51 Robins,* painted early in Warren's revived career, shows her backyard during winter. Migrating robins once stopped there on their way farther south and again a few months later, during their return. About the image, she says: "There would be literally hundreds of them at a time for about four or five days. Now we never see them." Perhaps this is because the orange grove that was behind her property—and that she thinks offered the migrating birds refuge—gave way to a housing development.

Warren's paintings are unlike Bettye Williams's work, in which a pastoral bliss seduces viewers; and Warren's seem antithetical to the visual exorcisms that Janice Kennedy undertakes in her painting. Another painting seems to reside beneath each of Warren's lovely images. Some viewers may be charmed by the artist's skill and patience or by the ethos that the paintings describe. Others might consider that the painted veneers represent her hopes, dreams, and regrets.

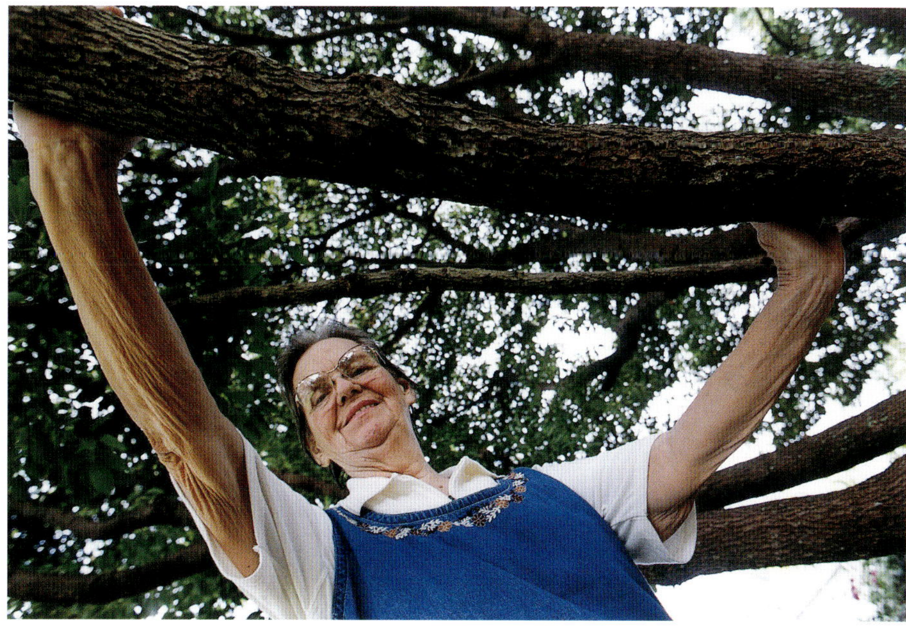

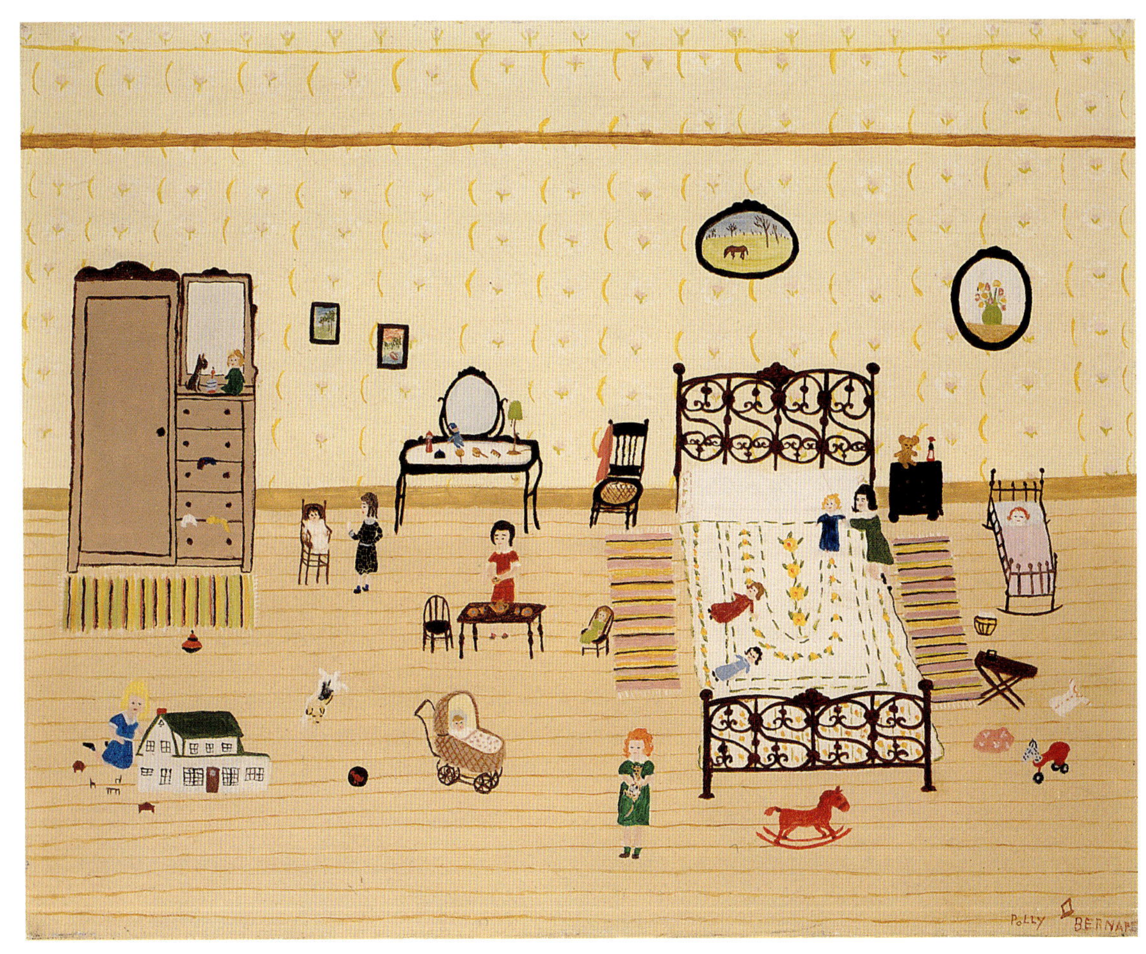

Polly Bernard. *Girls Playing House.* 1978. 16" x 20".

POLLY BERNARD

b. 1925

Polly Bernard is a pleasant, matter-of-fact lady, and her memory paintings are nonjudgmental recollections from her youth. They are reconstructions of the observable world, the facts of her childhood. She does not examine herself or reveal her feelings. There is poetry, though, in her very evocative paintings. Her isolated people and objects come together to reveal a private reality. "Painting brings back a lot of nice memories," she says as she sits in her Floral City home, the one-traffic-light town's former post office and general store. Built in 1883, it is similar to the places she depicts.

Working from family snapshots, each painting becomes a surreal album; a collection of vignettes forming a portrait of the artist's past. Mostly, Bernard's art appears charming, consistent with her primitive style and her fondness for the past. There's something bittersweet, too, which perhaps results from her approach: "When I paint my memories, my mind and vision go into the room; I'm right into the room or area with the people I paint. Maybe this is 'extra vision.'" Bernard populates her images with friends, passersby, and relatives from her youth. Sometimes she uses a bird's-eye view to delineate things clearly—perhaps depicting them as a child might imagine his or her world. This technique creates a sense of the artist's detachment. In stasis, the world exists beyond the frame in all dimensions. Perhaps what she's thinking about is not the stuff of polite society. Bernard reveals this much when discussing her painting *Christmas Memories*:

> I can tell you about any person in the painting. That's Aunt Jeanette. She was in her twenties, in the 1920s. She had tuberculosis. She got healed from tuberculosis but she had a ruptured appendix. And it was her monthly time. In that time doctors didn't operate on women when they had their menstrual period. The poison went into her body. She died. The doctor cried. She was going to be married, after the healing of her appendix. So my mother and my aunt were working on a wedding dress and her wedding dress turned out to be her shroud. I see her sometimes. She comes to me sometimes in the night. I'm psychic.

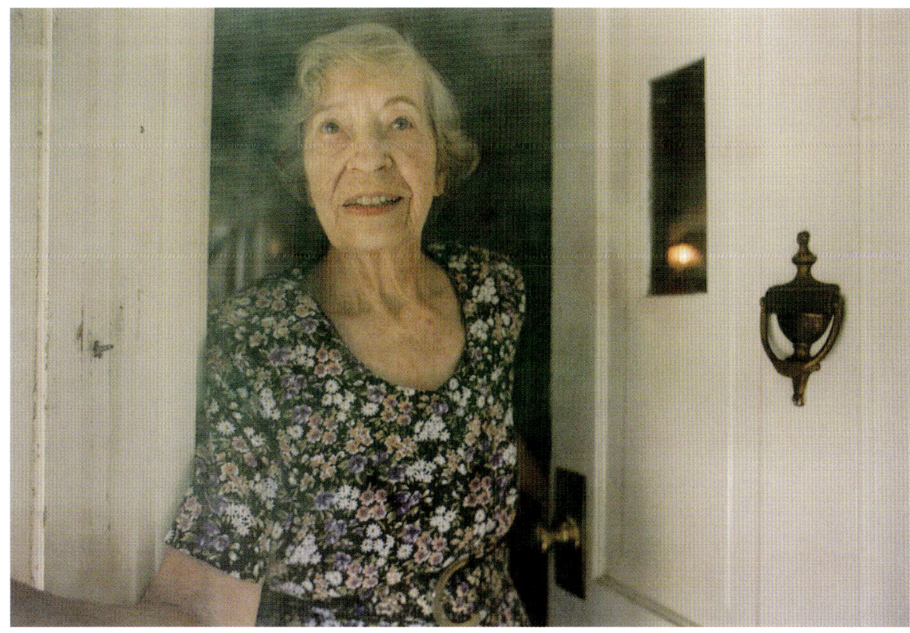

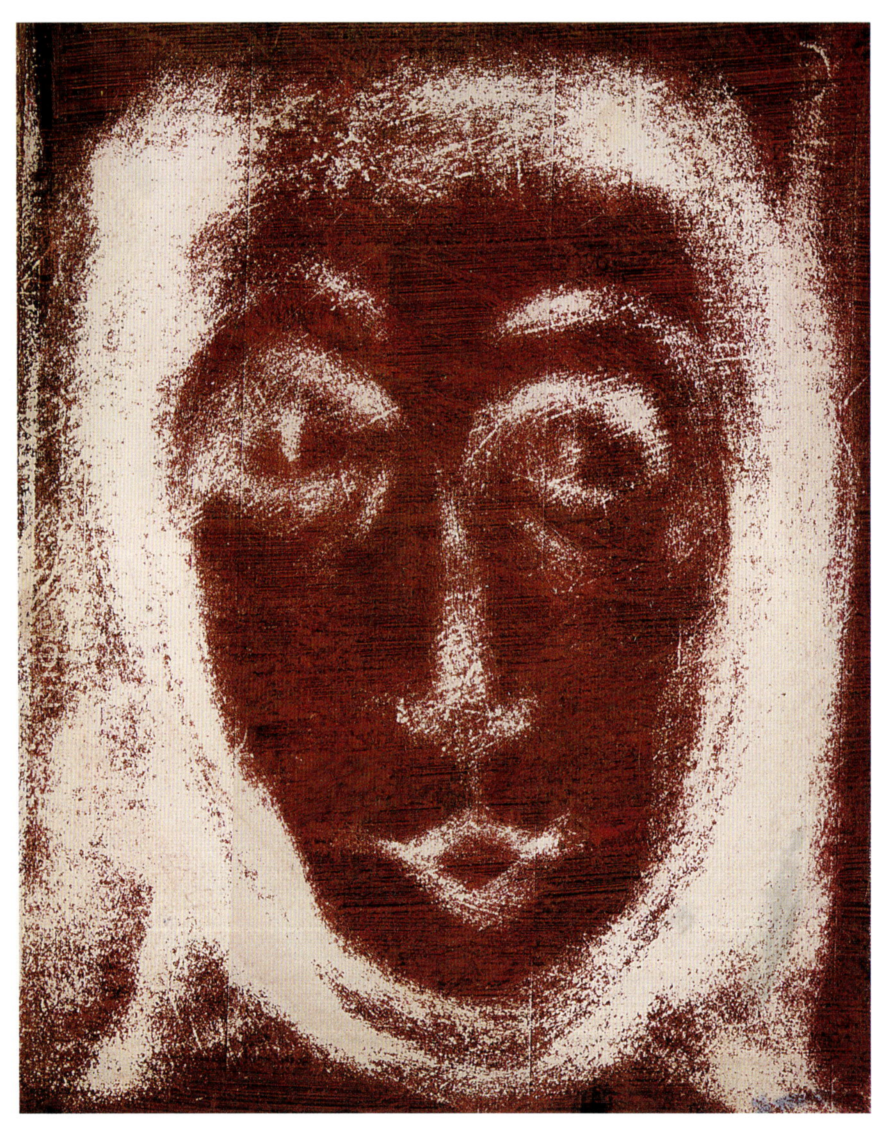

Trish Gullett. *Outside—Inside.* 12.25" x 9.75".

TRISH GULLETT

b. 1942

When Dwaine Gullett used to head an international oil company, he and his wife, Trish, maintained an apartment in London, another in Manhattan, and a vacation home in the mountains of North Carolina. However, when Mrs. Gullett began to study psychic phenomena and Spiritualism—a religion based on the belief in the continuity of life and communication with those who have passed on to the Spirit Plane—the Gulletts' life began to change. Today they live in a villa in a tennis and golf resort at Wesley Chapel. Their days and evenings spent in this "sacred space" are quieter and more reflective than those of their former jet-set lifestyle.

Because of her ability to empathize, Trish Gullett has since earned her mediumship and now "reads" for people, encouraging personal responsibility and spiritual growth. In addition to her work as a medium, Gullett creates "portraits of and from the other side." Trusting in the higher power of her spirit guides, she allows the images to come forth, acknowledging that the paintings "aren't totally me [mine]" but are rather a collaboration in which the spirits direct her. She begins each portrait by tracing an unseen sign of the cross, dragging paint from eye to eye and down the length of the nose as a blessing and a prayer. She blots the paint on cardboard and moves the pigment around with her fingers. Then, by sponging (usually) purple acrylic to blend and absorb excess material, an image is formed. She is directed to scrape the paper with steel wool, transforming the picture in a way that makes it look like a photographic negative.

If energy fails to flow through her hands, the colors become muddy or blend poorly. Otherwise, the faces that appear are portraits of those who have passed away. Sometimes, the spirits identify themselves to her.

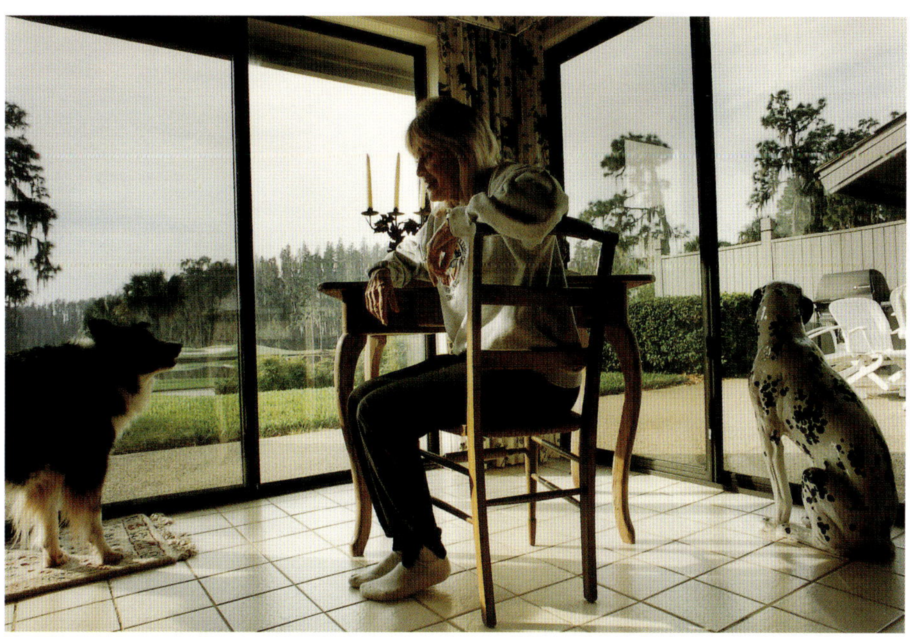

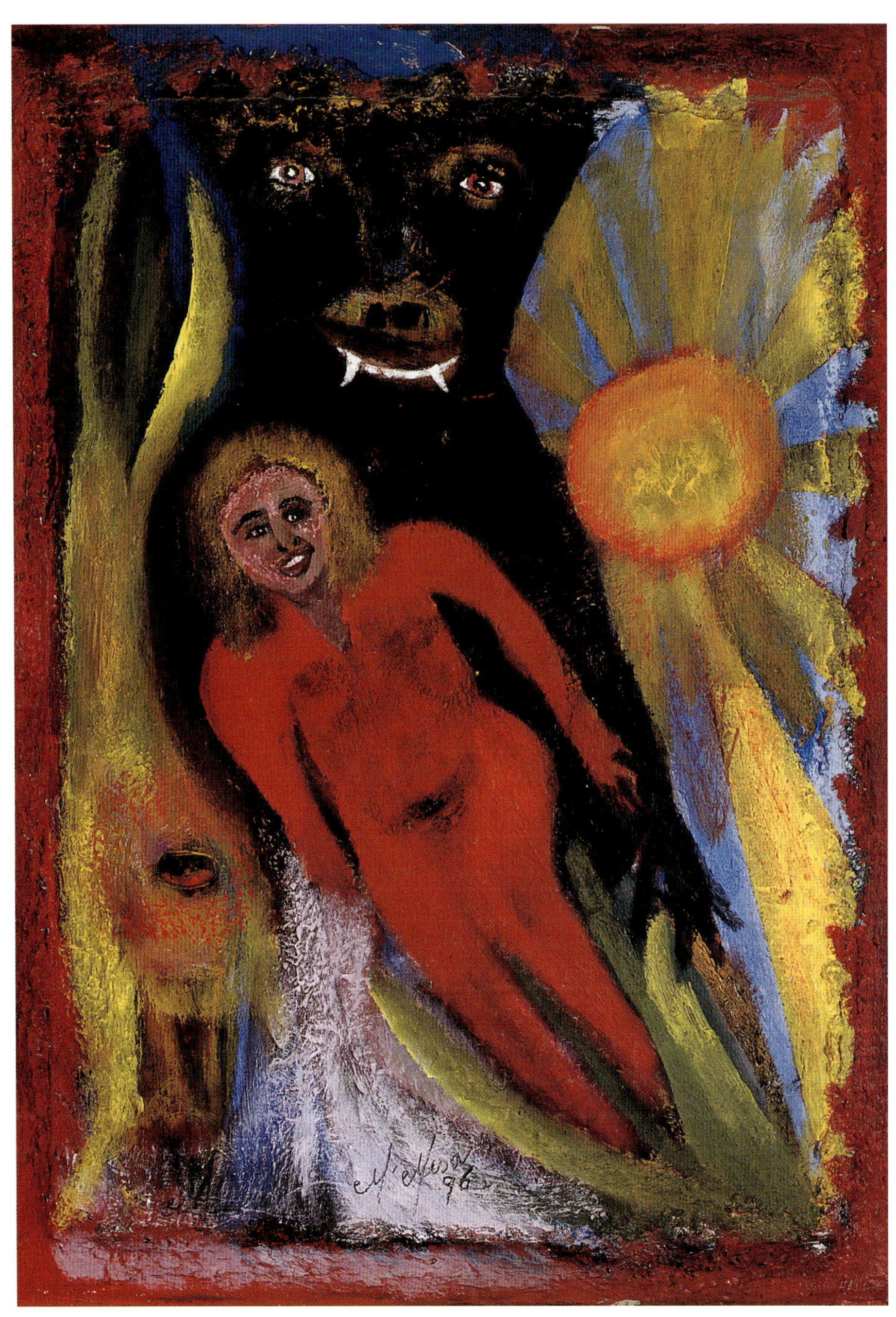

Mario Mesa. Untitled. 27.75" x 19.5".

MARIO MESA

b. 1928

Mario Mesa was among the 125,000 Cubans who fled their homeland on the Mariel Boatlift of 1980. He now lives in Miami's "Little Havana." When an emotional crisis led to his hospitalization in 1991, he began his creative journey. Mesa paints every day "to do something good for society." He proclaims, "I don't believe in the existence of anybody who doesn't give something back to society."

When Mesa closes his eyes, he sees things—things that spirits bring forth. He paints what they want, not what he wants. He says that he is possessed; spirit comes to him and imagery emerges through him. Although the pictures derive from his unconscious mind—if not from another realm altogether—"almost everything is real." Overtones of fantasy and wonder, a form of magic realism that is free flowing and unbridled, intensify the reality.

Mesa paints jungles with a woman's face and a fierce catlike creature peering through the leaves. His figures waft around and rise like smoke. They are abundant, fecund like tropical fruit. His paintings are sublime and surreal, dreamy but with an edge. Mesa's paintings are rooted in the everyday lives of his neighbors, and he offers codified and morally pointed messages for them. For instance, the devil symbolizes the physical illness and social problems brought on by drug abuse.

Mesa understands why his warnings are seldom heeded, why "they never change," and why they cannot. The artist believes that "all that has happened has happened before." His experiences and sensitivities give weight to his observations, especially as they are transformed through the mysterious process of painting. Mesa taps into something primal that helps to communicate his meaning. Maybe his position can be expressed by André Gide's observation that "art is a collaboration between God and the artist, and the less the artist does the better."

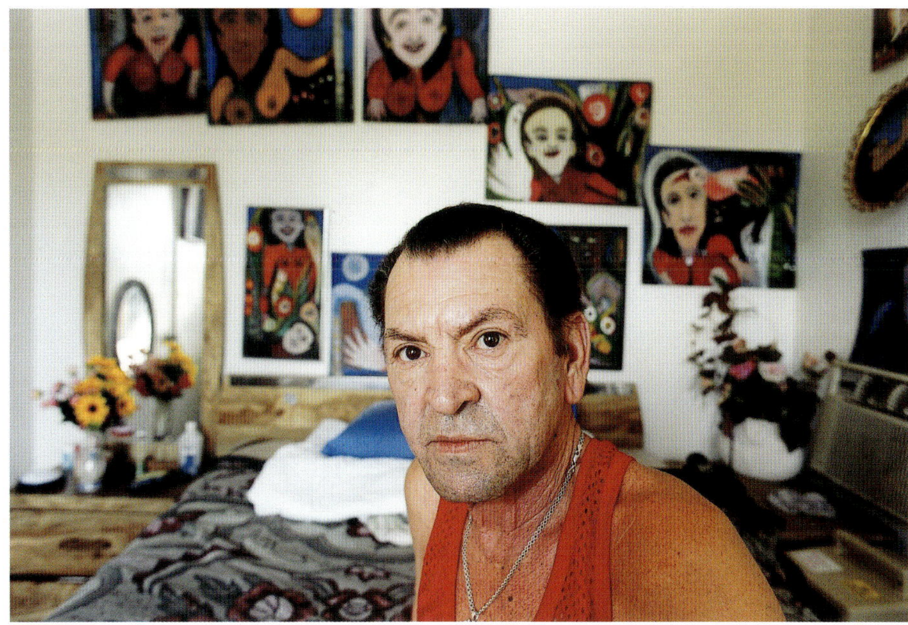

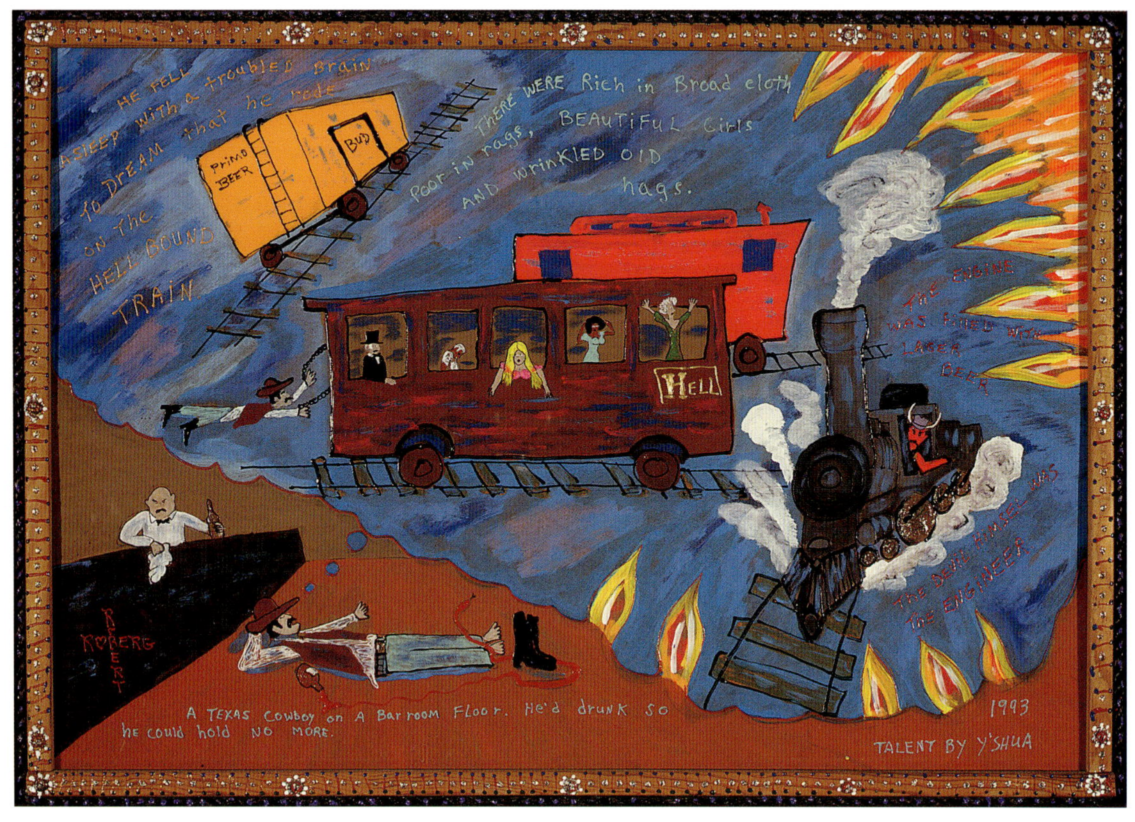

Robert Roberg. *Hellbound Train.* 1993. 22.75" x 32.5".

ROBERT ROBERG

b. 1943

Religion and religious tales inspire many self-taught artists, but Robert Roberg's paintings pay homage to Christian tenets with a vengeance. An unimposing, gentle man, Roberg was more often abused by people than listened to when he preached on street corners in Nashville, Tennessee. He once had worked at making art but then destroyed all his drawings because he viewed them as sacrilegious. But one day he picked up a piece of chalk and drew a visual reference to Scripture on the sidewalk to "tell them how to find their way into Yah's Divine Empire." Passersby stopped, looked, and listened. Their attention to this visual communication rekindled Roberg's interest in painting.

Roberg now lives in Palmetto, a depressed town on the Gulf Coast. Even though his work is about socially abhorrent behavior such as the dangers of alcohol, he is plagued by the fear that recognition or financial reward could undermine his commitment to paint in the Lord's service without compromise. He signs his name in the shape of a cross and notes "Talent by Y'Shua" on each painting, taking no credit for the vision. A written message, like a Commandment, completes each piece. The Book of Revelation inspired his recent work, apocalyptic scenes painted on a van that he intends to drive across the United States to further spread the Word.

Still, Roberg appears angst-ridden as he wonders why, with such clear messages and graphic delivery, people are still confused about how to live their lives.

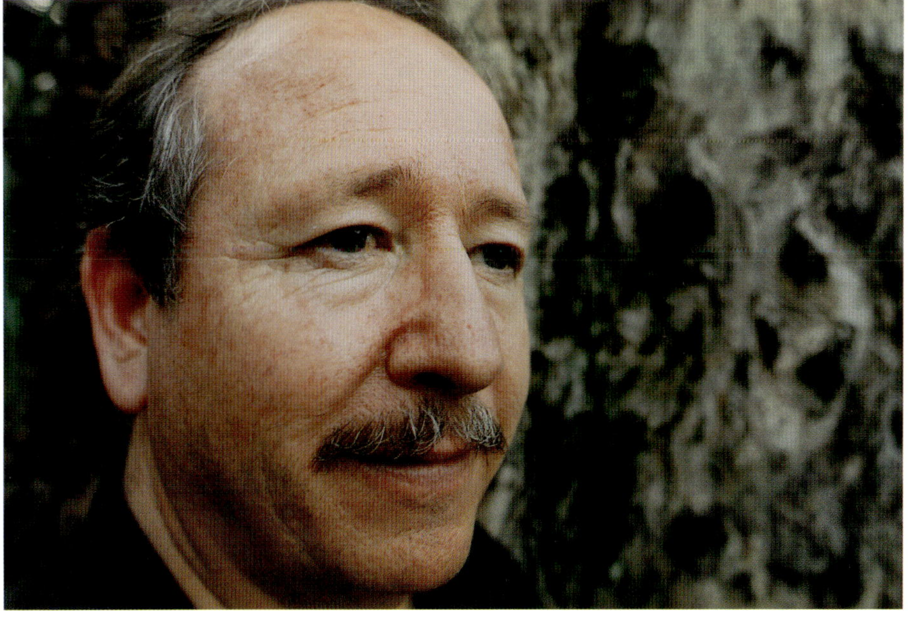

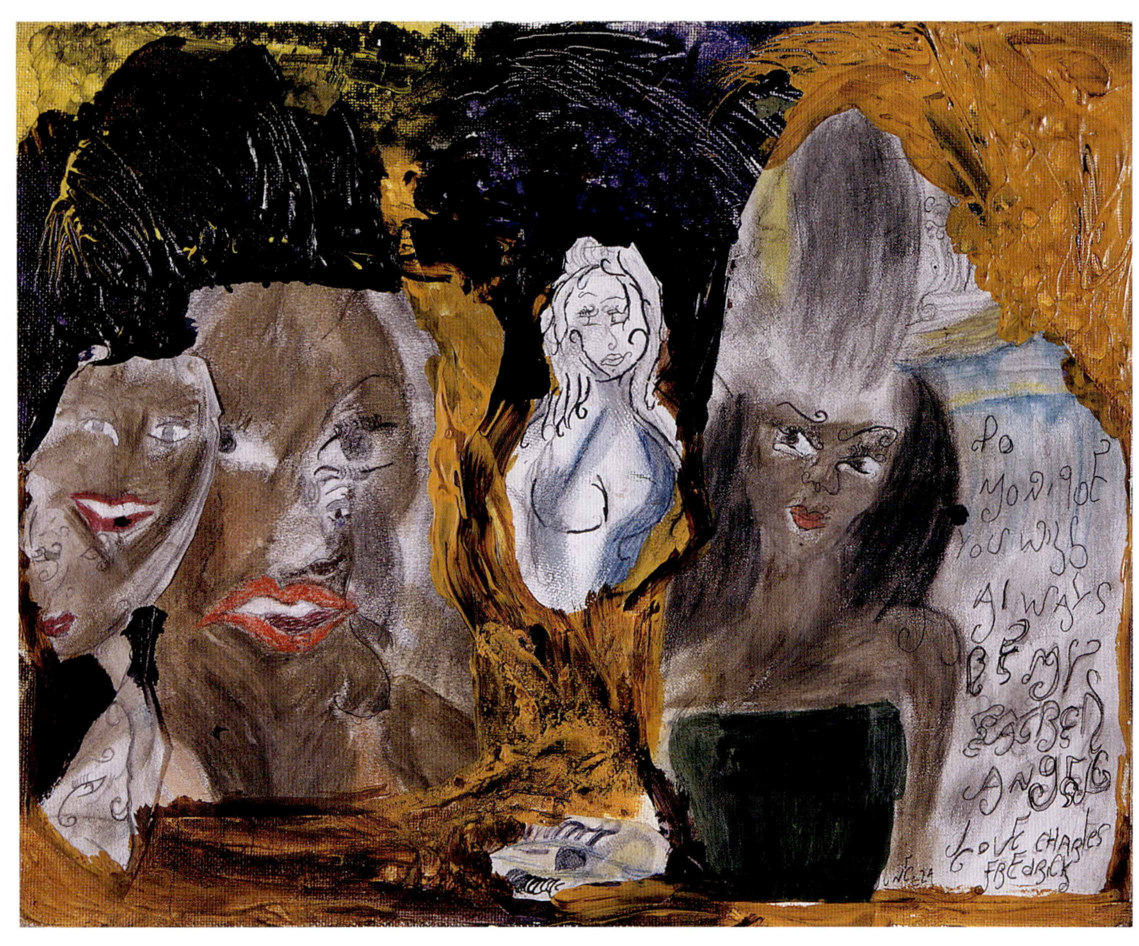

Charles Courtney. *Flames of Passion.* 2001. 11" x 14".

CHARLES COURTNEY

b. 1969

What his mother, Mary, describes as "pretty scary visions of naked women and very strange planetary stuff," Charles "Chuck" Courtney says is going to make him famous one day.

Mary claims that her son "uses his art to bandage and communicate his frustration in dealing with a world that sees him as different." To this he replies, "No I don't!" Perhaps he doesn't see himself as different; he has an aristocratic air—not stuffy but unconsumed by worldly concerns. He has, of course, the same desires as everyone else. An attractive young woman named Monique, he says, "is my muse." In spite of her recent marriage to another man, he still cares for her. He smiles, seems to shrug it off, perhaps giving in to *his* reality.

When Courtney was twenty months old, he opened the front door of his grandparents' home and wandered outside and into the path of oncoming traffic. He was struck by a van. Massive skull fractures caused by the terrifying accident left him speech-impaired and paralyzed on his right side. After enduring every parent's nightmare, his mother can proudly say that her son "is focused, self-disciplined. If there's something he wants to do, he keeps after it." He does it with good cheer. Although the paralysis is gone and he has learned to speak, there are hard times brought on by remaining neurological damage. And it's likely that his art is a way of coping or coming to terms with his disability.

He writes elegantly, exposing himself freely:

> I remember when I said; all I wanna do is make you happy, she said: you should make yourself happy, I should have said; what if making you happy does make me happy? Man! I am 33 yrs. old, never been kissed on the lips by a woman. I feel like as if I were a volcano ready to erupt.

Courtney refuses to sit on the sidelines. He draws and paints in a small Tallahassee house that he and his mother share. His mother is probably correct; he creates to express himself, to cope and to grow. Courtney's own reflection confirms her observations: "I used to write gothic poetry; now it's all about love and emotional frustration."

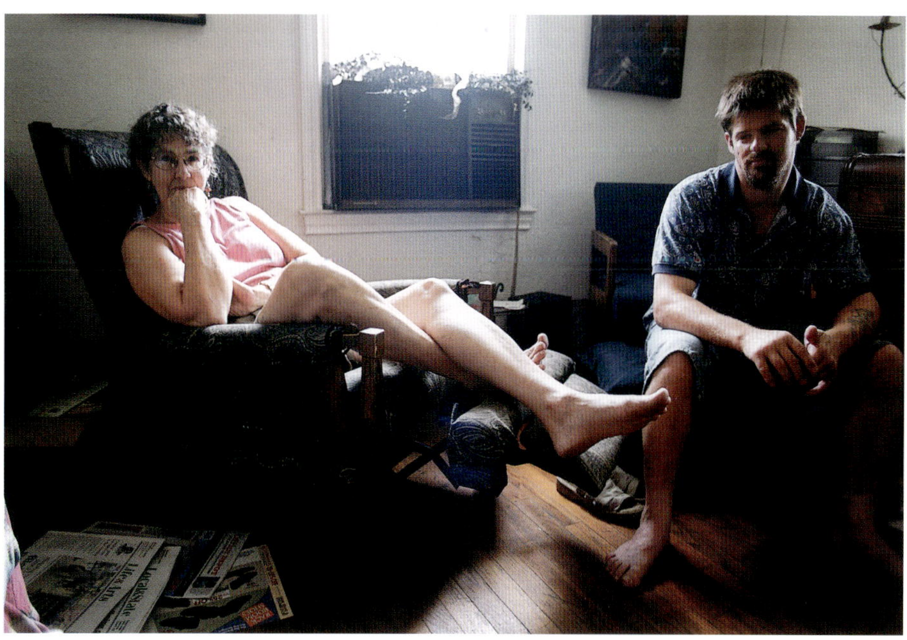

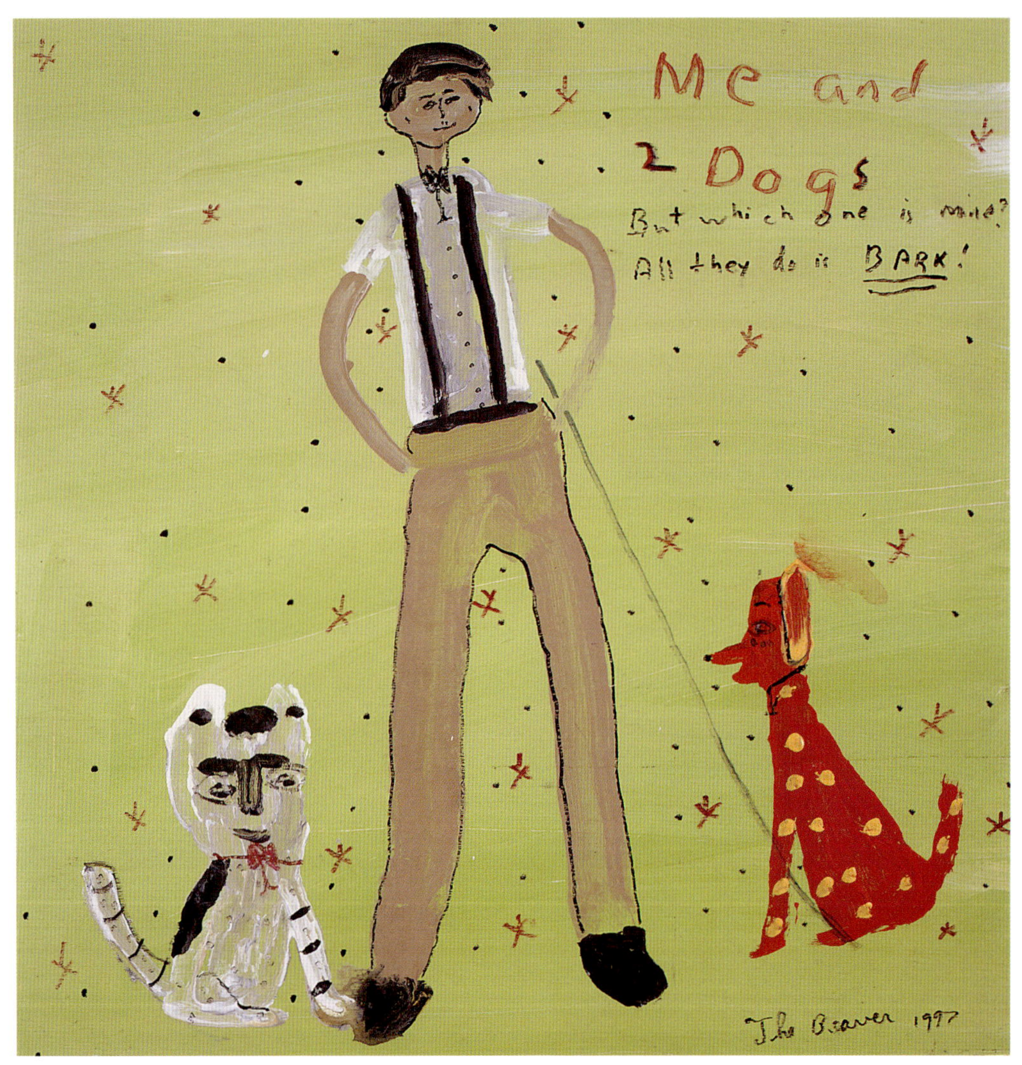

Robyn Beverland. Untitled. 1997. 24" x 24".

ROBYN BEVERLAND

1957–1998

Robyn Beverland, known as "The Beaver," was born with Wolfram Syndrome, a genetic disorder that he shared with fewer than seventy other Americans at the time of his death.

In spite of, or perhaps because of, the blow that fate had dealt him, Beverland appeared to have been able to rise above the confusion and existential musings that have so often plagued other creative minds. His sense of humor and irony often made it difficult to engage him in serious conversation. As Craig Pittman of the *St. Petersburg Times* once remarked, The Beaver is "always shooting off wisecracks like a man without a care in the world. Ask him how he started painting and he'll joke, 'I was born with a paintbrush in my hand.'"

Actually, The Beaver began painting in 1990 when his father, Jerry, gave him art supplies in the hope that making art might have some therapeutic value. At the time of his death eight years later, hundreds of paintings were stacked by his work table and along the walls of his studio in the backyard of the Beverlands' bay-front home in Oldsmar.

Family portraits, roosters, and dogs—all with iconic presences—were among the artist's favorite subjects. Once he envisioned a picture, it took only a few minutes for him to achieve the crudely rendered but striking image on squares of plywood. His subjects are presented without context, without even a horizon. At times he painted on long planks, a format that did not facilitate the use of conventional perspective or traditional pictorial structure. These techniques give Beaverland's work an immediacy and clarity that it might otherwise lack.

Asked about his palette, Beverland once stated that he chose his colors by reading the labels on the cans of house paint that he used. He explained that since he was colorblind (as well as legally blind), that was the most expedient way for him to deal with color. However, according to his mother, Wanda, the hues that her son selected were generally reflective of his mood.

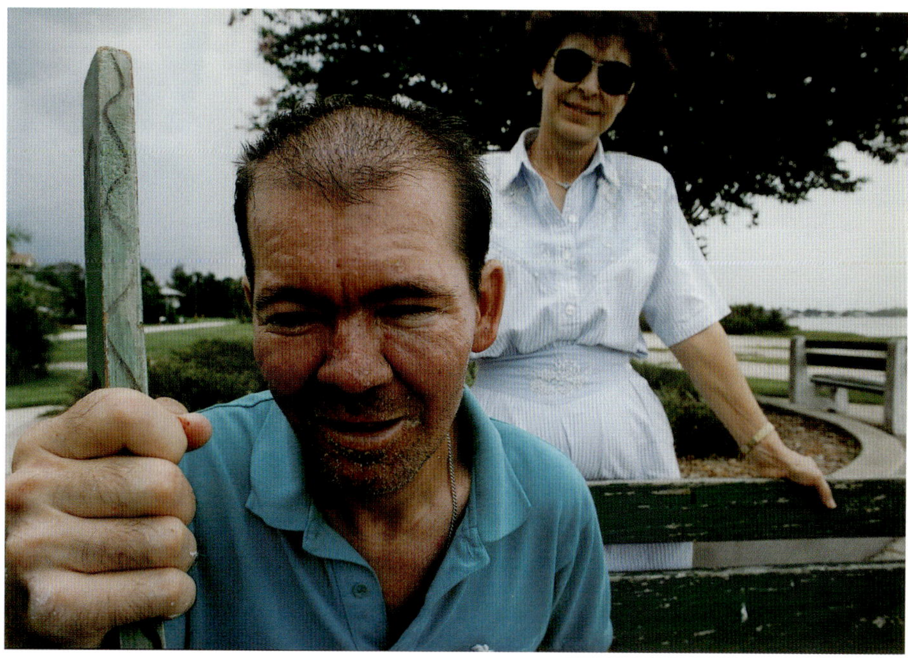

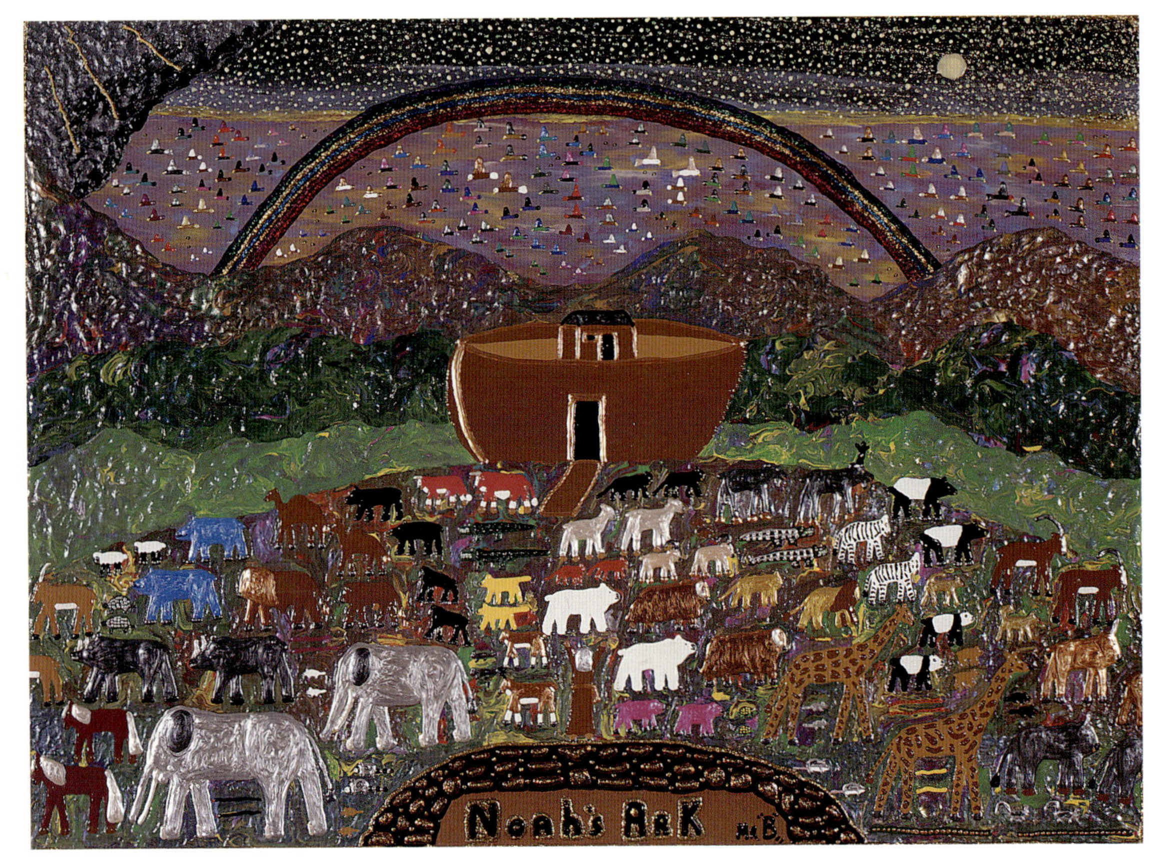

Jack Beverland. *Noah's Ark.* 25" x 34.5".

JACK BEVERLAND

b. 1939

When Jack Beverland, The Beaver's uncle, was ousted from his middle management career in 1990 at the age of fifty-two, he vacillated between thoughts of suicide and murder. Feelings of "worthlessness, shame, confusion, embarrassment, and depression" led to an obsession for revenge. He literally polished his guns and planned the assassination of the corporate executives whom he held responsible for his "forced early retirement." He credits his brother Jerry with his survival—for taking him under his wing for more than a year, never letting him out of sight, and helping him rise above the horror that he was living.

Since art had helped The Beaver achieve emotional balance, Jerry suggested that painting might also help Jack to resolve his deep-seated anger. Jack's first efforts were simple, moralistic, and, not unexpectedly, violent. However, with time these crude and obvious visual outbursts became more reflective, even poetic, and, eventually, beautiful.

Today, Beverland continues to paint away his desperation; he has come to believe that "art should be a way out." To facilitate his escape, he often paints himself into the pictures, assuming various personas, such as "The Enforcer," who is "here to make your life miserable." At other times he appears as a gray-haired older man. When he sees through younger eyes, his hair is blond and he often smokes a pipe. Occasionally he dons Native American dress. Regardless of who is on watch, all of his paintings are signed "Mr. B," and he always sports a beard. If there are no people in a painting, his pet opossum, Big Guy, stands in.

When he takes a break from painting, Beverland finds solace in the garden of his Citrus Park home, where he has planted an Edenlike tropical jungle intended to distance him still further from the cruelties of an uncaring world.

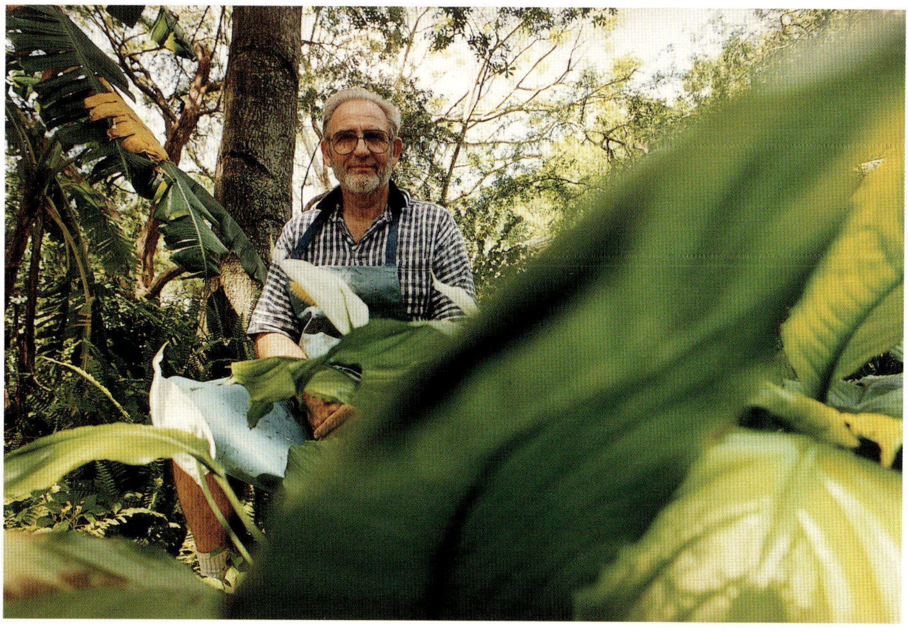

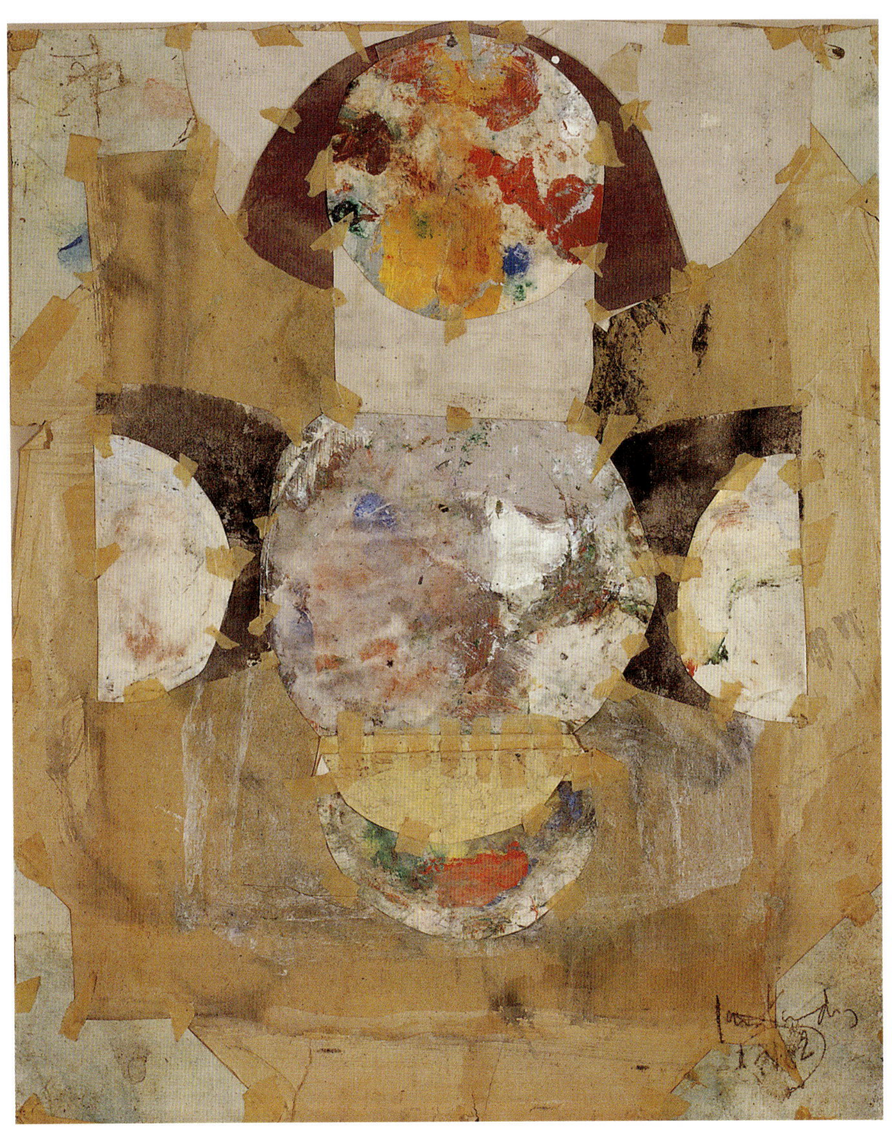

Jan Kardes. Untitled. 16.75" x 14".

JAN KARDES

b. 1949

Jan Kardes, admittedly incorrigible, dropped out of school when he was thirteen years old and left home. He grew up in the counterculture, immersed in the seedy world of urban cowboys and hookers. But Kardes was attracted to the arts. He found comfort among artists and took refuge in their studios, where he drew pictures incessantly. Still he wandered the streets, eventually settling in Key West; the southernmost city in the United States became his "personal environment." Kardes's lifestyle hasn't changed much over the decades. He's still a drifter working menial jobs, floating back and forth "between Key West and wherever." "I come here to lick my wounds," he says.

Painting has overcome drinking as his prime pursuit. He is intellectually transported by the creative process—"like astral projection"—to get a detached look at his own circumstances and worldview. A recovering alcoholic searching for clarity, Kardes developed a cosmology that he calls "Thought Fire," which he expresses in beat generation stream of consciousness. His theory holds that there is a universal pulse that, although undetectable through traditional measuring devices, binds all living things. "The constants from history to the present and into the future" are accessible only through the arts, he contends.

Painting is an education for Kardes, "part of a toolbox" with which he can discover life's essential qualities in order to learn about himself and about nature. The act of rendering sharpens his ability to perceive: "Drawing is like being able to read minds," he says. On his search for illumination, Jan Kardes uses his saliva to hold and better manipulate ink and watercolors and, more important, to identify his creations. "My DNA is in every one of my drawings," he says. Like amber encasing the secrets of ancient life.

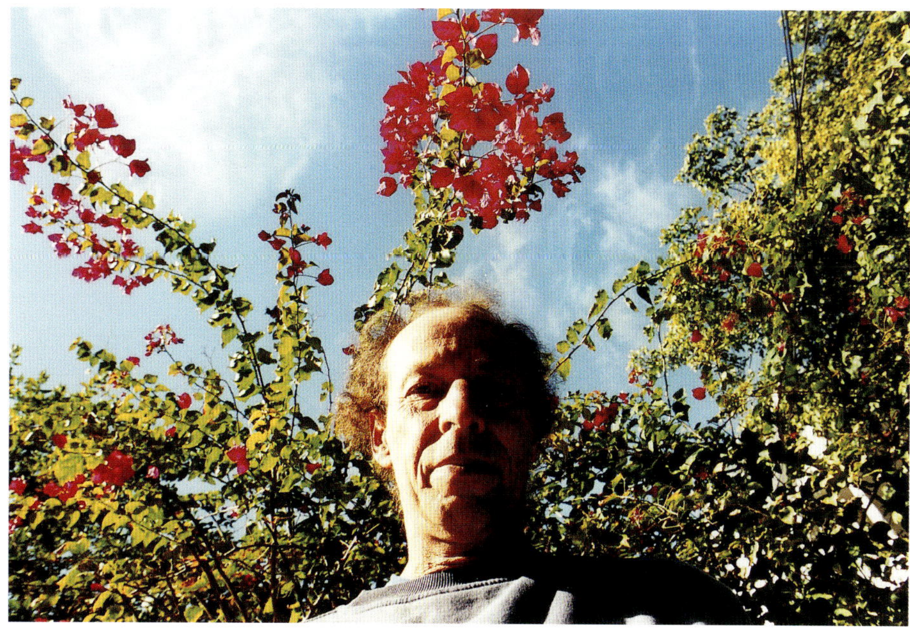

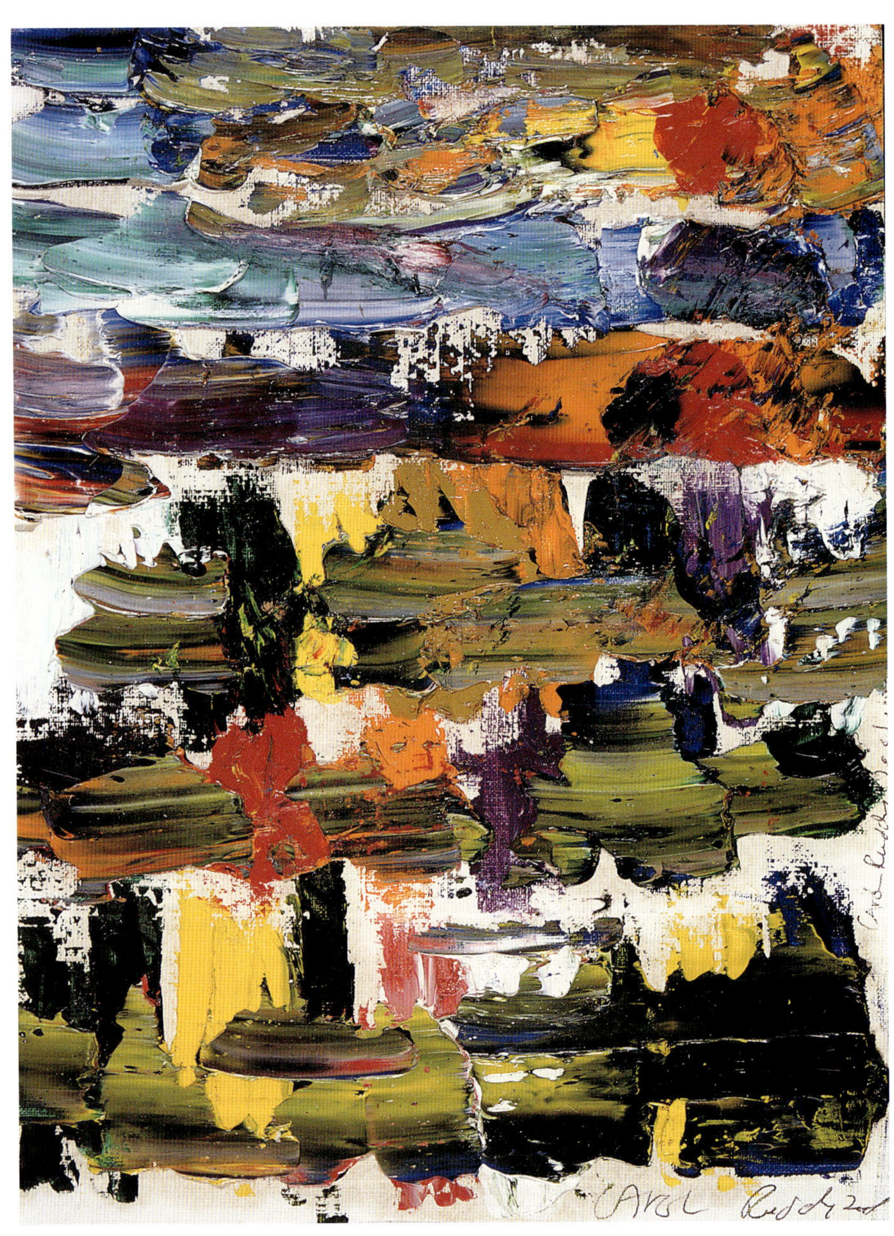

Carol Ruddy. *Mardi Gras.* 2001. 11.825" x 9".

CAROL RUDDY

b. 1950

Carol Ruddy's parents do not accept a doctor's diagnosis of schizophrenia for their daughter, but they suggest that maybe too many drugs during the late sixties, the death of a close friend, a bad split with her boyfriend, or all of these events, led to a nervous breakdown. In 1982, Ruddy committed herself to a psychiatric hospital. "Whatever the physicians gave me made me high as a kite. I was high for ten years. . . . Been on a trip ever since," she chuckles. With the help of her dedicated parents, a trusted psychiatrist, and her art supplies, Ruddy has developed self-esteem. When someone observed how very attractive her sister-in-law looked in a perfect family portrait, she added without a second's hesitation, "Yeah, but she can't paint."

While institutionalized, Ruddy was allowed to take a painting class. "But in the nut house I had to draw realistically. Made some pretty nice place mats," she jokes. Attracted to Salvador Dali, she recalls that "I wanted to be surreal, but nobody wanted to be surreal with me. It was a problem." Matisse appealed to her too. But when she saw the work of Jim Dine, Ruddy said to herself, "If he can draw a shovel in a box, I can paint!" Realizing the limitations of structured art classes, she took her last one in 1988. Now she works in a corner of the garage in the family's upscale, impeccably kept Port Orange home.

Looking at the work of Saul Steinberg for the first time, she asks, "What kind of dope is he on?" The drugs that she takes daily keep her well. No longer physically agitated or belligerent, she now can concentrate. Ruddy has no particular artistic goal, which she thinks is a result of not knowing good from bad art. But she does know that "art is my life work. It's all I have. It's like having pets."

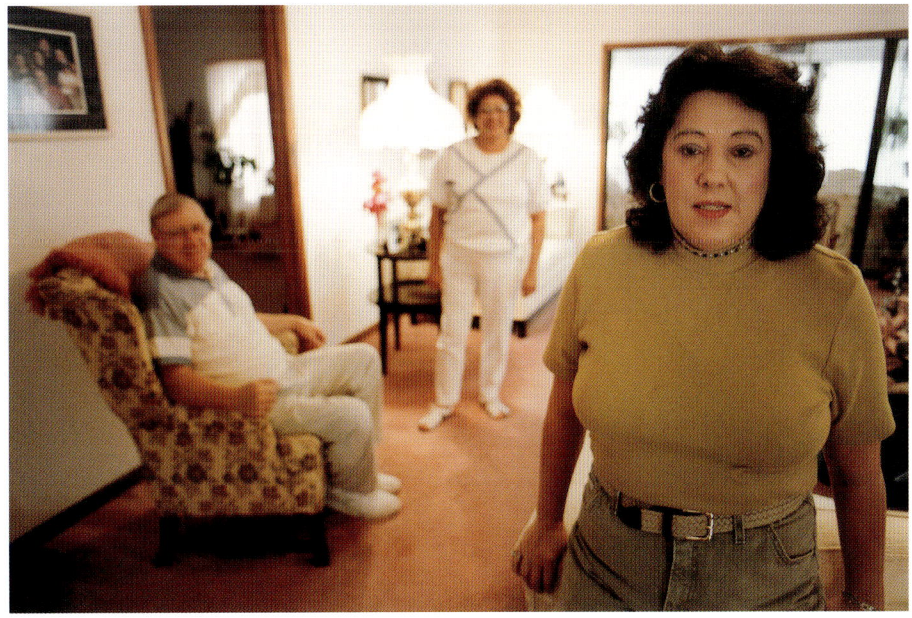

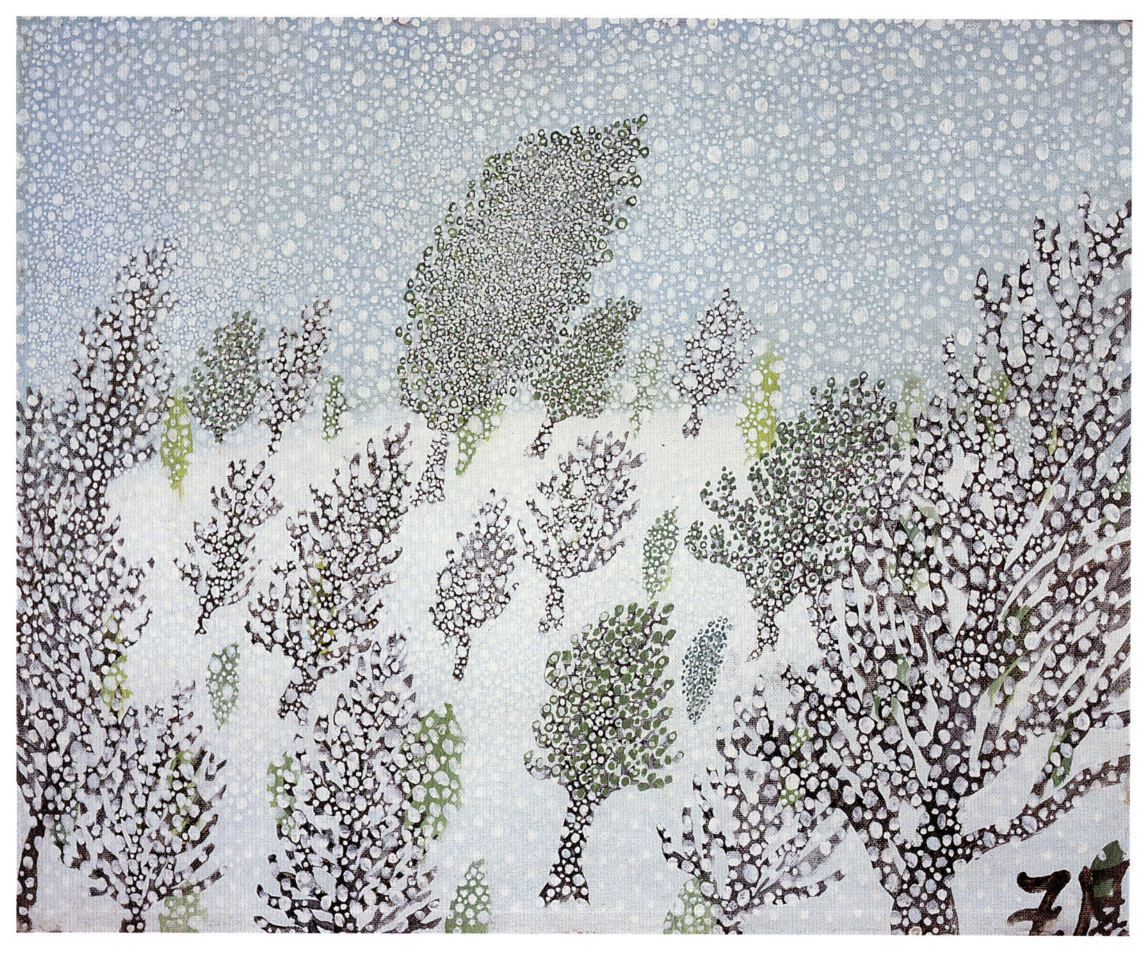

Frank Ritchie. Untitled. 16" x 20".

FRANK RITCHIE

b. 1941

Frank Ritchie lives with his parents in their modest Ormond Beach home. His father is restricted to a wheelchair or an electrically operated La-Z-Boy. A floor lamp separates the lounger from a matching chair for his mother's comfort. She recalls that Frank was very artistic as a child, but that he did not "get serious" about painting until after he was diagnosed as schizophrenic.

When Ritchie becomes nervous or if his mind begins to wander during a conversation, he makes up songs by putting the other person's words to rhythm. He sings these songs to himself while the person continues speaking. Ritchie attends Mass every morning and has recorded an album of gospel music, *He Is the Way,* for which he wrote the lyrics. He also authored a book, *How to Find Your Perfect Mate,* which outlines his theories about "blushing, speechless love." His physician and his priest denounced the book, and the album failed to sell, but Frank Ritchie's faith in God has served him well over the years, helping—along with the correct medication—to keep his spirits high.

Ritchie paints landscapes that are constructed with dots representing leaves and falling snow. His precise and intricate technique has less to do with pointillism than with the sheer joy of engaging in the process and satisfying his compulsion. He begins by painting the sky, and then he lays the ground. Next he lets his index finger "droop" over the canvas board until it gets hot, as though warmed by a candle. At that point, he plants a tree trunk. It is unclear whether the heat radiates from his finger or if flash points strike from the picture plane, but this process accounts for Ritchie's compositions. His mother points out that as a youngster her son wanted to become a meteorologist, and she speculates that an early interest in the weather might explain the artist's many snow-covered scenes.

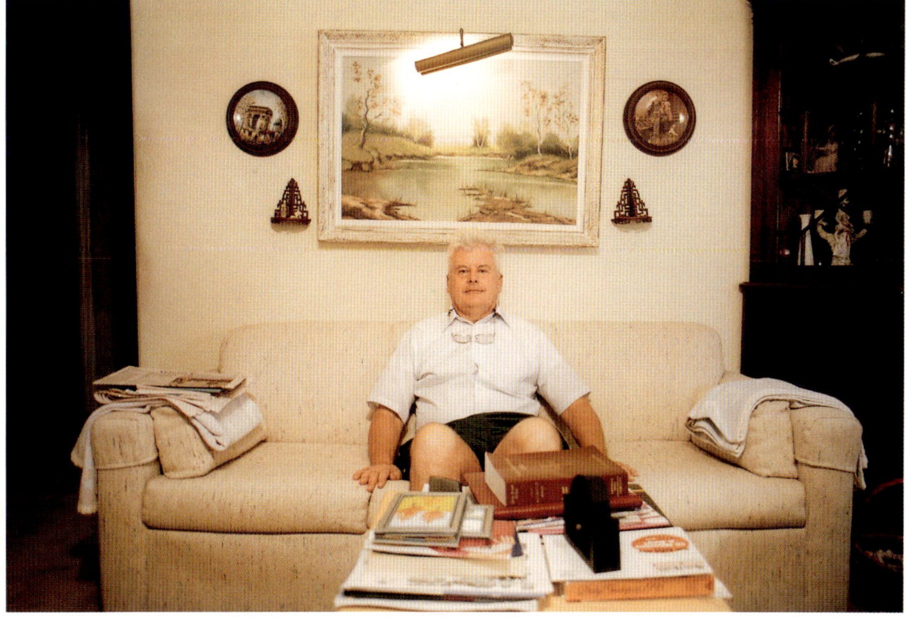

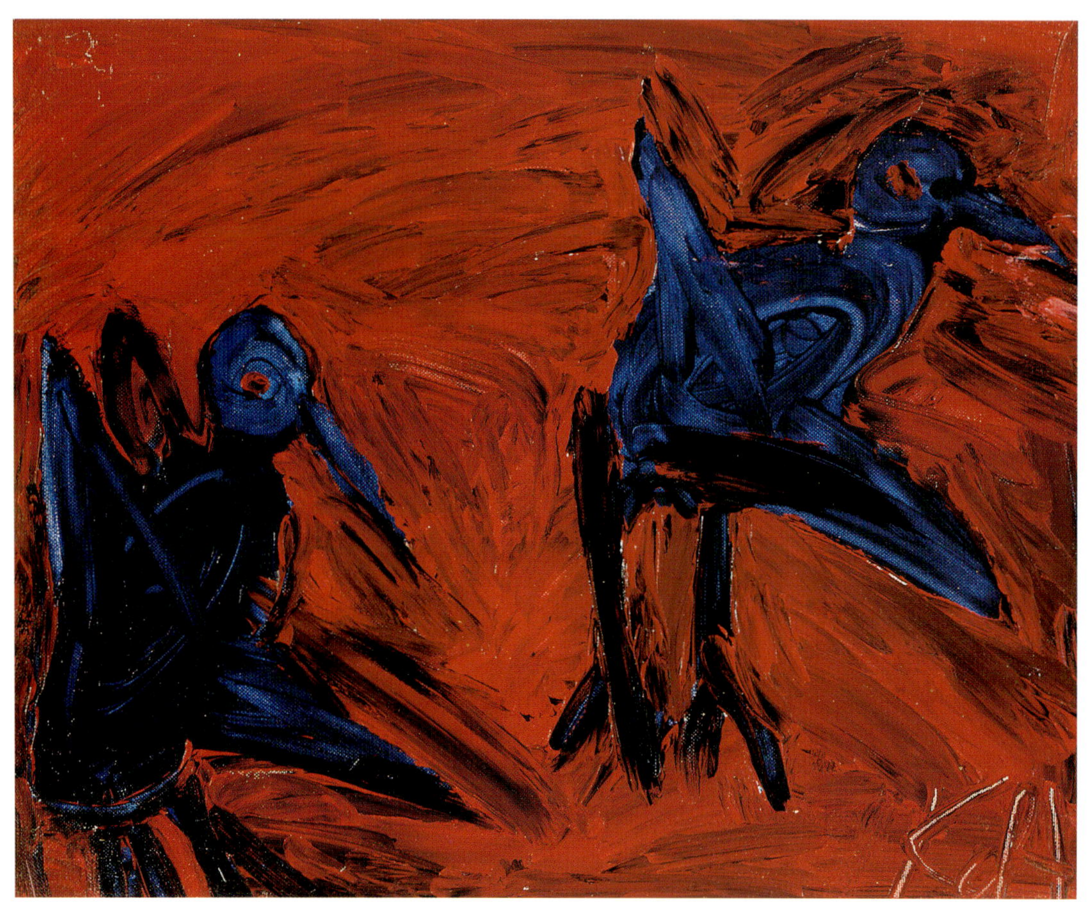

Kathy d'Adesky. *Gates of Hell.* 15.5" x 19.5".

KATHY D'ADESKY

b. 1953

A few weeks prior to graduating with a bachelor's degree in literature from Harvard University, Kathy d'Adesky ingested a substance that spiked a bowl of nonalcoholic punch at a student party. She believes that the substance was LSD. Tests never conclusively identified the drug, but the result was permanent emotional and neurological damage. She now lives with her father at their home in Ormond Beach.

In her art, as in her life, little comes between her thoughts and her actions. Audacious and hyperactive, d'Adesky acts out her paranoia and anxiety. Her paintings are bold and uninhibited, showing little concern with delicacy. She applies her paints to canvas or poster board quickly and densely. This technique is especially effective in her portrayal of flowers—a regular motif—that are always freshly realized, immediate, and invigorating. Her portraits are also powerful, capturing the person depicted with uncanny insight and expressionistic zeal. In an *Orlando Sentinel* article about d'Adesky, Vicky Koren got it right when she wrote that "colors collide and images stand out, while eager brush strokes give a continuous motion and rich texture to each piece." Yet even this vivid description is almost an understatement.

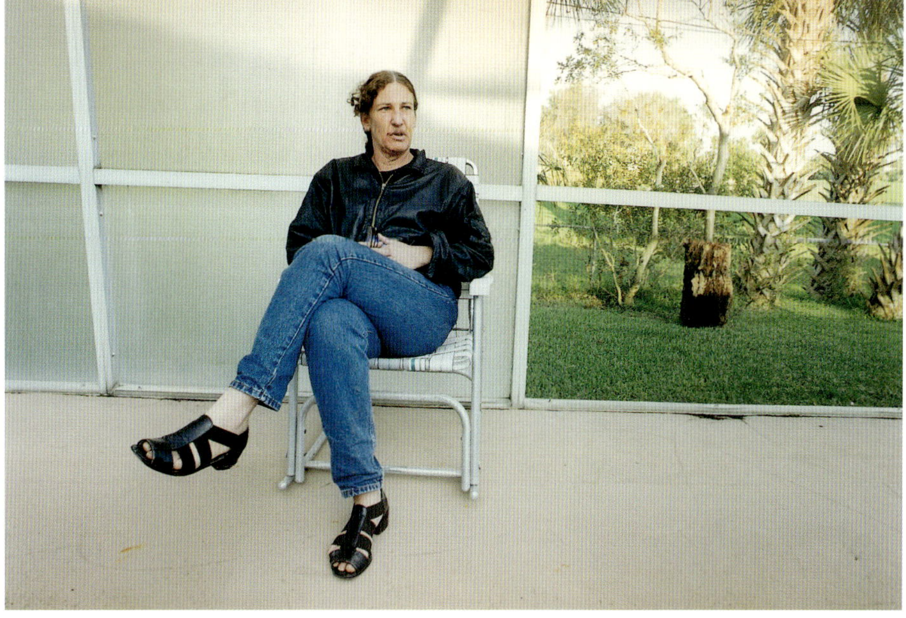

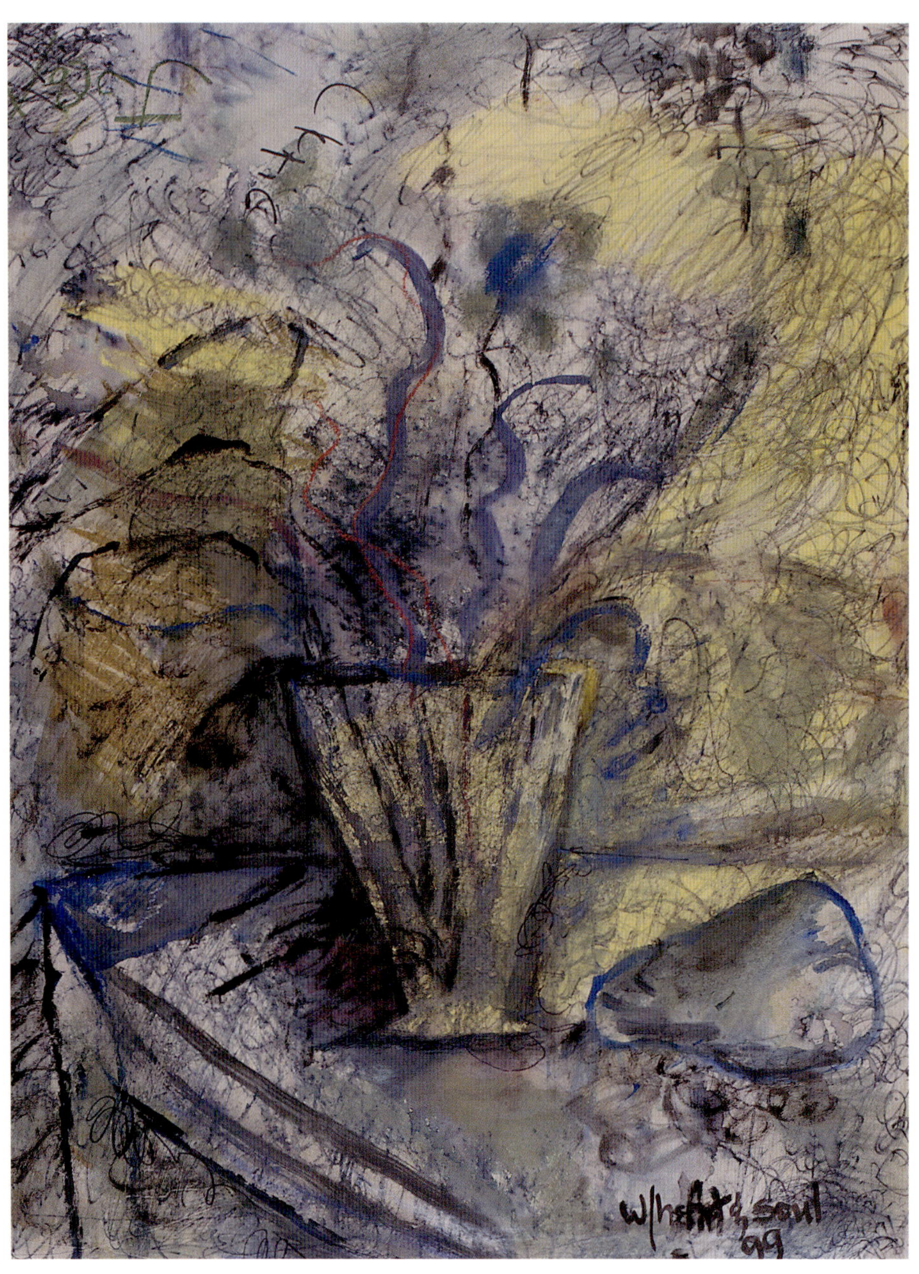

The Studio of Patricia Calamari. Untitled. 22.825" x 16.75".

PATRICIA CALAMARI

b. 1955

"Art speaks to the best part of who we are as human beings," Patricia Calamari says, while around her the artists she serves—all of whom suffer from profound mental and physical disabilities—paint under her watchful eye. In her nonprofit *heArt and soul studio* in Fort Lauderdale, art therapy in the traditional sense is abandoned along with most other conventions. Calamari's innovative creative strategies make her something of a renegade in the eyes of the art therapy establishment. She shudders at the thought of mindless, labor-intensive activities such as "making nice place mats."

While those who would dismiss the idea that the disabled possess creative potential might devalue the disparate markings of her artists, Calamari believes in these artists' potential. "Theirs is pure art," she says, explaining that these individuals communicate expressively and without ulterior motives. Calamari's process involves two or three people working on a single painting that is completed during several sessions. By understanding which artists' mark-making strengths can be best utilized to complement works-in-progress, she orchestrates the compositions by moving, turning, and positioning the paintings and pastels among the participants. With rock music blaring, the images gradually come alive. She thinks of herself as a choreographer and can identify which artists are responsible for the components of every painting.

It is difficult to know whether the creative energy in the studio originates with the teacher or the students, or whether it perhaps results from a synergy of all involved. Yet as seamless as the pictures appear, they are composites of very different artistic impulses. Even with the most literal images, it is likely, for example, that what seem to be boats are but erratic stragglings, hair a fixation with yellow, clouds a suppressed anger.

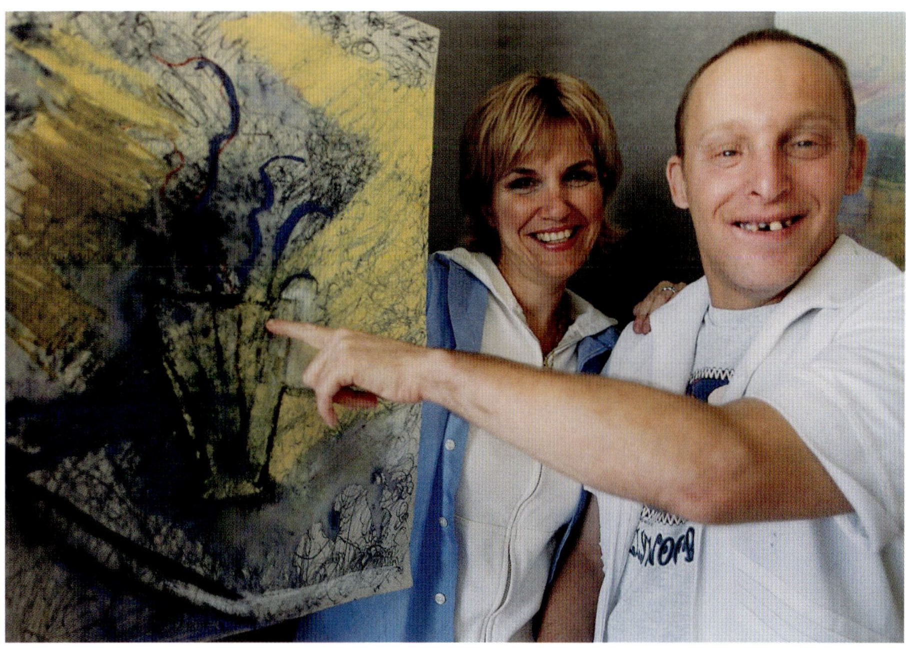

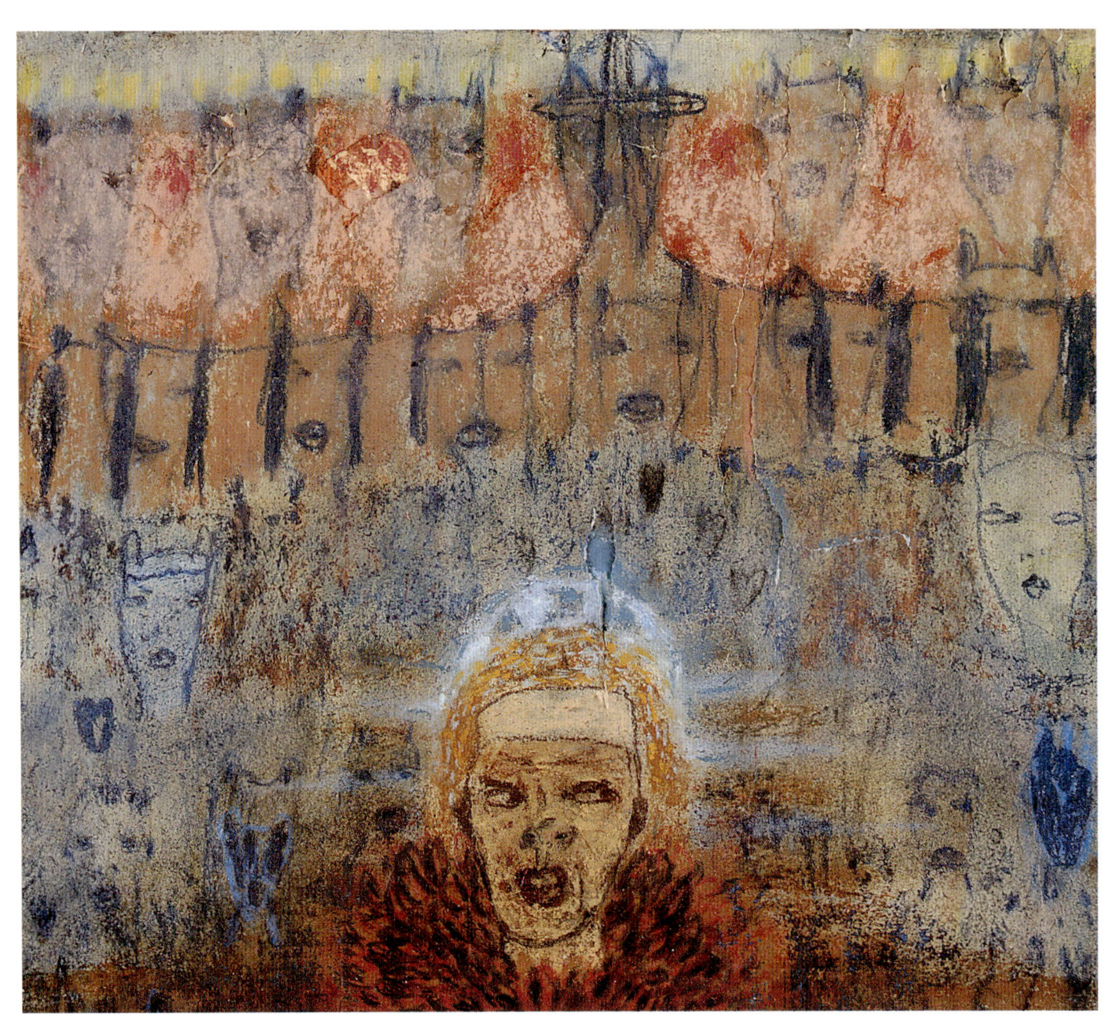

Susanne Blankemeier. *Reasoning*. 2001. 9" x 10".

SUSANNE BLANKEMEIER

b. 1953

"I learned how to keep secrets, even from myself," says Susie Blankemeier, referring to her youthful suspicion that her charismatic stepfather was involved in southern California's cultlike network of pornography and drug distribution. Living her youth in fear, she was unable to talk with her siblings about it, and isolated herself from her entire family soon after beginning one of her own.

Blankemeier began molding clay and painting in oils while in her early thirties but switched to pastels "out of curiosity" ten years later. Then she began figure drawing, and her work became introspective. The drawings speak about the abuses that her stepfather and his associates inflicted on her and on others, and how this made her feel. "The work kept coming out," she explains, a healing process that released her buried feelings and dark memories. Her pastels illustrate "how my psyche organized itself so I could cope." About coming to terms with her subconscious mind, she says, "I need to work with it, otherwise it might overwhelm me. It's like carrying around a septic tank on your back."

Blankemeier is never quite sure what the process will reveal. She drags and blurs the somber-hued pastels. Sharp lines become soft. She often rubs out some of the images, which leaves a shadow of the portrayals. She says that "some of the characters that spring from my imagination and flow out of my fingertips take center stage during the later phases of the drawing. They're like surprise actors that pop out to help me tell my story."

She is uncertain of the symbols' meanings when they first appear. But some of her characters have become familiar. Her devilish girls signify whom she felt like at certain times. There is the transcendent black man, the harbinger of spiritual strength. He's strong and wise, a purifying force, a holder of darkness who frees the artist to become whole again. Distorted ears refer to secrets told or overheard. Dresses express darkness or purity.

As Susie Blankemeier sits at her work table in her upscale Winter Park home, she knows that "at the source of meaning there is going to be a picture, because we live in the physical world." In a Blakeian way, her imagery reveals her truth: "The truth is that mystery and beauty are often conceived in darkness, and if I can come close to achieving a sense of this in a drawing I feel a wonderful sense of relief."

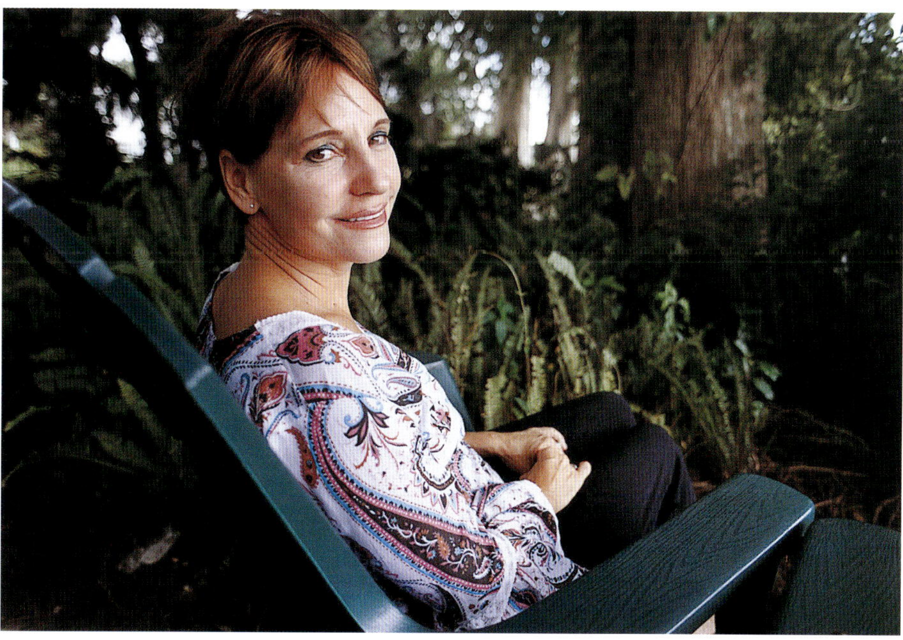

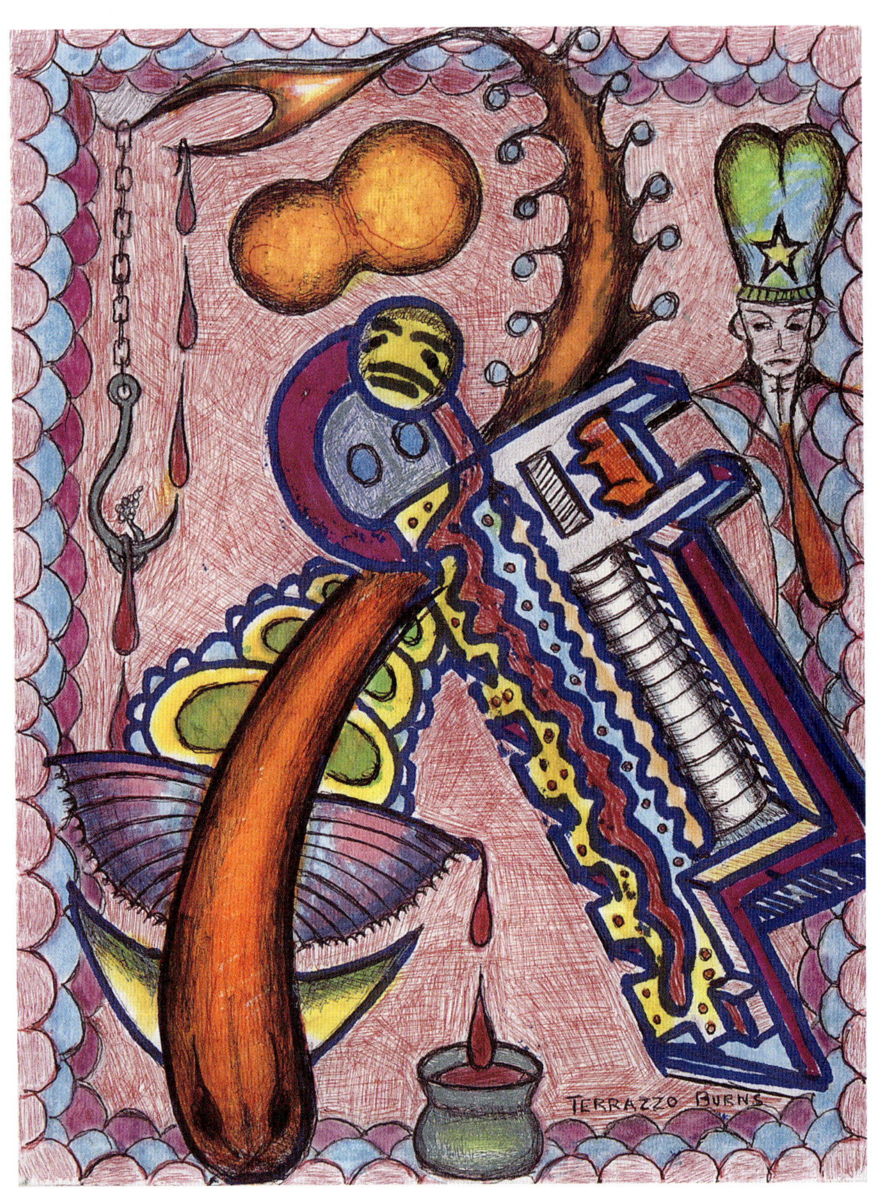

Steve Miller. Untitled. 11" x 8.5".

STEVE MILLER

b. 1942

Steve Miller's early sketches describe the wolflike creature—"Invisible Bird-man that arrived from another dimension"—who renamed him Terrazzo Burns. Its shamanistic presence helps him make sense of the world. By day, he lives in the bedroom of his small, nondescript Cocoa Beach cinder-block house. The television is always turned on, either tuned to a news broadcast or playing racecar videos. A bottle of vodka on the floor next to the bed is Miller's "liquid of inner dimension transportation." At night he comes to life and sings blues with a few local bands along the coast.

Signed "Terrazzo Burns," his drawings are macabre and adolescent: "You bang your head a few times and start thinking like this." He is only half kidding. He's jaded, his mind informed by death-defying experiences. Having grown up looking for fights in a motorcycle culture, he never thought that he would live to be twenty. Laughingly, he says, "Sheer blind luck, or bad luck, that I'm still living."

Miller's drawings suggest a soul not fully resigned to living life the way it is. Lines rove around the paper in search of design and order. Meaning, though, seems beside the point. To him, "drawing is like [using] a Ouija board"; it takes him to mysterious places of bricks, brains, guillotines, light rays, meat hooks, blood, and chains. Bright colors lighten the presence of the imagery but intensify its effect. A motif of swirling shapes leads his pencil to the next radical form. His architectonic modeling creates an iconic tenor and an iconoclastic terror. The repetition of a female pear-shaped form gives momentary relief from the emotional weight of his bizarre imagery.

Whether altering magazine pictures, mocking their relation to reality, or building biomorphic walls and geometric fields that acknowledge his social isolation, Steve Miller will not give in to what he calls "misplaced authority."

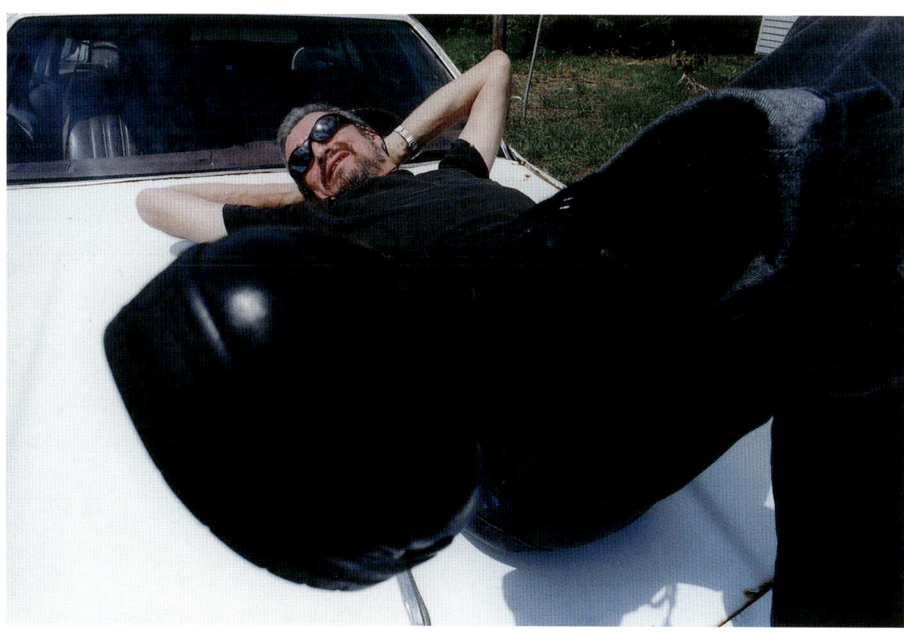

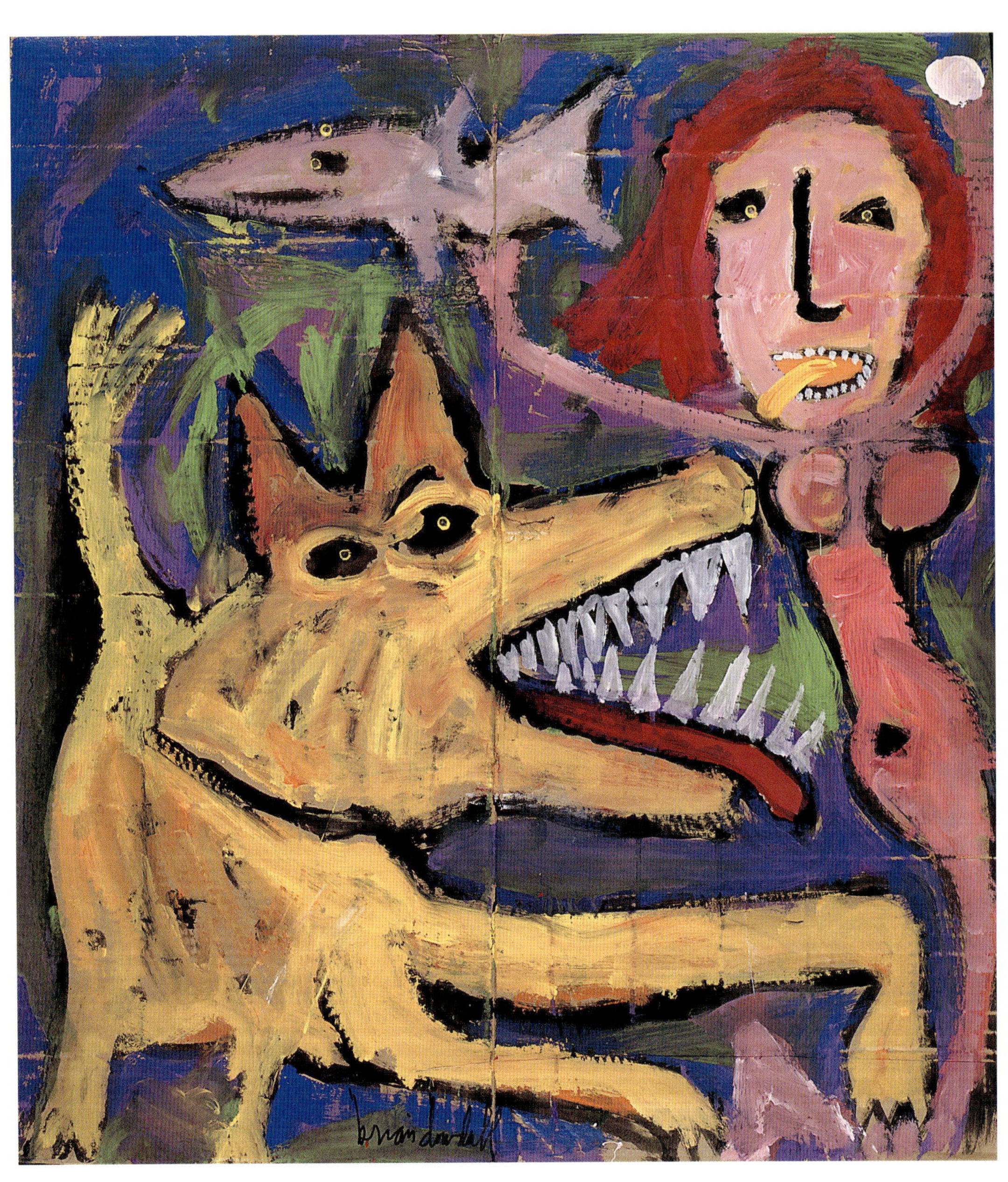

Brian Dowdall. Untitled. 2002. 36" x 33".

BRIAN DOWDALL

b. 1948

Along a strip of A1A in Cocoa Beach, Brian Dowdall lives with his wife, Julie, in a 1950s house originally built for the military. Inside, the Dowdalls' home is anything but standard issue. Besides his own paintings, the cramped interior is like a surreal cultural candy store, full of thrift store finds, art books, Mexican carvings, and the creations of other artists. Dowdall is a professional among self-taught artists, an artist with considerable dealer and gallery representation. The sales of his paintings are his primary source of income.

The artist's Animal Spirit paintings reveal his view that animals are "pure spirits of the earth." Intrigued by the wildlife found in the foothills and mountains of Anaconda, Montana, where he grew up, Dowdall has been painting pictures of animals since he was a child. But the roots of his life as an artist reach back to the mid-1960s, when he left home for Haight-Ashbury. There he lived a "dharma-vagabond existence," sleeping in San Francisco's Golden Gate Park and communing with other free spirits. According to Dowdall, the sixties were "an open and embracing time. Outside of the adobe mud hut where I lived, at night it felt like I could pull the stars off the sky."

Besides animals, Dowdall paints goddesses, whom he reveres as "supreme beings whose spirits are ever-present." He asserts that "we are not above the earth," and to prove his point he makes "sand paintings" by mixing sand, dirt, paint, and glue. His paintings are gestural, and the colors originate "from the sun, moon and fire, the earth, trees, and water." "Spirituality isn't locked up somewhere," Dowdall insists. "We're blind to beauty." Disdainful of the "lunacy" of modern religion's alienation from nature, Brian Dowdall considers himself "a born-again pagan."

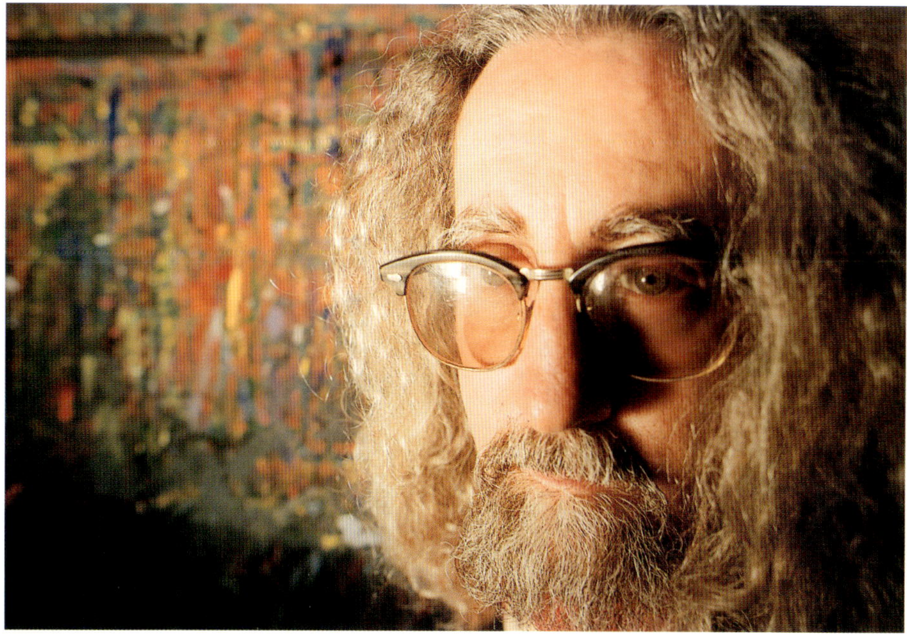

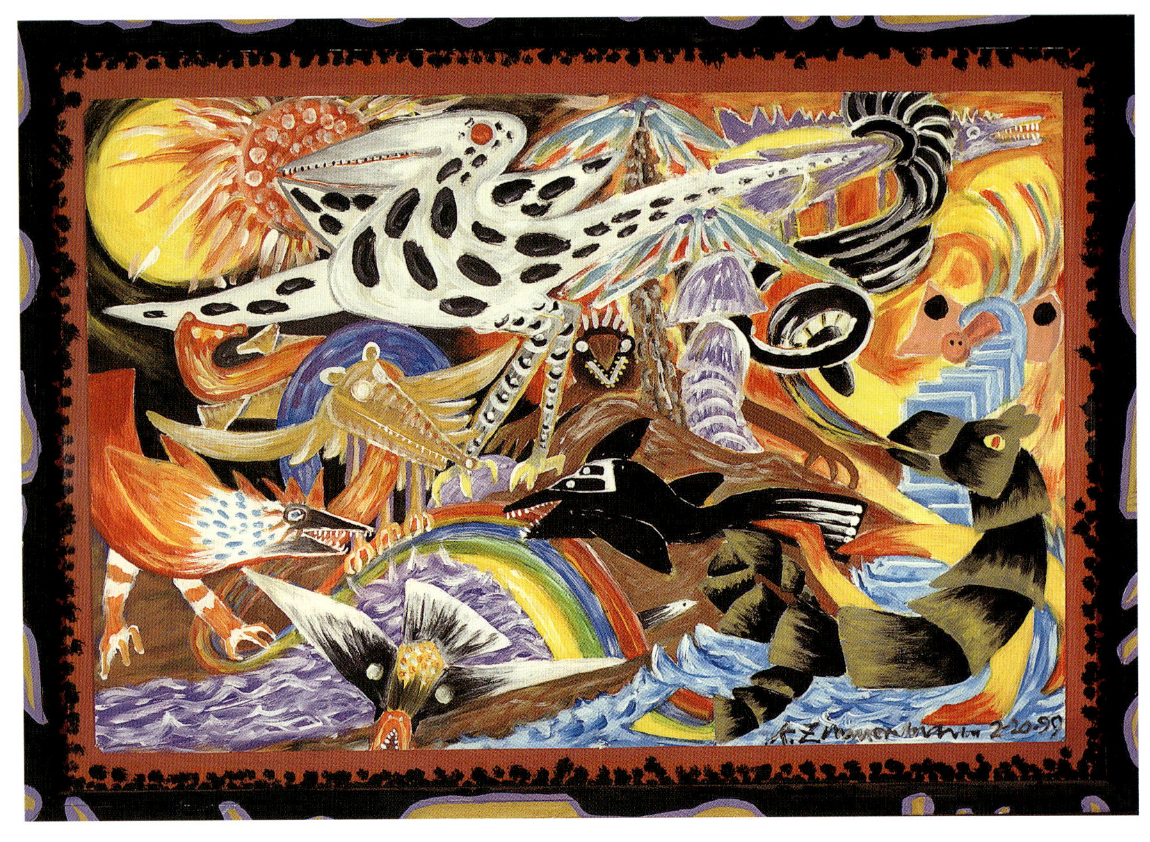

Kurt Zimmerman. Untitled. 1999. 31.75" x 45.5".

KURT ZIMMERMAN

b. 1925

In Cocoa, just inland from Brian Dowdall's home by the beach, Kurt Zimmerman also finds solace in painting animals, but his and Dowdall's motivation and understanding differ in important ways. Whereas Dowdall's pictures are joyful and of the Earth, Zimmerman's are angst-ridden and "of the cosmos." He enjoys the primordial sense of life around the Indian River that flows near his home. He studies the dead animals, birds, and fish that he finds lying by the riverside and paints their images from memory. He feels that he is bringing the creatures back to life, and he is, to be sure, creating a new reality.

Painting "expressionistically" and without deliberation, Zimmerman's pieces reveal his moral vision. Only upon completing a painting can he figure out how the image relates to his own life. His thoughts come alive as he describes wildlife, people, and outer-space images with exceptional painterly style. In his machine-based images, vigorous brush work crashes into his gearlike structures, hinting at Zimmerman's sense that the world is becoming "fragmented" and is "falling apart." He says, "In today's world, if you *don't* get stressed there's something wrong with you."

Although born in Germany, Zimmerman has spent most of his life in America. As fate would have it, he was drafted into the U.S. Army during World War II and flew thirty-five bombing missions over his homeland. The grief that this caused him intensified during his years of employment with General Electric doing work for the Defense Department. As a field engineer, he returned to Germany to work on a secret NATO project. It was then that he suffered a nervous breakdown. Later, while he was assigned to the Apollo moon mission at Cape Canaveral, the weight of his life took its toll again. He resigned from his position and in 1964 began painting as a way "to connect us all."

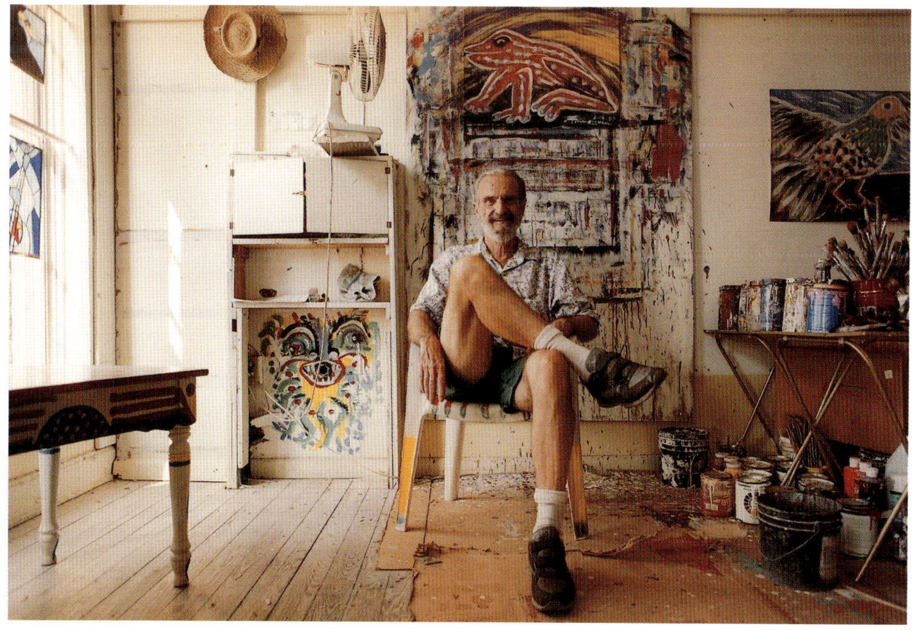

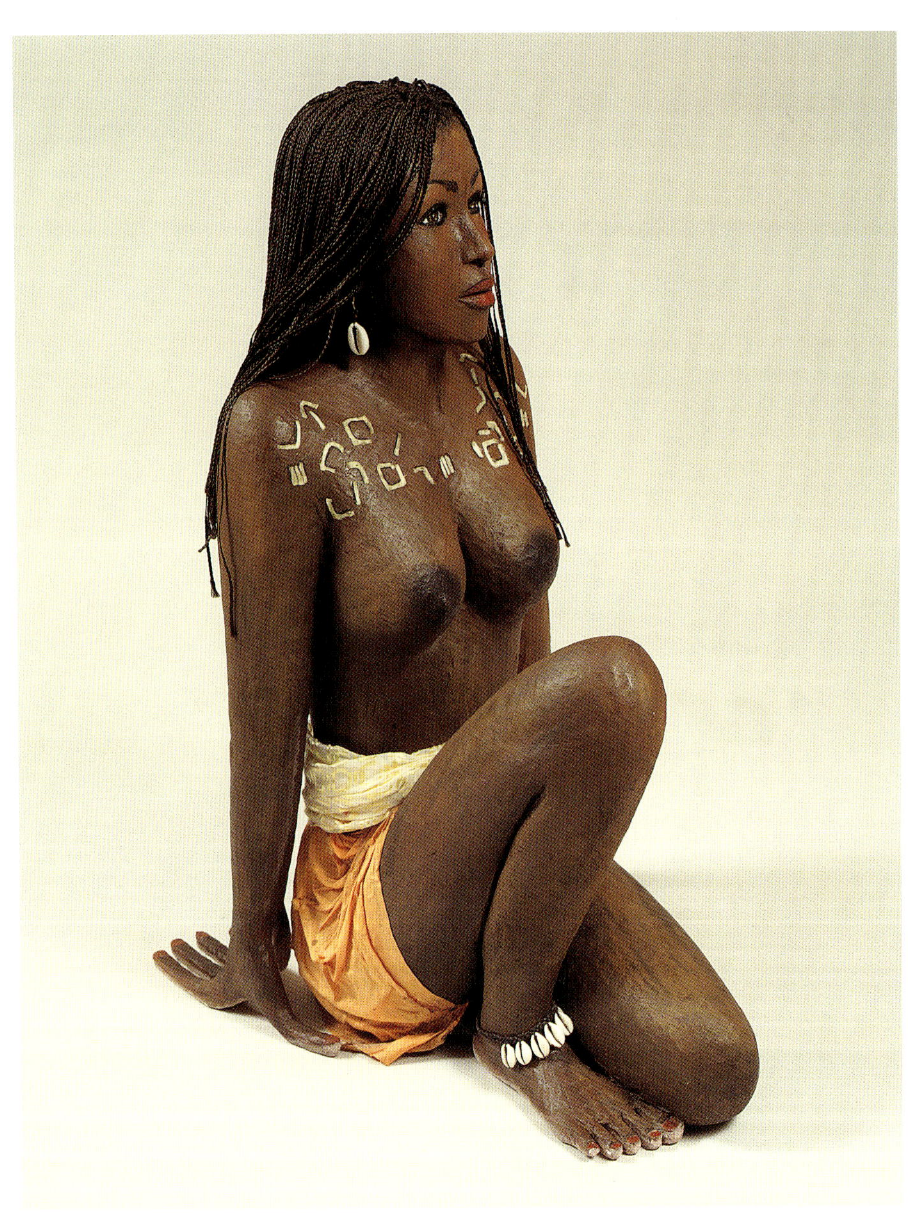

Rose Bilal. *Osun.* 2002. 34.75" x 17.5" x 25".

ROSE BILAL

b. 1942

Rose Bilal has been "hooked on art" since going on a school field trip to a Manhattan museum, but when she moved from Newark, New Jersey, to Philadelphia, it was to sing jazz. She traveled with her band for several years, but in 1969 she grew weary of life on the road and followed her family to Tampa. After seventeen years as a service representative with GTE, she was "screaming for consciousness." Her children were grown; she was forty-seven years old and ready for a big change. She has had to learn to live without some luxuries, but her "I'm a woman, I can do whatever I want" attitude led her to follow her heart. She now ekes out a living by singing in clubs, acting in local theater productions, and selling her artwork. "I can blame my lifestyle on anything—sanity or insanity," she says.

Bilal's art came to fruition when, as a student in a painting class, she learned about shading and proportion. Not content with two-dimensional pictures, she borrowed some books about how to sculpt papier-mâché figures. Using old newspapers processed to the consistency of mud, she forms ballerinas, actors, and athletes. The figures slowly come to life as she works beneath a large wood-framed bay window in her inner-city home. "Life is a dance," Bilal says with a performer's zeal. And the completed pieces confirm her optimism.

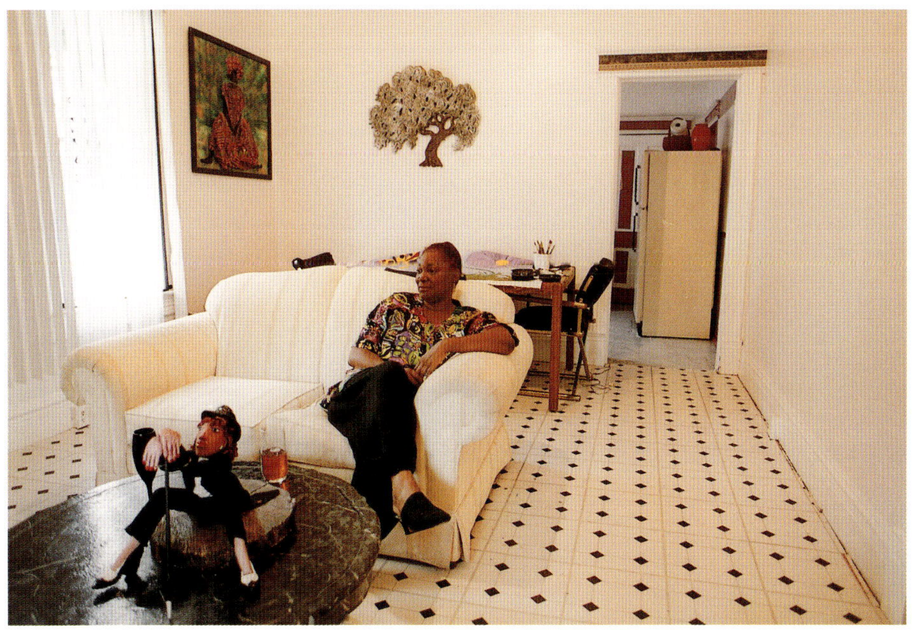

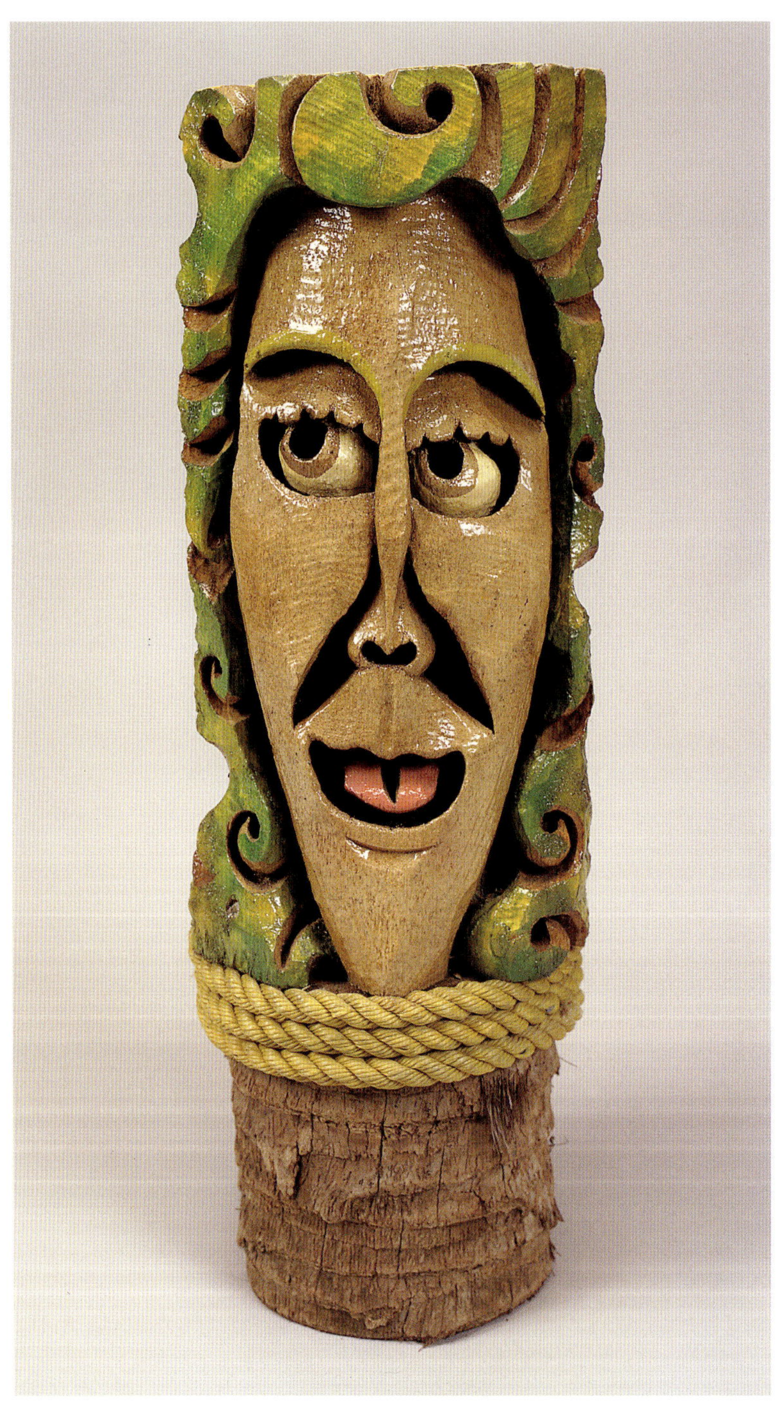

Ed Volonnino. Untitled. 2002. 31" x 10.25" x 11".

ED VOLONNINO

b. 1958

Ed Volonnino professes to have a "consciousness of trees." In order to carve his tiki heads, he has to know all about the sabal palms that he uses for his work. He likes to work with trees that have been dead for one-and-a-half to three years. Fronds still attached to a tree that otherwise might seem a good candidate for his carving let Volonnino know that it has only recently died, so the wood will be too "green"—hard and moist and prone to crack. If a woodpecker has gotten to a tree, he knows the wood will be too dry and apt to crumble under his chisel, since the birds like softwood.

Volonnino always knew that he would become an artist, even though his parents pushed him to get "a real job" after he graduated from Melbourne High School in 1977. He spent hours in the library looking at pictures, seeking inspiration and instruction on how to carve tiki heads. It took the aspiring sculptor a few years to find his way. He hitchhiked around the neighboring beach towns with his heads-in-progress and bucket full of lathe chisels. Determined to succeed, he asked his family priest to bless them. He vowed never to use a chain saw. Volonnino has been an independent artist since 1981, selling tiki heads along the area's roadsides.

He knows little about any Polynesian roots of tikis, having only a scant notion that they might symbolize gods and have religious meaning; Volonnino sees the tikis as ersatz totems of hedonism and escapism. When tourists ask him if he is carving idols, he replies with a blunt, "No." His creations are secular. He doesn't mind, however, if a buyer prays to one of his tikis. His are made, he says, for "fun-loving people, not for the snooty art guild types." He contends that onlookers' alcoholic consumption boosts his sales. A few drinks, he reports, "loosens 'em up a bit," making it more likely that tourists will take home one of "Ed's Heads."

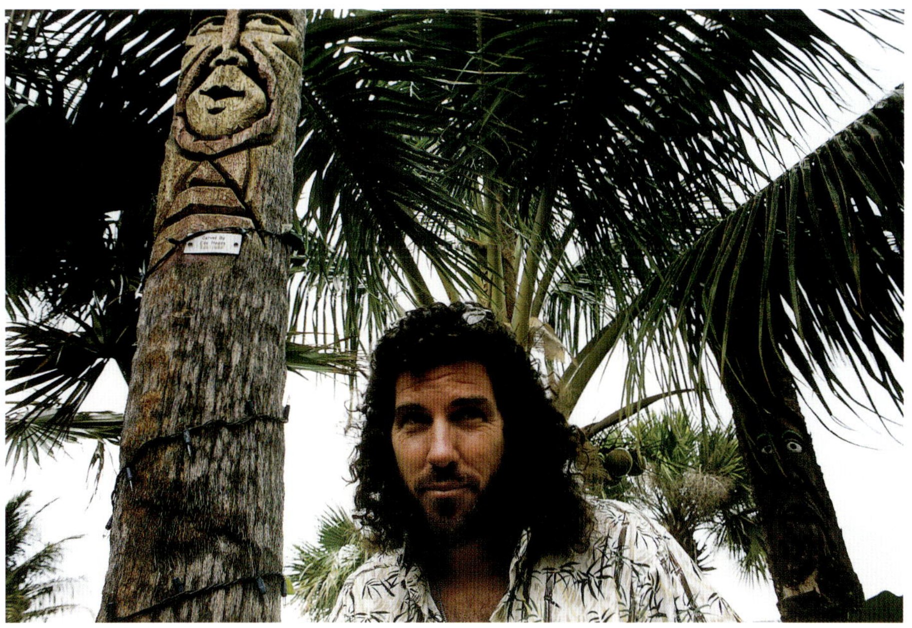

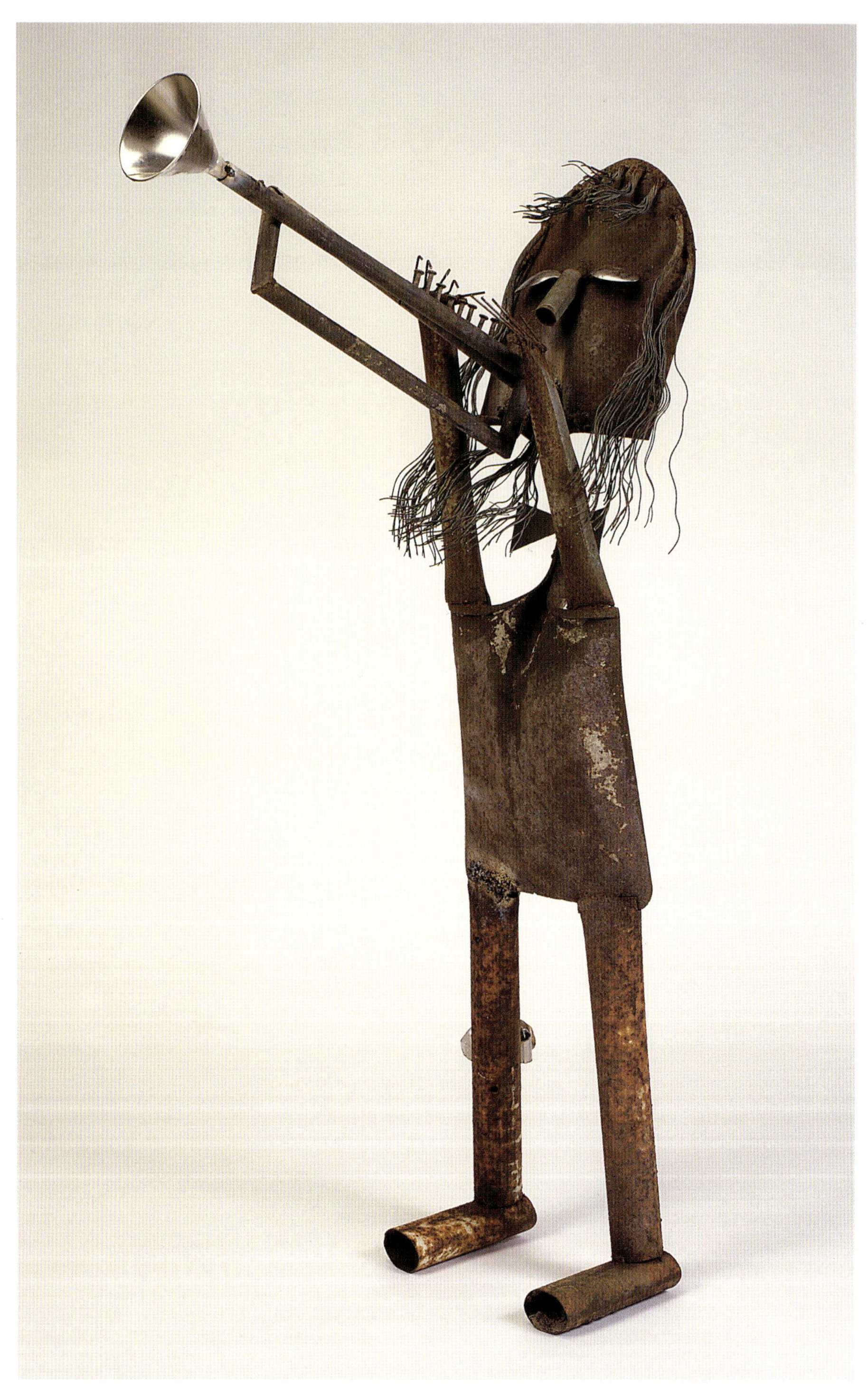

Ray Brown. *Trumpet Player.* 2002. 44" x 13.5" x 10.75".

RAY BROWN

b. 1943

In 1968, Ray Brown started tow boating, pushing barges along the Gulf Coast and Mississippi Delta as he worked his way up to captain. After marrying for the second time in 1989, he quit to stay at home with his wife. But the marriage soon failed, and Brown returned to the waterways. He chose to come back as a deckhand, not wanting the responsibilities that come with rank. But in 1997, Brown underwent open-heart surgery and has had to remain on land.

"I was kind of in her way," he says about his mother's urging him to make sculptures with the welding equipment that he had bought but never used. So, with recovery time on his hands, he tried it. He "gathered stuff to make stuff" and tossed it all around his weathered trailer, his Panhandle home in Freeport. Ray Brown was becoming a sculptor. "Whatever popped into my head while I was welding," he says about the origins of the whimsical array of people and critters that grew and rusted on his property. Mostly he made people from shovel heads: round-point for the faces and square-point for the bodies. Legs were formed from exhaust pipes, swing-set posts doubled as arms, with the figures standing between two and four feet tall. Spoons became eyes, socket wrenches became noses, and galvanized cable was used for hair. The twisting of the cable was how Brown found personal expression; with it he gave his people their personalities.

On January 4, 1998, while driving in his pick-up truck with his grandchild sitting by his side, a tire blew, and Ray Brown threw himself in front of the boy to protect him from the oak tree that he remembers coming at them. Brown was thrown through the windshield; the accident "pulled all the nerves loose from my shoulder." He lost the use of his right arm completely.

Brown hasn't welded since, but he has gained enough strength that he feels ready to begin afresh. In the meantime, he's been gathering junked cars and selling them en masse to a company in New Orleans that crushes, grinds, and recycles the metal. His friend Woodie Long says that the artist's brothers "would sell the sculptures for junk if Brown didn't hide his works from them." It's fitting that Brown refers to his sculptures as "Junk Yard Art" or "Hearts and Humor O'Rust."

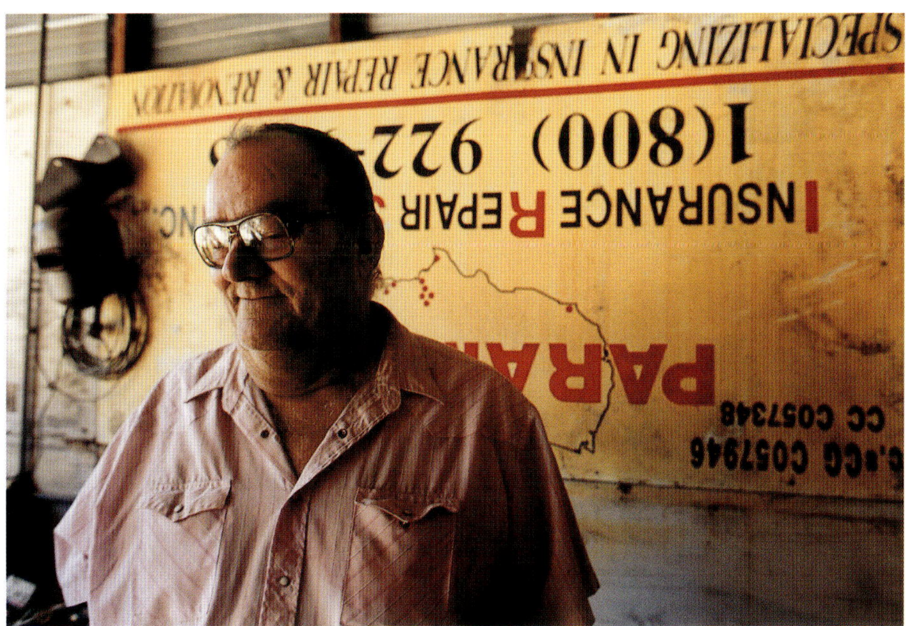

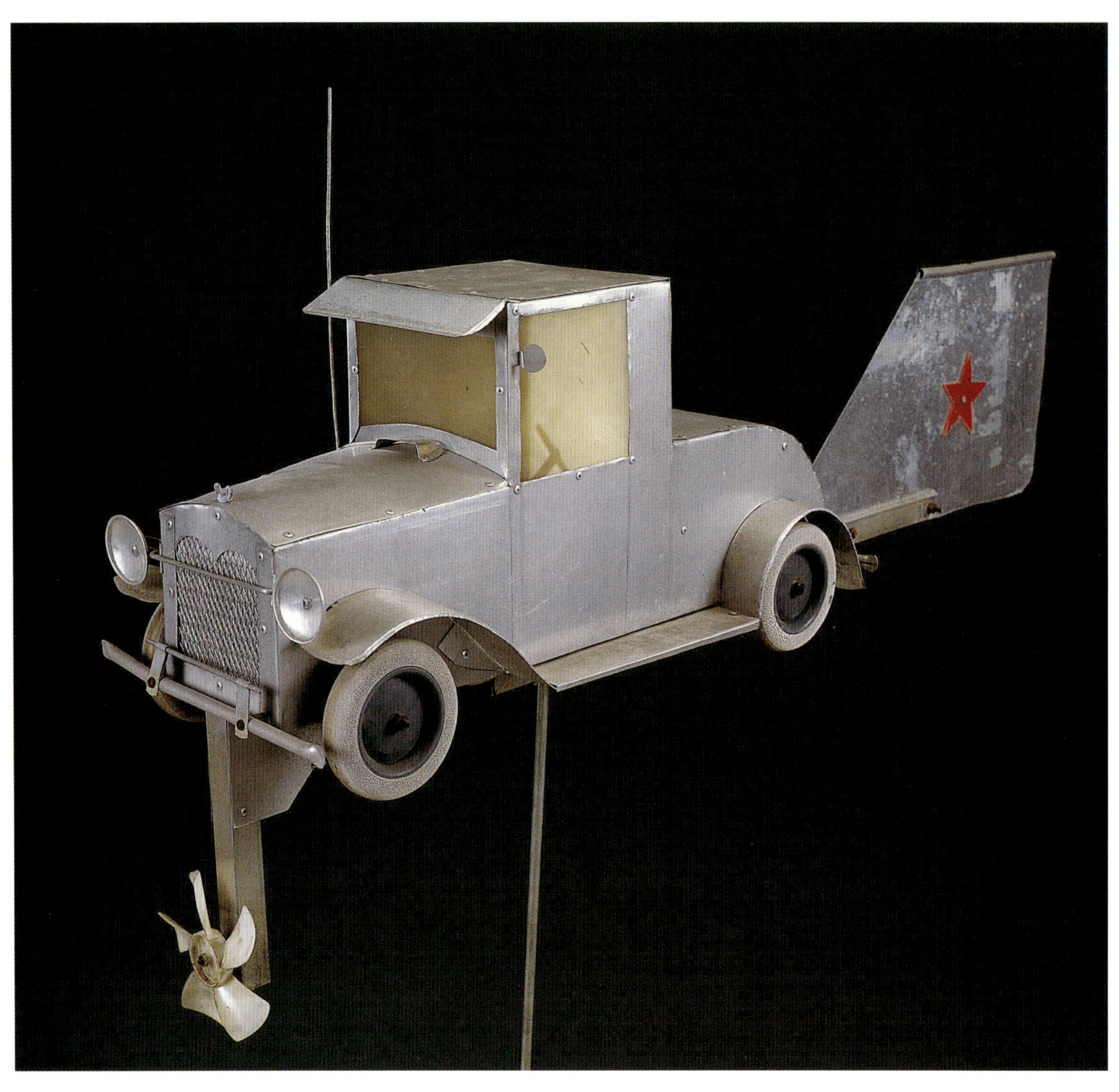

Melvin Thayer. Untitled. 48" x 13.75" x 12".

MELVIN THAYER

b. 1917

As cars zoom along Central Florida's old two-lane Highway 17, travelers can't help but notice Melvin "Pop" Thayer's garden of wind-driven whirligigs sitting on post tops alongside the road. Discarded items used as ornaments—toys, dolls, model cars, lawn decorations, plastic cows, ducks, flamingos, and action figures—bring life to the mechanically animated pieces. Here, an airboat heads into the wind causing its propeller to spin; there, a two-dimensional Wildlife Patrol officer points his gun toward the sky. Nearby, a Ferris wheel made from the spokes of a wheelchair stands next to a merry-go-round on which a Felliniesque party is in progress.

The Thayers moved to Seville in 1973, and six years later, when Pop began collecting Social Security, he started growing his metallic garden. The complex sculptures are cut from scrap aluminum. In a tone more matter-of-fact than proud, Thayer points out that there are no blueprints for his creations: "I think something up and see if I can make it," he says. After a moment's pause, he adds, "Movement makes them more attractive than if they sit there."

Melvin Thayer considers himself a "half-assed auto mechanic," not an artist. He says that he makes the whirligigs for his own pleasure. It's a hobby; he's not interested in selling the sculptures he creates. He adds that he doesn't want to worry about county officials looking over his shoulder for fees and taxes, either.

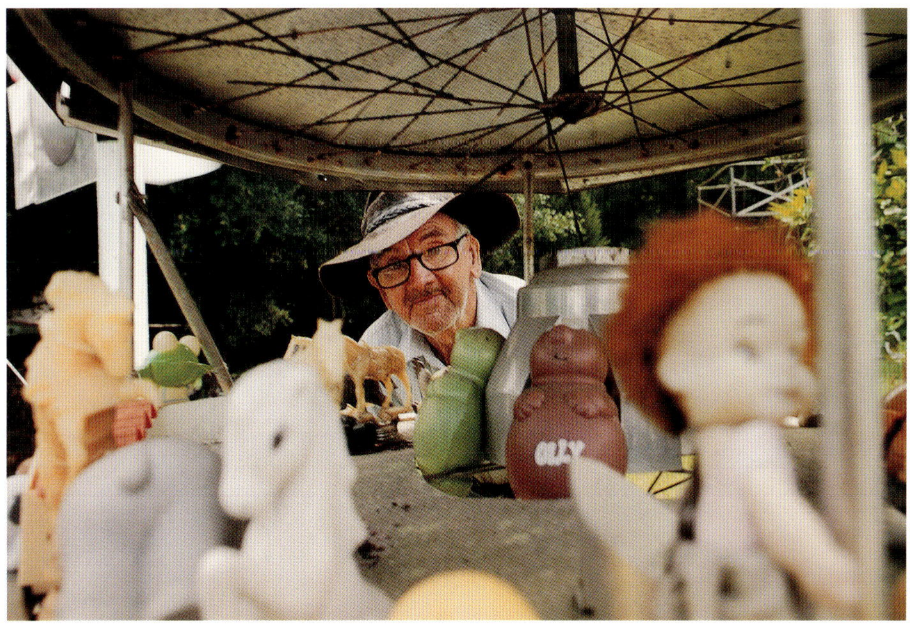

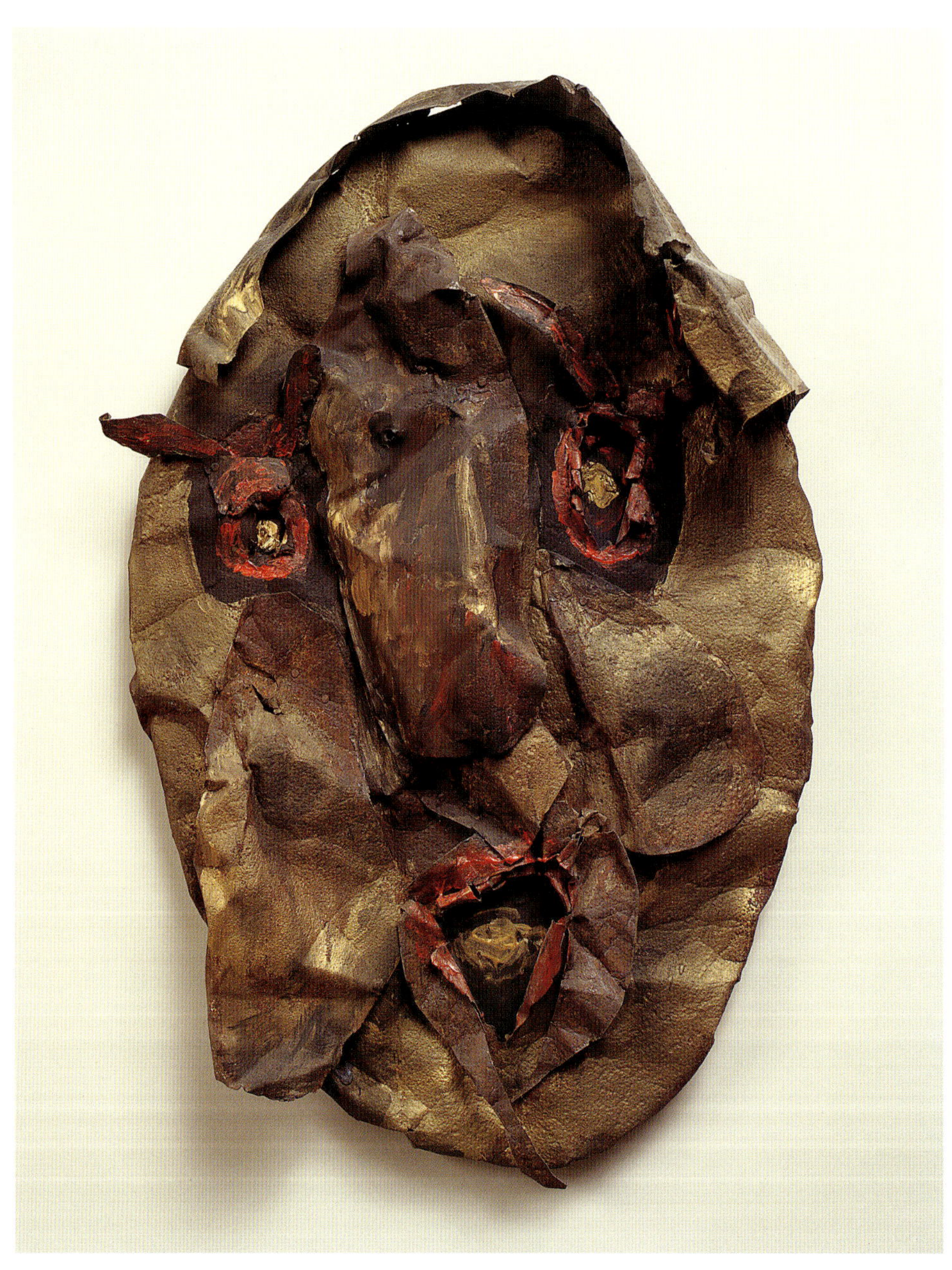

Jerry Coker. *The Prince.* 1995. 18" x 12" x 3.75".

JERRY COKER

b. 1938

Gainesville artist Jerry Coker believes that art comes forth from an unknown source, that it emerges naturally from the unconscious mind. The artist is, in effect, a channel for the free flow of creative energy.

Coker's "identity masks" are meant to illuminate the 388 most interesting people that he has met. Many of them are people from his youth in Arkansas. Fabricating the masks from rusted pieces of tin covering wood shaped as a face, Coker folds, mallets, and secures the pieces of metal to form the features. Noses are often long, protruding strips that stem from the forehead. Mouths and eyes may be cut out or formed by tucking some tin under another layer of material. He occasionally contends with a tuft of hair. The faces are often elongated, pushed and pulled to reflect distinct personalities. "Masks," he says, "are my calling."

Whether he captures the spirit of an individual is unknowable and even largely irrelevant. And whether that spirit even exists beyond the artist's imagination matters only as much as it propelled him to perfect the image. Because Jerry Coker sees an artist as a medium, he is quick to point out that he or she is a distraction once the work is completed.

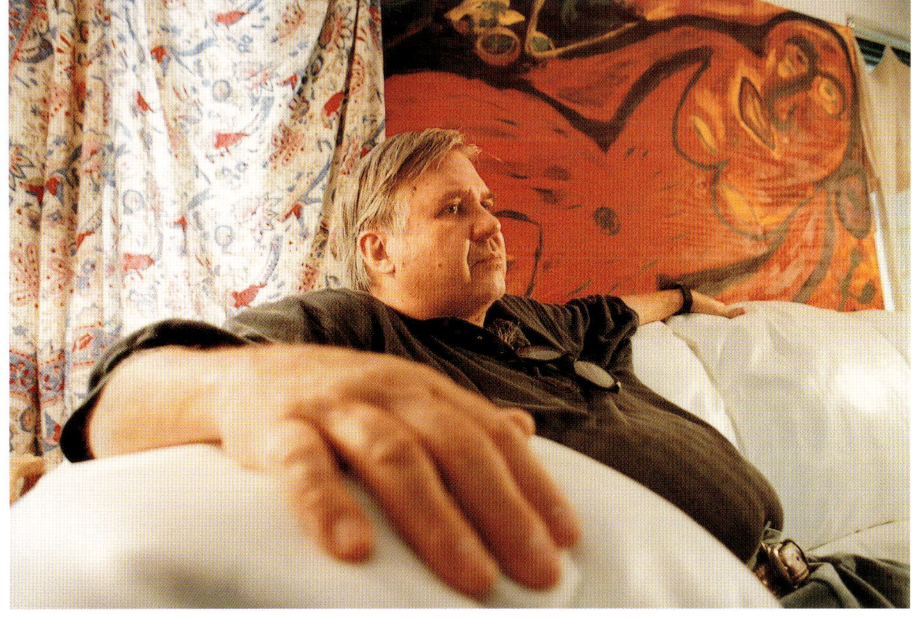

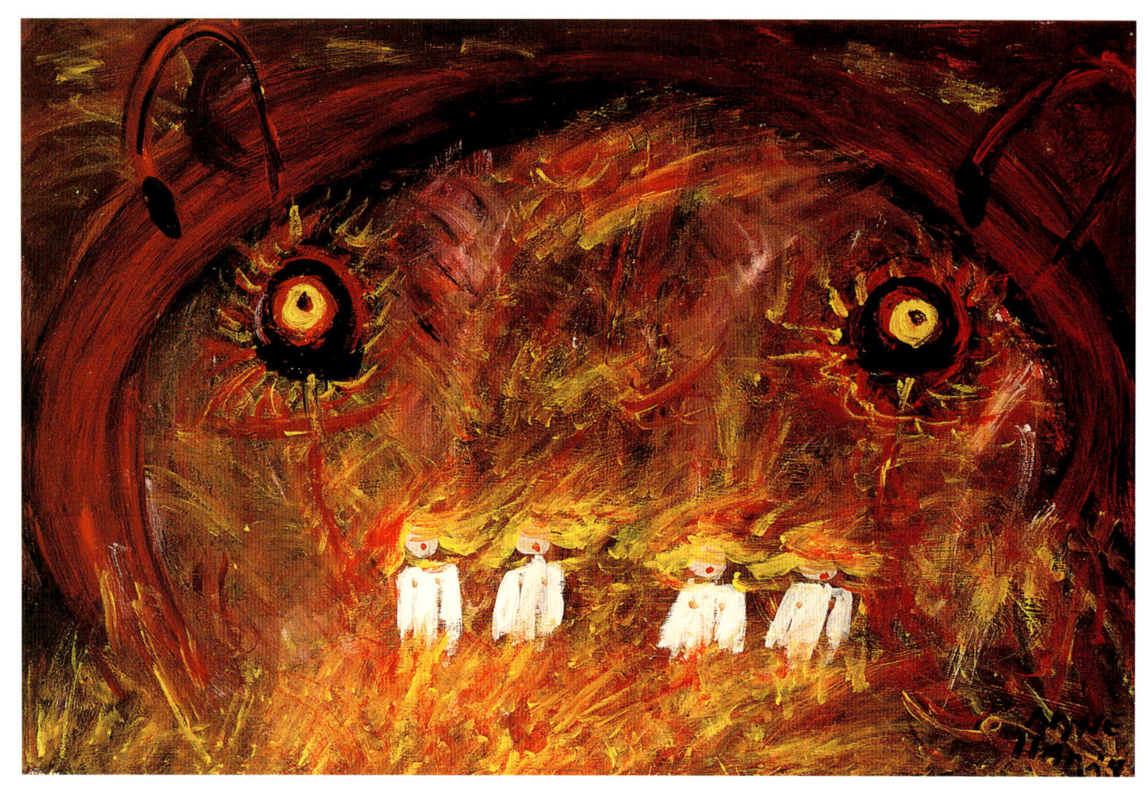

Alyne Harris. *Devil Devouring Angels.* 1988. 24" x 36".

ALYNE HARRIS

b. 1942

Alyne Harris epitomizes the idea of the artist as conduit. She compulsively mixes and feverishly applies paints to canvas boards, oblivious to the pieces she has produced once they are completed. Her subjects include landscapes, slaves, and churchgoers. She also paints "haints," devilish creatures whose open mouths sometimes reveal angels.

When Harris attended a painting class at Santa Fe Community College in Gainesville, her instructor, Lennie Kesl, was impressed. He considered her a "born painter." "Alyne would come into class and just paint her heart out," Kesl recalls. "She paints like her father owns a paint store." Being unencumbered by artistic theory may release the creative spirit from the material world, allowing primal urges to flow into natural forms. Although cryptic, the forms are a font of information. For Harris, the content is as clear as day.

"I paint the friendships of people's relationships," says Harris. Many of her paintings refer to the church, especially to preachers. "Once the preacher was revered and people would set the dinner table for supper with him," Harris says. "Now people talk about the preacher like a dog. Attitudes have changed. Things could be better." "Beauty," she says in her turn-away voice, "is different for everyone. Somebody much likes lamb chops. I don't. I like chicken. Tomorrow I'm barbecuing drumsticks."

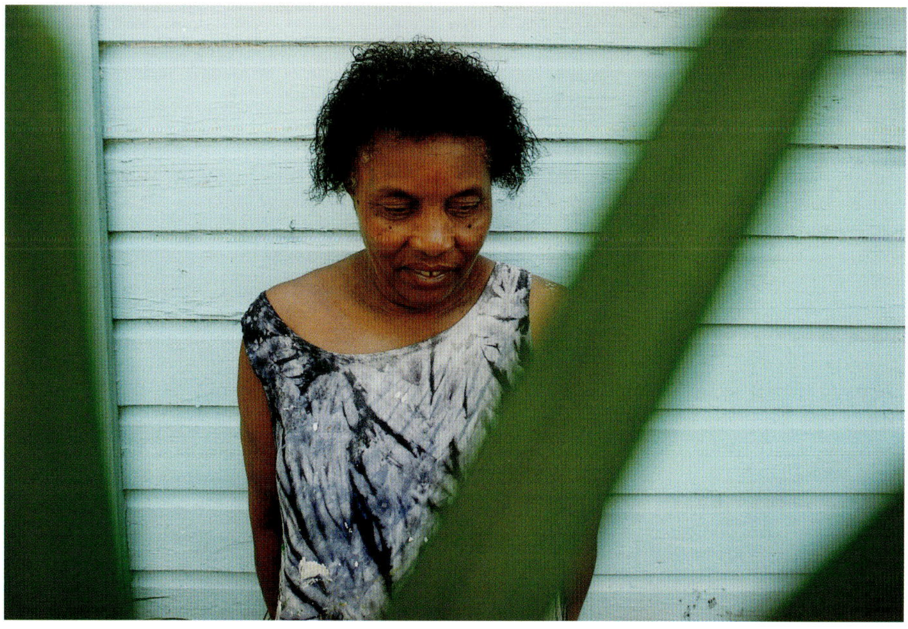

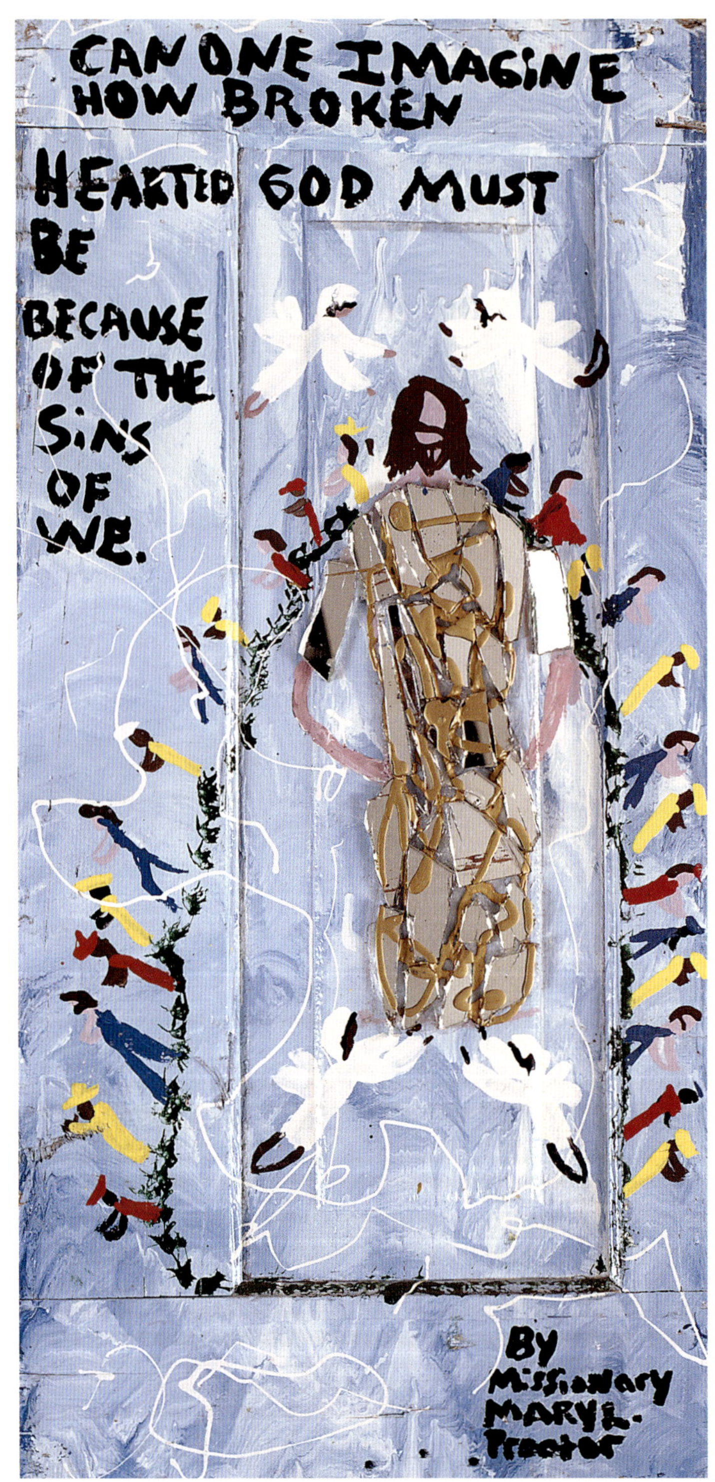

Mary Proctor. Untitled. 30.5" x 14.5".

MARY PROCTOR

b. 1960

The death of Mary Proctor's grandmother, aunt, and uncle in a house fire in 1994 threw her into a depression. She "didn't know which way to go" and resorted to fasting and prayer. Her pleas for guidance were answered in February 1995, when "the Lord gave me a vision. He told me to paint on a door." She grabbed cans of blue and white car paint that were on hand and went to work. "Blue like the sky," she remembers, "like walking outdoors and being overwhelmed. Awesome."

Before her vision she had never painted, but now she cannot stop. She paints on garage doors, on old windows and their frames, on small squares of wood. She paints only a few themes but varies them, enhancing the images with shards of mirrors, glass, fabric, and buttons. Mostly she paints on doors, all day long and everywhere.

Proctor believes that God uses her to communicate His love for humankind, and she sees her painting as a way to "go deeper." In His service, she signs her paintings "Missionary Mary Proctor." She explains that "the message needs to be out there." Room after room of a former house on the outskirts of Tallahassee has been transformed into a showroom containing thousands of her paintings, while more than a hundred of her painted garage doors are stacked in the yard. Nowadays, when people come to view her artwork, the reverend charges admission to her museum.

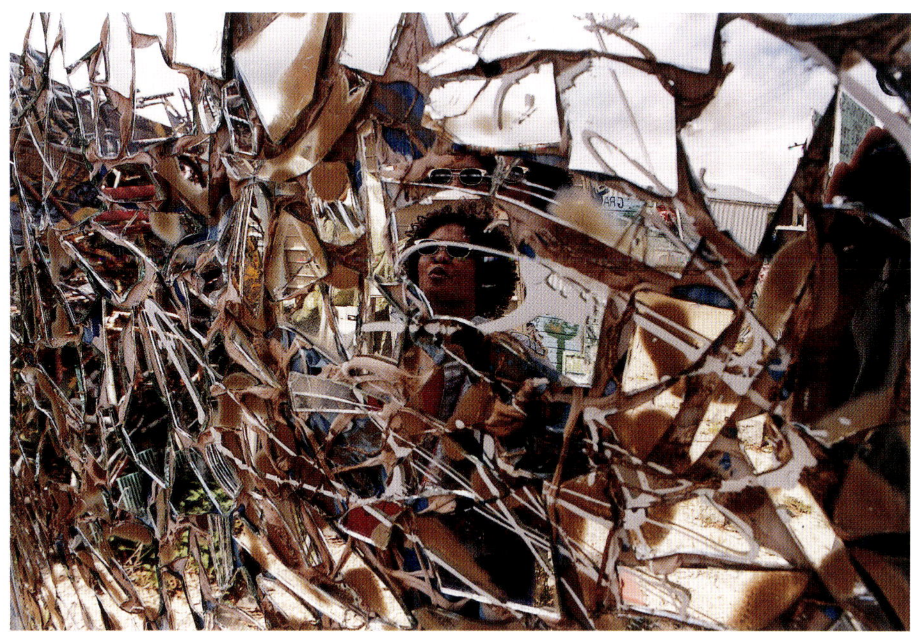

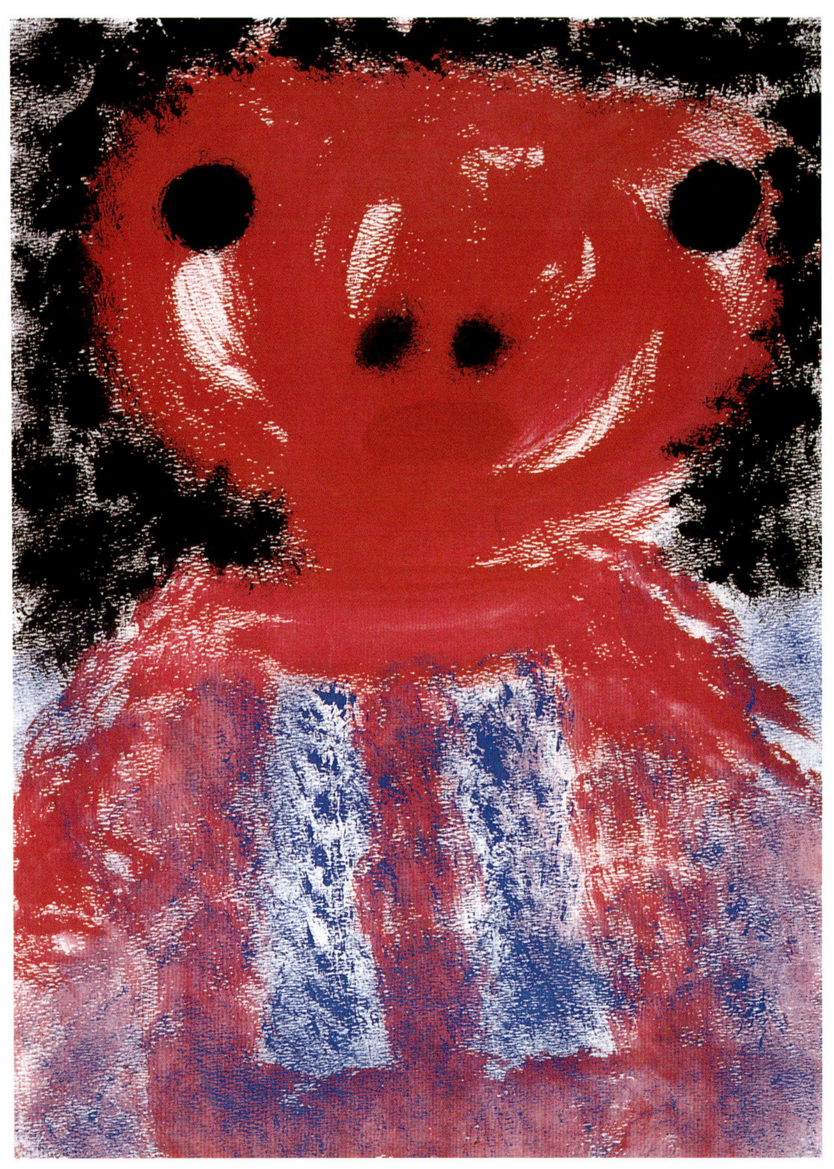

Aurelia Johnson. Untitled. 15" x 11".

AURELIA JOHNSON

b. 1918

Aurelia Johnson has "doodled" all her life, but she says that she is unworthy of being called an artist. "I don't brag," she says, "because I know my Bible." Indeed, there is a feeling of spiritual warmth about her small, freshly painted, shotgun-style house in St. Petersburg. Welcoming visitors into her home, she points out sculpture-dramas; fashioned from discarded toys, they are positioned on Styrofoam packing materials. "Mama Johnson" acknowledges plastic detergent and shampoo bottles that have been transformed into dolls that she calls her "missionary girls going out to do good." She often talks to her dolls, mostly chastising them. "Ain't nobody going to want you," she tells them. "You so ugly." Jeanne Kronsnoble, who represents the artist, suggests that these may be her alter ego.

Johnson draws with colorful felt-tip markers. Her forms are childishly outlined and filled with unending circles that spiral and overlap. The lines continue beyond the forms across the paper to go nowhere and everywhere. She pays little attention to traditional technique. When given stretched canvas, she draws on the back, using the wood molding as a frame. With acrylics, she attains half-inch, dry-brush, dotlike patterns that seem to blot up the papers' white surfaces.

Best known for her "missionary girls," Mama Johnson also draws "aliestos," her endearing term for *aliens.* She renders fish, snakes, and flowers too. "I love flowers," she says. "I don't care how they look." She is surprised that people are interested in her images. "People say they're beautiful," she notes and then adds, "but I think they're ugly."

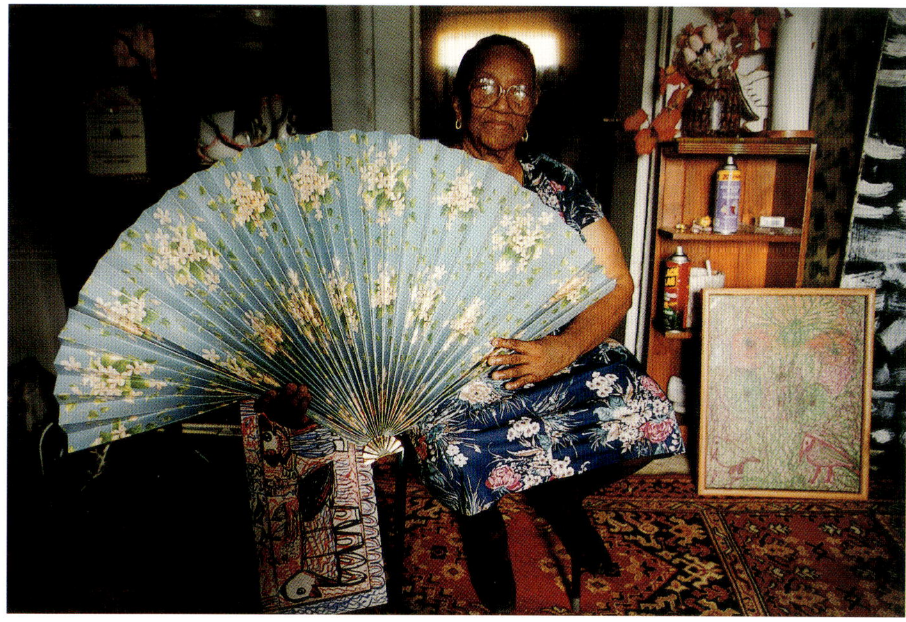

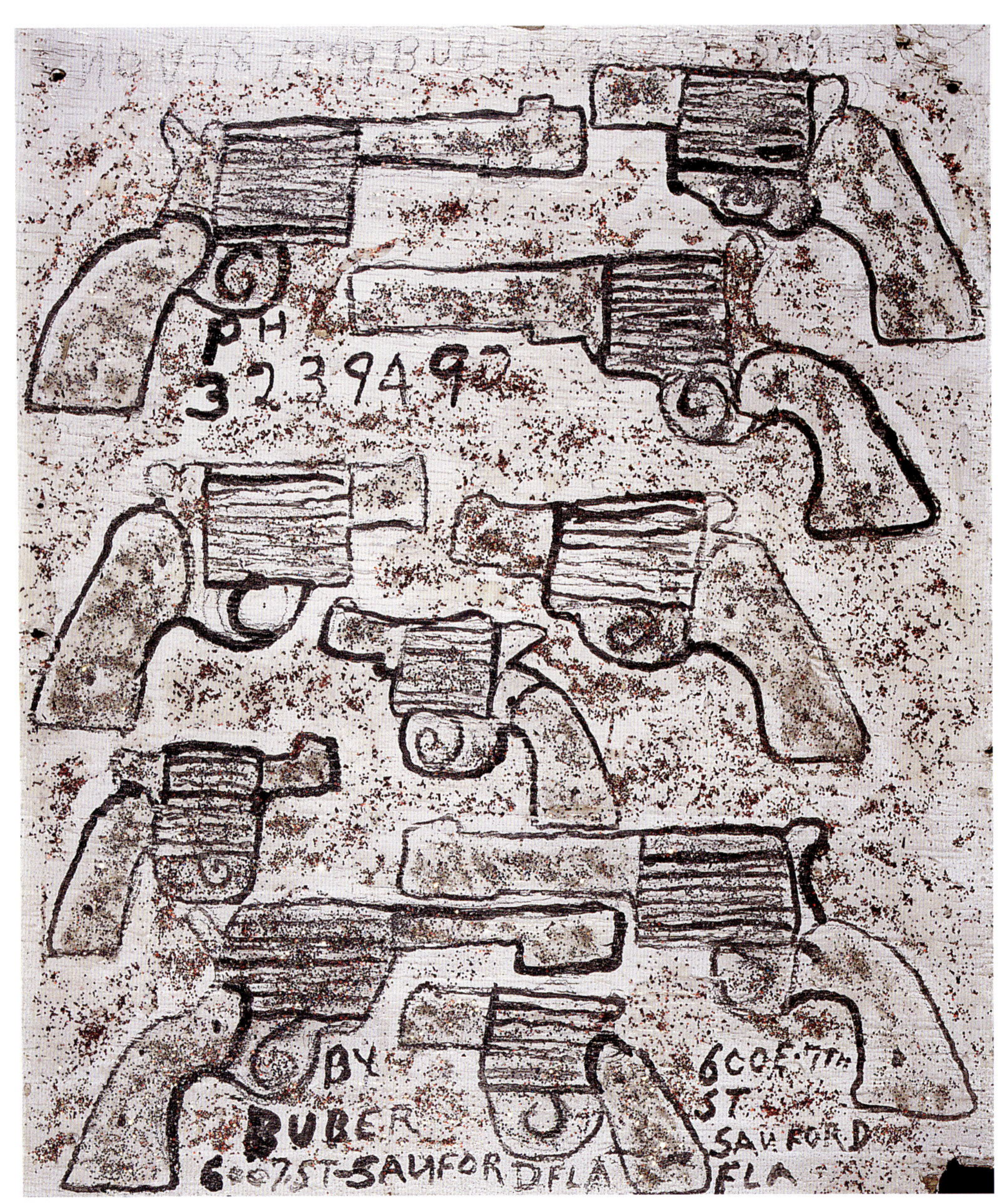

Bryant Gowens. Untitled. 20.75" x 18".

BRYANT GOWENS

1918–2003

Bryant "Bubba" Gowens made images of guns. There is no attempt at narrative. He drew as many guns as he could fit onto the pieces of scrap plywood that he used. The guns are crudely outlined, their symbolism more potent than pictorial artifice. He added glitter to give the guns additional presence.

Although one might be tempted to interpret Gowens's guns as a protest against the rampant violence that has become a part of American culture, he saw them as a homage to the weapon. He was not a violent man, but he did love guns, which were a part of his life since childhood. "My daddy always kept guns over the door," he recalled. Pistols hung from nails on his bedroom wall. A weapon was never out of reach. "I wouldn't want to live in a house without a gun," he said. "Need it for protection."

His daughter, Betty Jean, suggests that her father's gun panels were constructed as warnings, and they do look more like signs than art. Placed in the yard or visible through a window, they may have served to ward off potential thieves. Crime in his Sanford neighborhood was a constant worry, especially with "people out there doing crack cocaine." Gowens was known to "shoot up a box of cartridges a week" in his yard, reasoning that it might scare away anyone who might be lurking in the dark. "The cops never come by [to investigate the gunshots]," he chuckled, "not in this neighborhood."

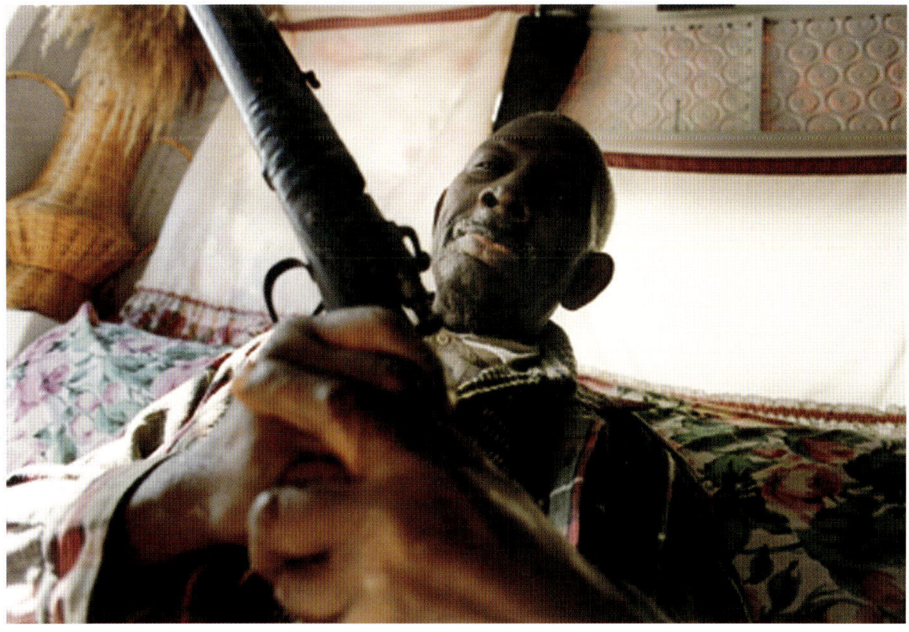

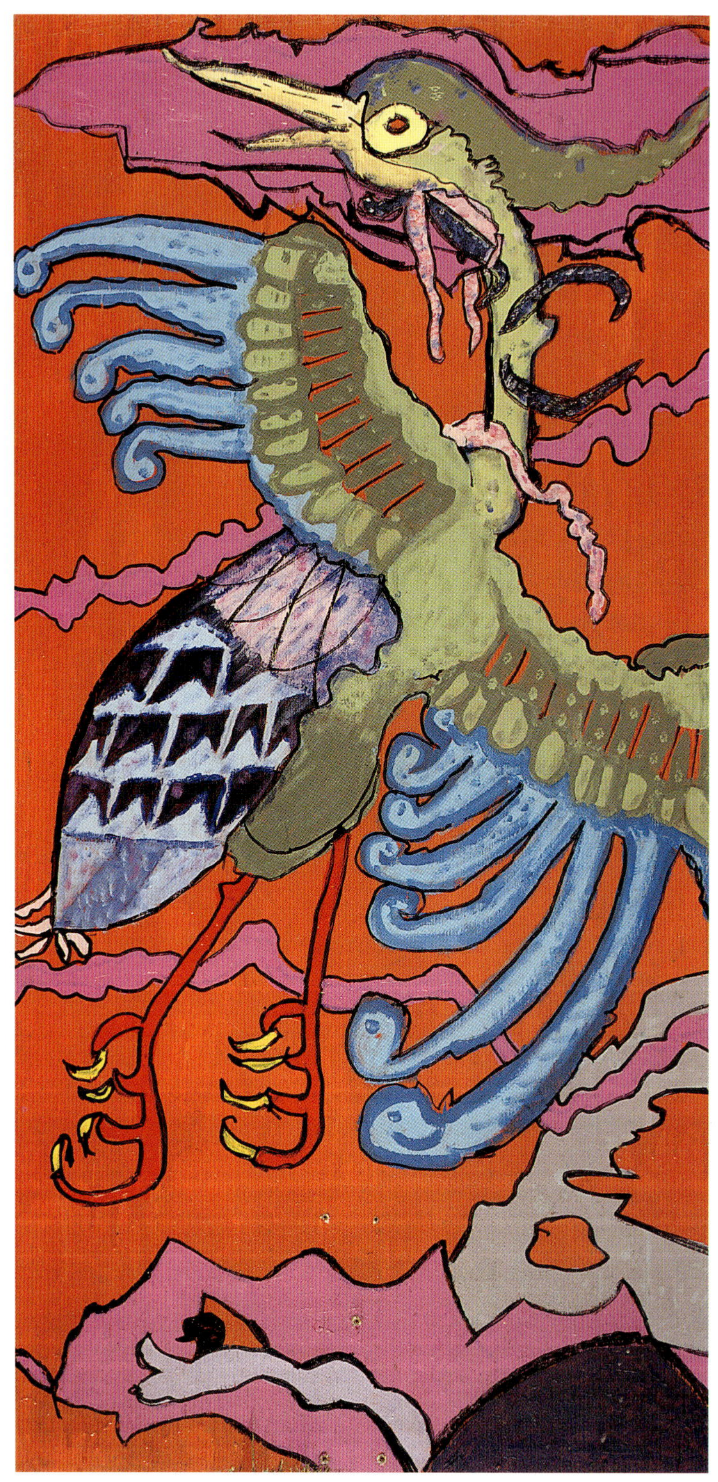

Duane Locke. *Mystical Firebird.* 48" x 24".

DUANE LOCKE

b. 1921

Since he began painting in February 1997, shortly after his wife's death, Duane Locke's new world has sprung to life. It flourishes with fifty two-by-four-foot paintings on plywood that are mounted on two-by-fours to rise from the ground like totems in the yard of his inner-city Tampa home. Recent paintings of flowers and birds and images referencing classic literature line the house's dark interior. Locke's otherworldly home is strangely inviting, its foreboding atmosphere enhanced by its unkempt foliage and Locke's garden of paintings and found objects. Cats roam freely throughout the house, which resembles a movie set; encapsulated by dust and decay, fenced and abandoned-looking, it echoes the surreal nature of Locke's art and life.

Duane Locke is the quintessential outsider. He has created a world apart from the mainstream—intellectually and emotionally—and makes no pretense of being part of the academic community from which he has retired. His learned but unassuming nature led him to appreciate the inherent "intense and exalted" pleasures of the arts. Believing that reality exists *within* the individual, he stresses emotions and thinks of absolutes, generalizations, and logical analysis as falsifications of truth. His observations seem less contrary than enlightened. Perhaps this is why the word *mystical* is part of all of the titles of his early paintings. Locke thinks of his art not as mimetic but as musical. He says, "I paint to be heard."

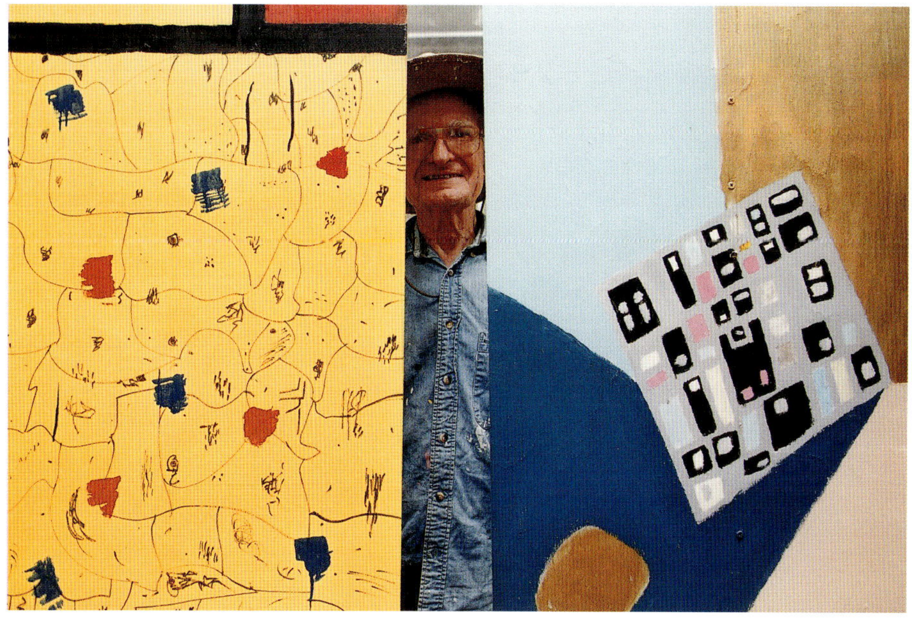

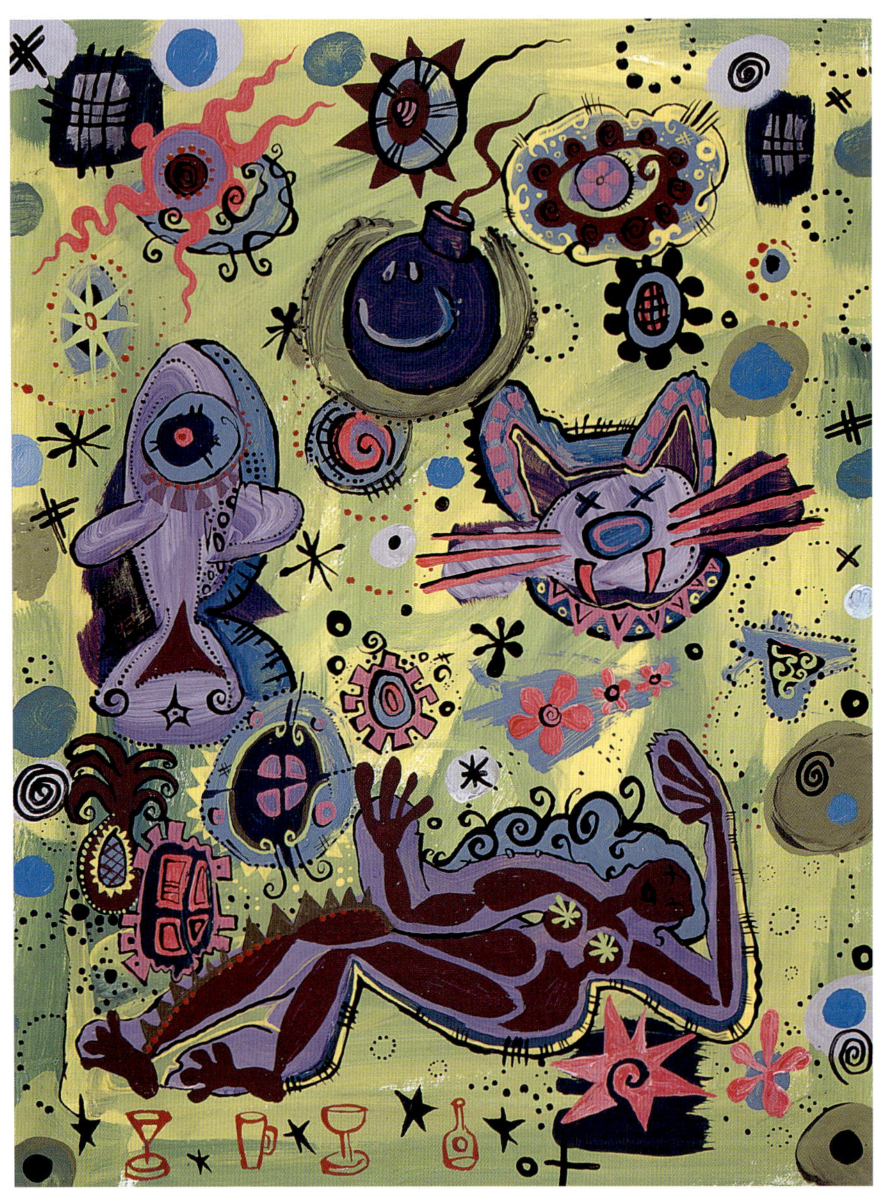

Morgan Steele. *10 Million Dead Southern Baptists.* 2000. 11.625" x 8.625".

MORGAN STEELE

b. 1968

Much of Morgan Steele's oeuvre deals with images that suggest nothing in particular and that are appropriated without regard to their origins. An odd juxtaposing of cars, rats, planes, cows, roosters and fish, Steele's comic icons just don't add up for conventional viewers. He practices a sort of "cartoon surrealism" in which the formal quest of "just trying to fill the space" is similar to killing time at the Orlando bird refuge where he lives.

Using a process that he calls "embellishing," Steele alters existing images by adding meticulous designs and applying his unique color sensibility. He spends hours that turn into days patiently transforming imagery borrowed from popular culture and classical painting into a type of contemporary clip art. His mark makings coalesce as encryptions that, like hieroglyphs, appear codified and impenetrable.

From "those years of reading *Mad* magazine," Steele has acquired a satirical edge. His work *The Last Supper* could be viewed by some as sacrilegious, but his lighthearted treatment may help him avoid the wrath of religious conservatives. Steele's intention is not to be contentious; he just feels that "Christianity is a little too serious."

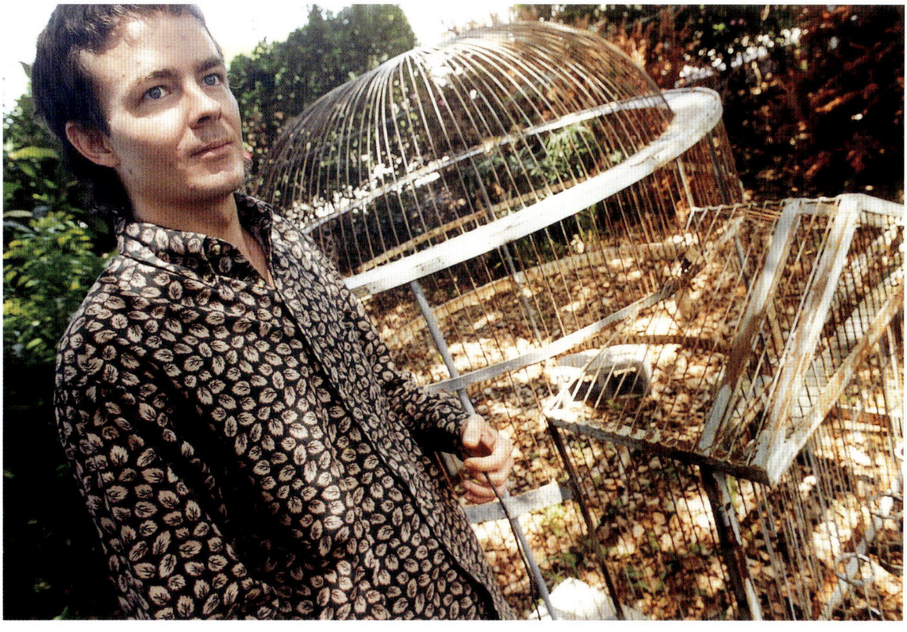

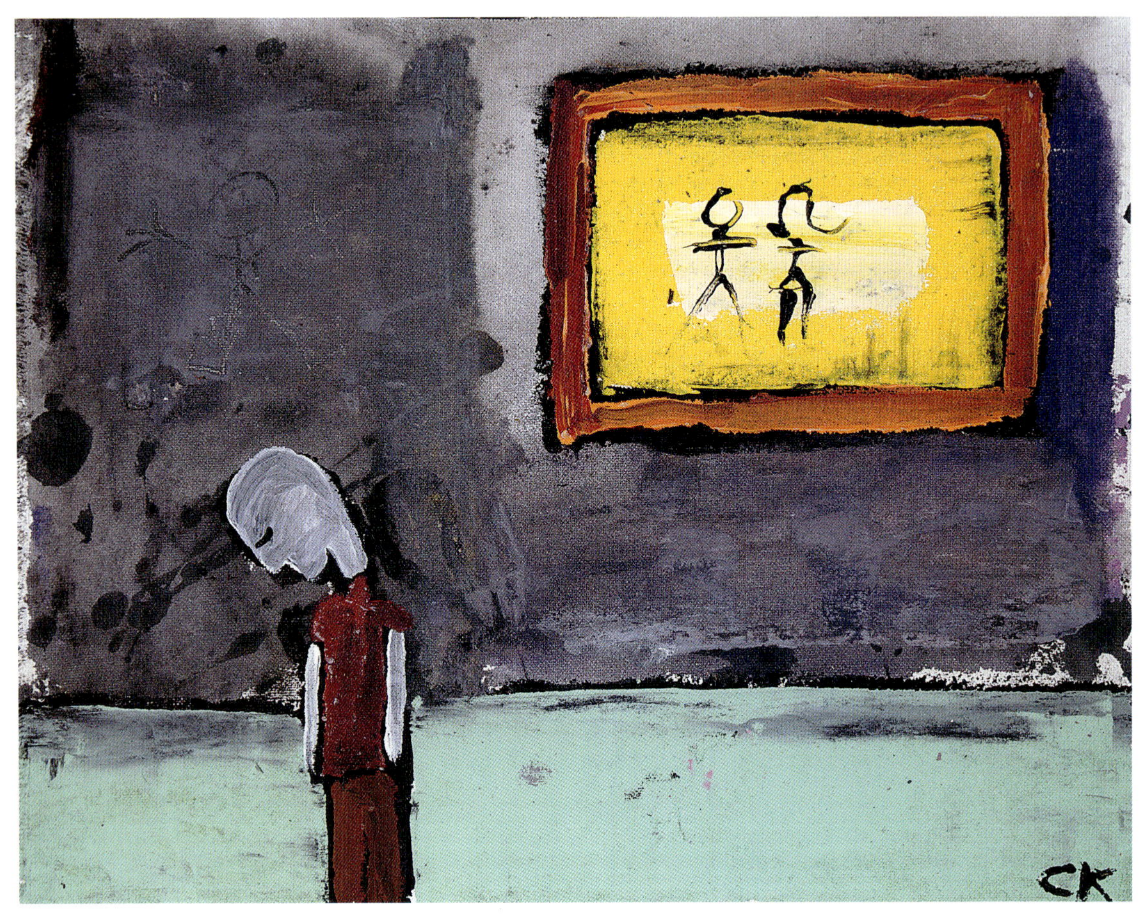

Carl Knickerbocker. Untitled. 12.5" x 16".

CARL KNICKERBOCKER

b. 1954

Carl Knickerbocker refers to his art as "suburban primitivism," a blending of folk forms and pop influences that carries with it the weight of his sociopolitical observations. He is a spokesperson for the liberated Dilberts of the world. His large canvas commentaries engender smiles, but as *Orlando Weekly* columnist Lindy Shepherd put it: "You laugh because you get it. Then you sober up because you really get it." His intellect is cleverly concealed behind his humor. His art is content driven, and it has a point to drive home. Art for society's sake.

Knickerbocker came of age at the end of the tumultuous sixties. His social concern is evident in the *Onstage* and *Spectator* series that are about self-identification—how we perceive ourselves and how we perceive what others perceive about us. His colors are as rich as the magenta hues of the azalea plants that form the shape of a giant flying saucer by the lake at his home near Chuluota. His cast of characters is cartoonish and drawn very much from contemporary symbols that are familiar yet perplexing. *Ethnocentric Dogs* is a series of paintings that depict blue and green dogs in conflict. The green dogs usually come out on top.

With their unique blend of whimsy and provocation, Knickerbocker's paintings become an antidote for what ails us in our fast-paced, often frightening society. As people of developed cultures search for meaning by trying to replace the models that modernism trusted and postmodernism mocks, Knickerbocker's art provides us with a paradox that is simultaneously entertaining and enlightening, thus transforming the prosaic into poetry.

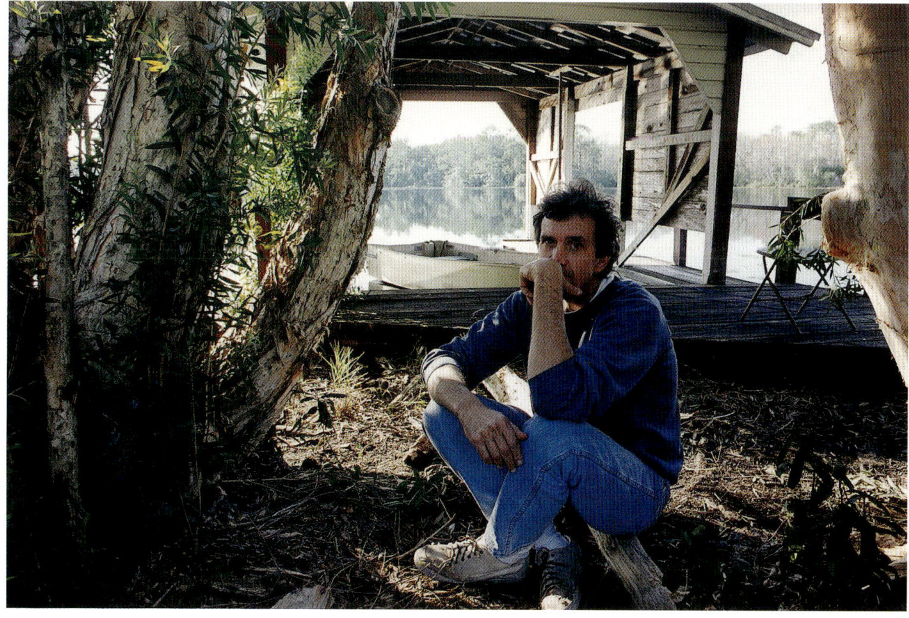

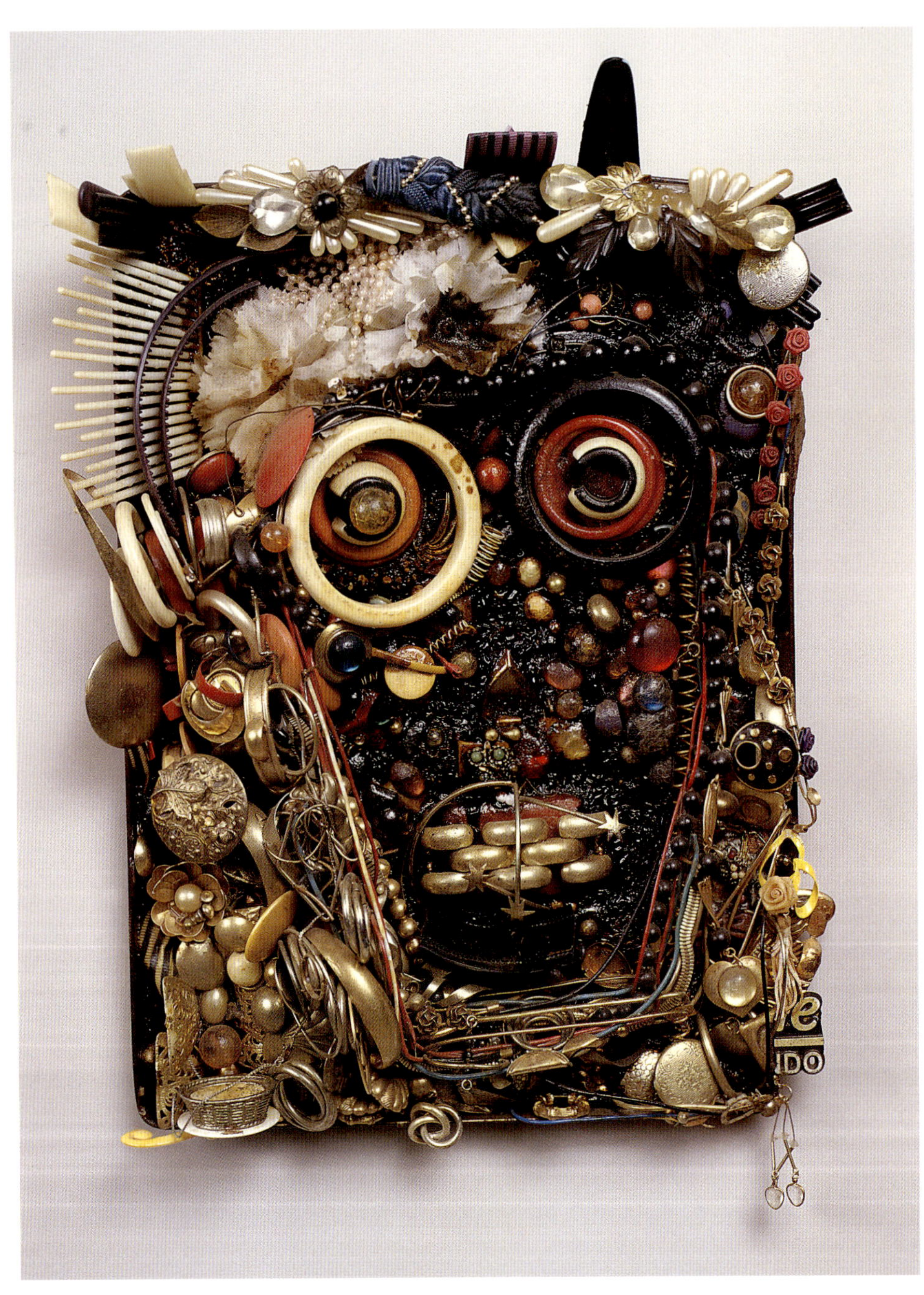

Tony Garan. Untitled. 17" x 14" x 3.25".

TONY GARAN

b. 1962

Tony Garan's art is a metaphor for our fractured world. The hard edges and vivid colors that he often utilizes might easily be mistaken for decoration. He would like viewers to believe that the work is just what it appears to be—a way of keeping busy in which technique *is* image. It may even be that he believes this himself. He creates while cloistered in his room in his mother's Orlando home. He has no ax to grind, no influence to peddle, no agenda. But haunting the straight lines, extreme applications, and witty designs is a muted clamor that suggests that Garan's works are manifestations of his own troubled psyche.

For example, the character "Otto" came to Garan while he was thinking about "mechanical beings." Otto is emblematic of the artist's view of contemporary society as cold, predictable, and yet impenetrable. "I have this really weird dream where I'm stuck in a shrink-wrap machine," Garan explains. He is practiced in the art of deception; his flowers, figures, and assemblages conceal the artist's pain with their visual charm. Assessing the content of Garan's art is a lot like asking the proverbial question about the noise a falling tree makes in a deserted forest. It might be easier to agree that his art is substantial, that the artist is searching for significance. Whether or not it is intentional, Tony Garan's work probes the social insanities of our seemingly dysfunctional world.

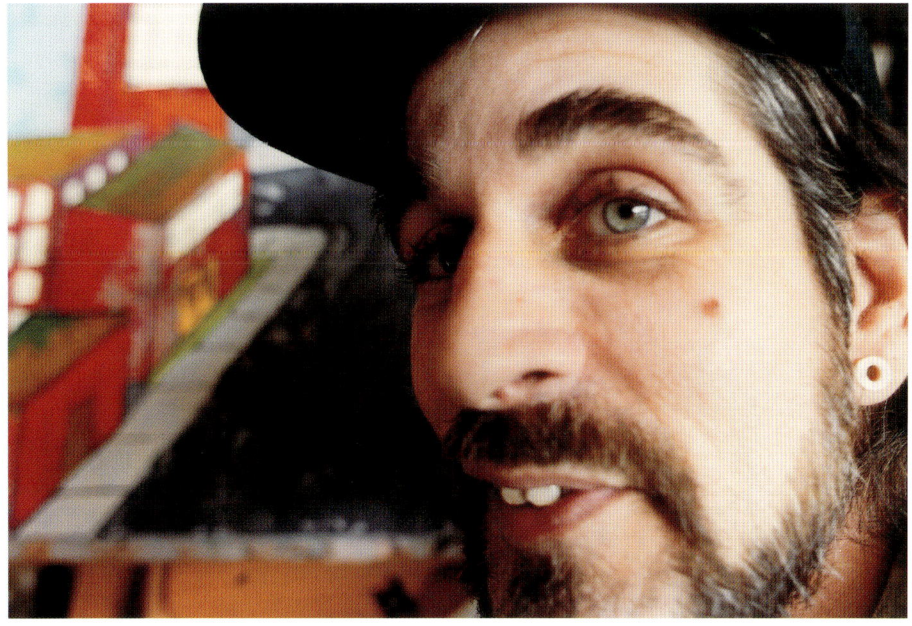

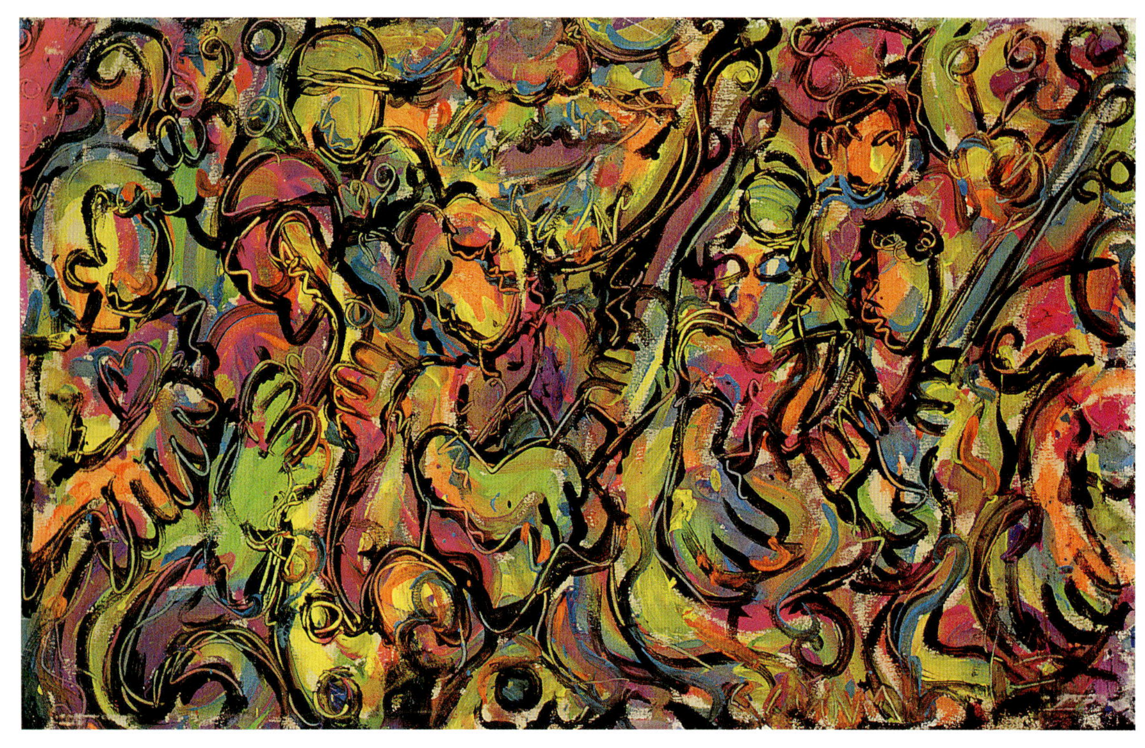

Keith Campbell. *The Other Ones.* 1998. 25" x 40".

KEITH CAMPBELL

b. 1964

Keith "Scramble" Campbell lives in a worn trailer off a dirt road in Altamonte Springs, between the migrant farmlands of Central Florida and the bustle of Orlando's business corridor. The artwork that is piled throughout and around the trailer, including his psychedelically painted Volkswagen van, suggests that a hippie lives here in bliss. And that is not far from the truth. Scramble has created a retro-sixties world. He is the spiritual center for Orlando's underground artists, including Steele, Knickerbocker, and Garan.

A few years after discovering Salvador Dali's art in 1986, Campbell's mission became clear. He wanted the duality of his "perceptions and depictions of life's puzzling meanings" to be a pathway to a collective consciousness. Common ground is the sixties—where looking at paintings about "things within things" would be "entertaining and absorbing"—when the world seemed on the verge of becoming a better place.

He practices "live art" (action painting) with bands and refers to his work as "painted music." He wields a brush on stage while rock, jazz, and punk bands play. His improvisational brush work keeps the sway of the rhythm. He dances "to the energy of the music" while painting, and since the crowd is often far away from the stage, his movements are sure and exaggerated. Performance painting brings the entire process alive because the shared energy of the music involves the audience: "I feel the vibration in the music and it makes me dance." And paint. Scramble's palette resembles tie-dyed shirts, and his paintings appear hallucinogenic. Forms swirl and colors bubble, like in a lava lamp.

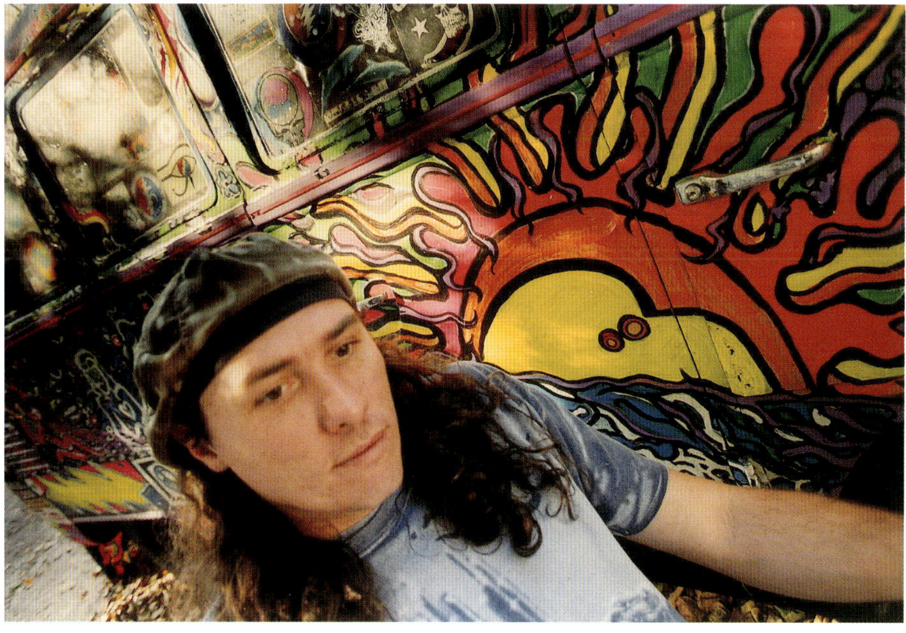

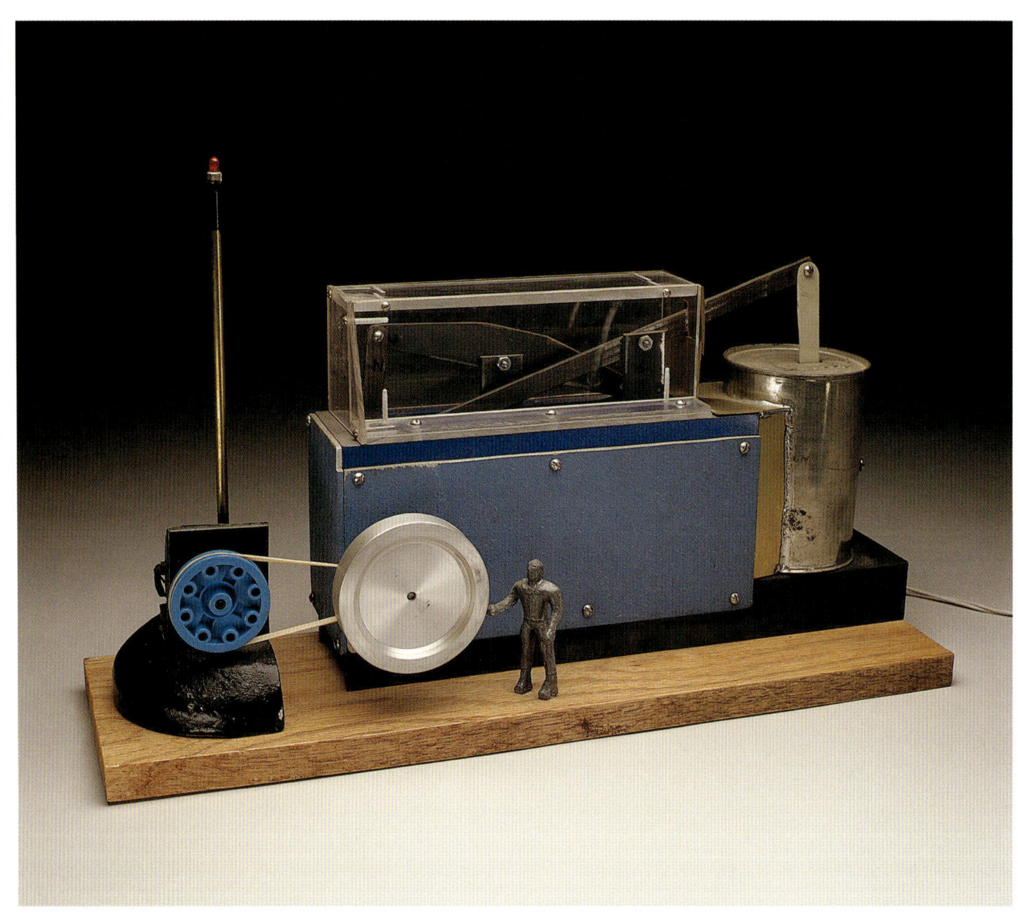

Mark Miller. Untitled. 11.75" x 19" x 5.75".

MARK MILLER

b. 1959

In his youth, Mark Miller saw things that he couldn't possess, including the robot in the TV series *Lost in Space.* Since there wasn't a model he could buy and assemble, he built his own robot from scratch. Miller has made countless variations since; not just robots but piston-driven machines in every size and shape. Miller casts the metal that houses his hand-built motors. He molds and forges the details that distinguish them, including the people and trimmings that define his 11 ft. by 30 ft. environment *The Big City,* a frenetic community that he built from the ground up. Everything in the artist's life is kinetic and revving at high RPMs.

Adjacent to his trailer on a large rural lot near Tallahassee is his "War Room." It looks like a bunker. Surrounded by a high wooden fence and camouflaged tarps, the sign over the portal reads "Foundry." He enclosed his hand-built furnace with bricks "to keep the shop from burning down." His shop seems like a Willy Wonka Chocolate Factory for a mad scientist—a Disney World gone bad, where hundreds of cast iron machines that would impress Rube Goldberg sit on shelves. Standing around are sculptures housing clocks that he has built but that, by design, do not keep time; that wasn't their function. The clanking noise that the gears make excites the inventor.

He has little interest in the completed pieces. He never casts editions but keeps producing new models because "copies can never be as good as originals."Fascinated by the loud, driving repetition of the engines, with their moving armatures revealing their form, he has made thousands of precise and exquisite machines.

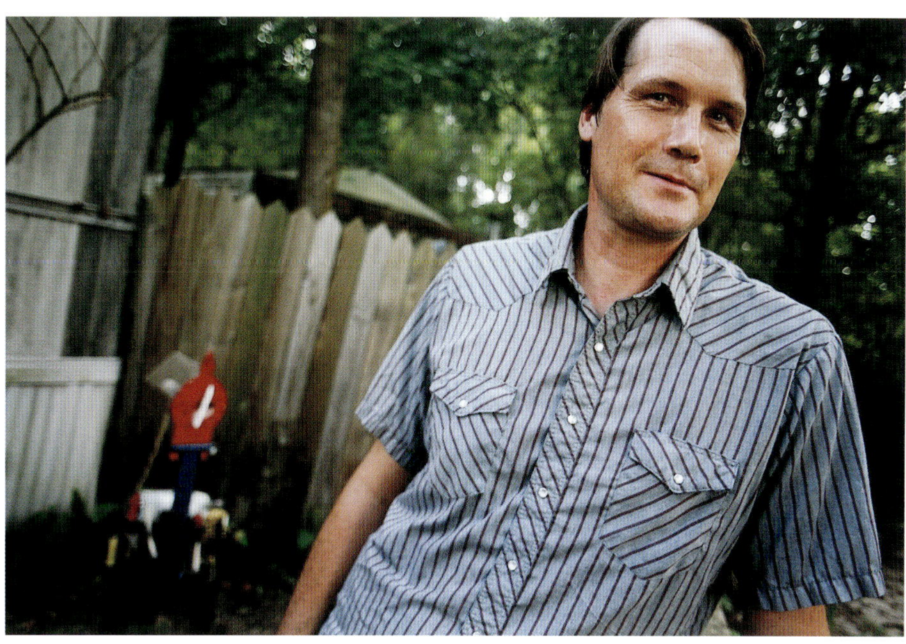

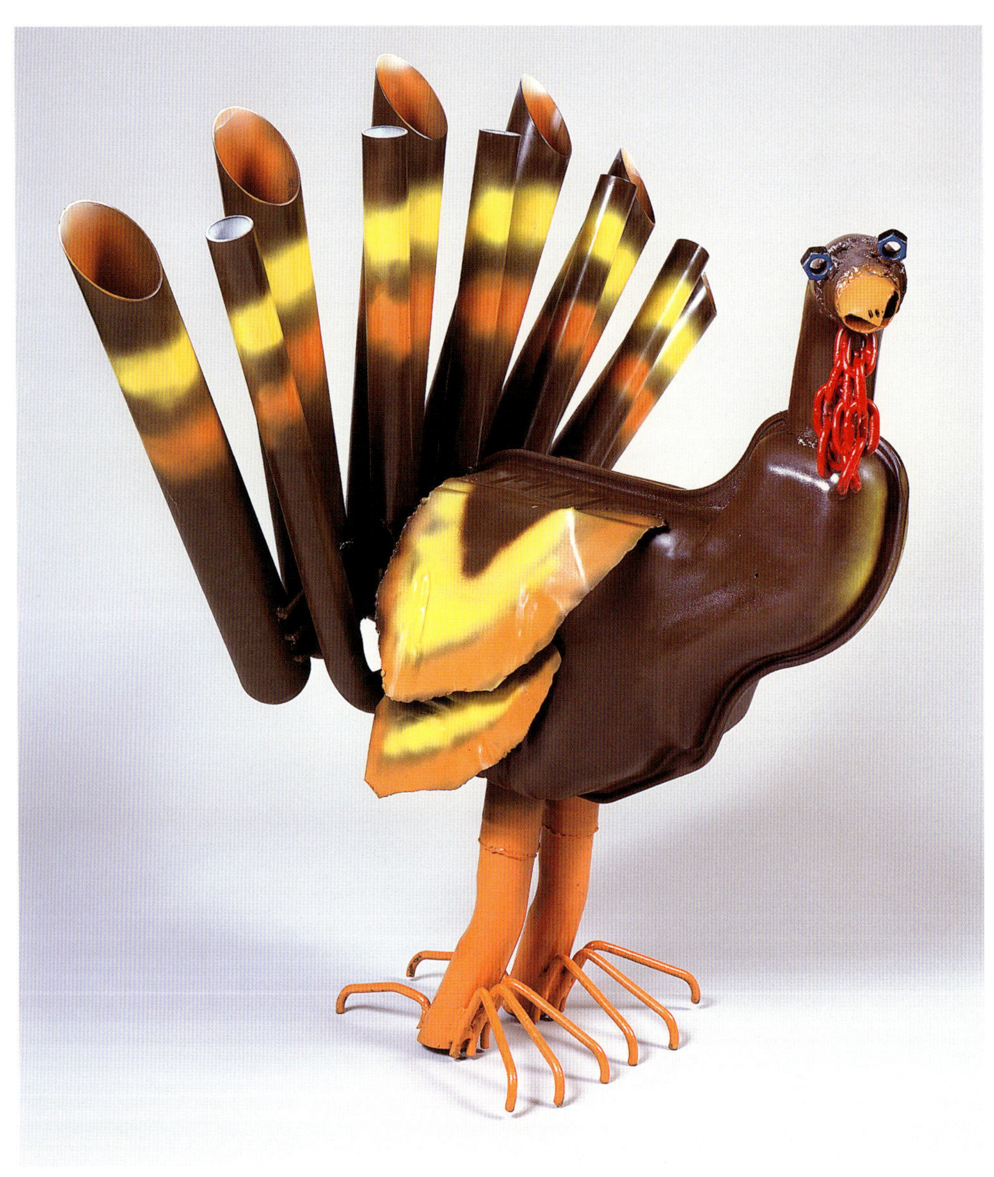

Kevin Doyle. *Turkey.* 2002. 40.5" x 42" x 32".

KEVIN DOYLE

b. 1954

There is dead time in the muffler business, time spent waiting for mufflers to go bad. Kevin Doyle, of the town of Davie, is co-owner of Mad Hatter Mufflers. He sculpts as an avocation. He smiles a heartwarming smile. Doing business with him must be a pleasure because the shop is generally busy. A conversation may go like this: "It's a secondary muffler. Dogs are $150; the tailpipe is 85." His conversations are mixed with laughter. Although he sells many of the animals that he makes, his roadside animal farm is always well populated, invigorating the otherwise desolate urban landscape and offering cheer to countless motorists.

All mufflers are created different. So anticipating what animal or form each muffler suggests excites Doyle as he removes it from the underbelly of the vehicle. Honda mufflers are short and round and "make great heads. GMC Suburbans' [mufflers] make good bodies." Tailpipes are good snakes. Doyle is concerned with materials too. Because he installs many high-performance mufflers for car enthusiasts wanting to replace factory-installed mufflers, he enjoys an unending supply of like-new "body parts."

Most of the animals are domestic and made with an artisan's sense of craft. They are creations without any of the hidden meanings that people suppose permeate works of art. Kevin Doyle likes to make "fun stuff." He tries his best to represent the animals realistically. "A dog looks like a dog. If it doesn't, I didn't do a good job," he says. He has tried four shades of brown Rustoleum in search of the right one for a Chesapeake Retriever. Recycled, buffed, and primed, Doyle's sculptures emerge from a palette that is bright and right out of the spray can.

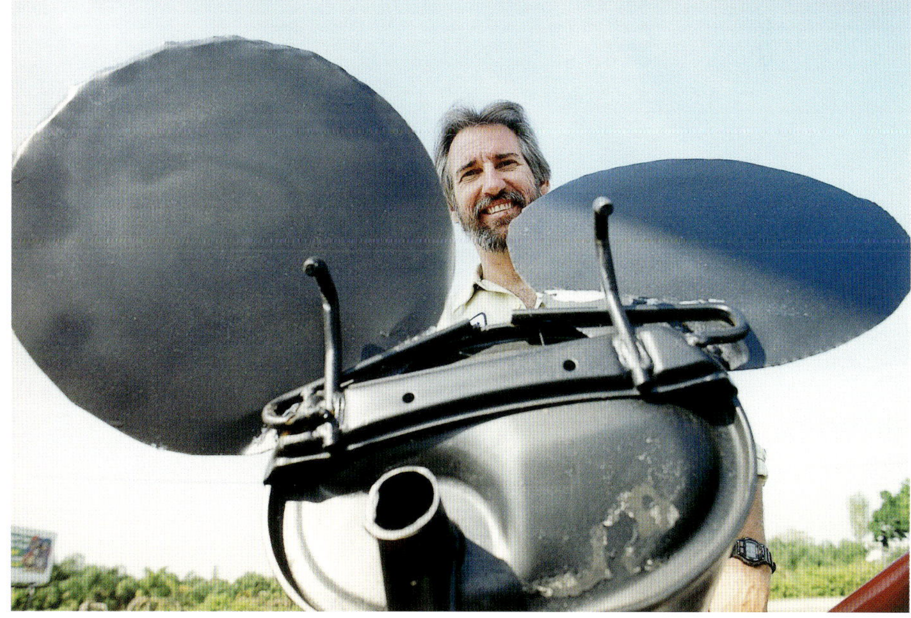

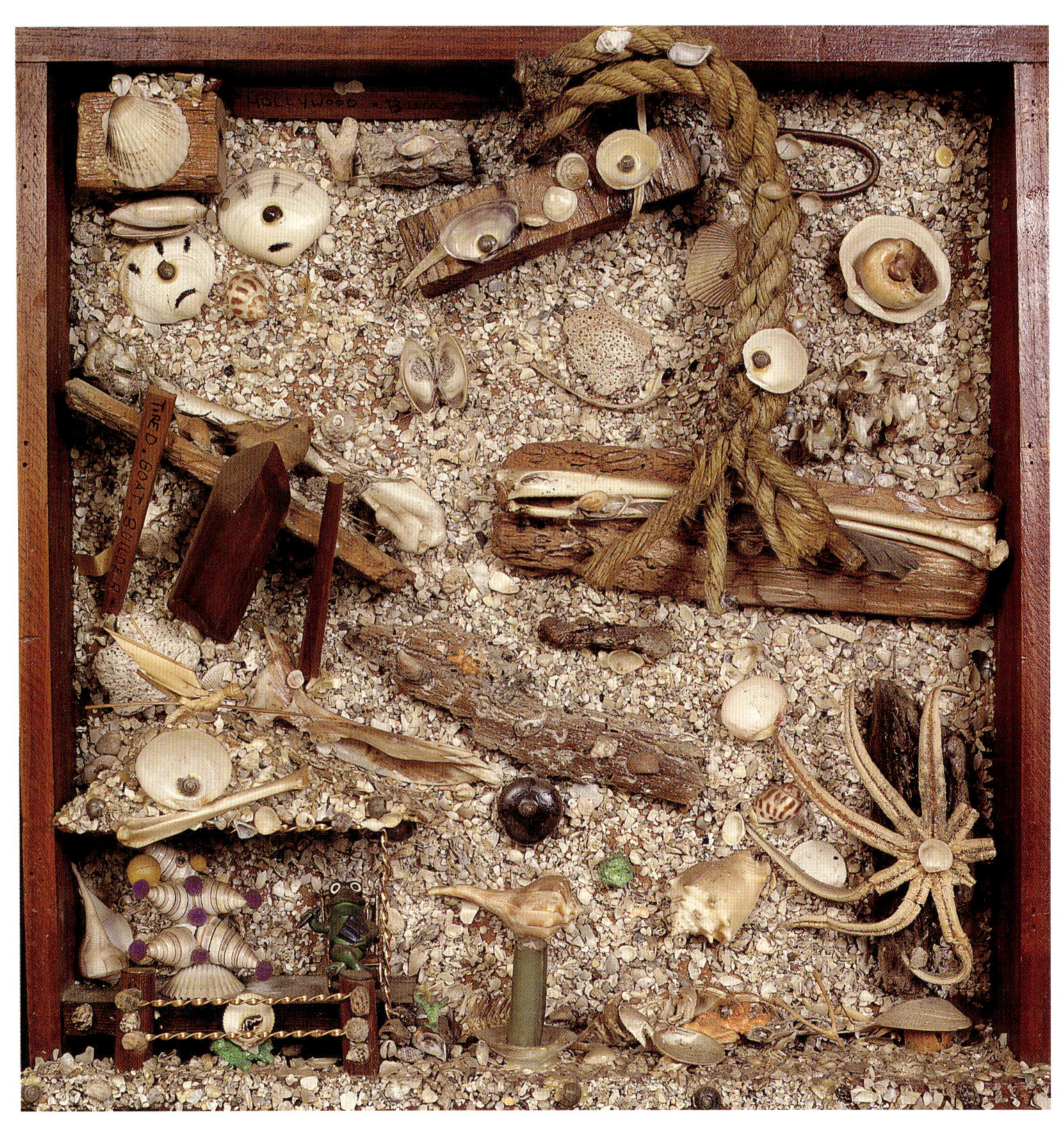

Arthur Desillier. Untitled. 24.5" x 24" x 4.75".

ARTHUR DESILLIER

b. 1922

In Fort Pierce, Arthur Desillier created a pleasant environment in his otherwise bleak existence. With a meager Social Security check augmented by cash earned from recycling aluminum cans, and surrounded by neighbors whose behavior he deplored, Desillier made another world for himself. For much of his life, he was an amateur clown and performed in hundreds of parades.

In the narrow front yard of Desillier's rickety home were numerous structures cordoned off by makeshift fences that were unified by lush plantings. Three shrinelike structures, each about five feet high and almost as wide and deep, contained model houses. One is tempted to relate these objects to concepts of home and family, which Desillier never had. He explains that each edifice took a year to make. A sign posted in the yard of one of the homes read, "For Sale as Is." He says, "It is my idea to make a different place."

Throughout his rented old house were odd assemblages of debris—including shells, sticks, seaweed, and corks—glued onto beach sand–covered boards. These pieces were without motif or message; they were anti-art, if art was a concern at all. It was not. He has also made large, geographically oriented dioramas showing highways and mountain roads that heighten a sense of traveling or passing through or being passed by.

When his home was condemned—only to be demolished—Desillier unceremoniously carted all of his creations to the Salvation Army, keeping just the bare essentials that would fit into the boardinghouse room he moved into.

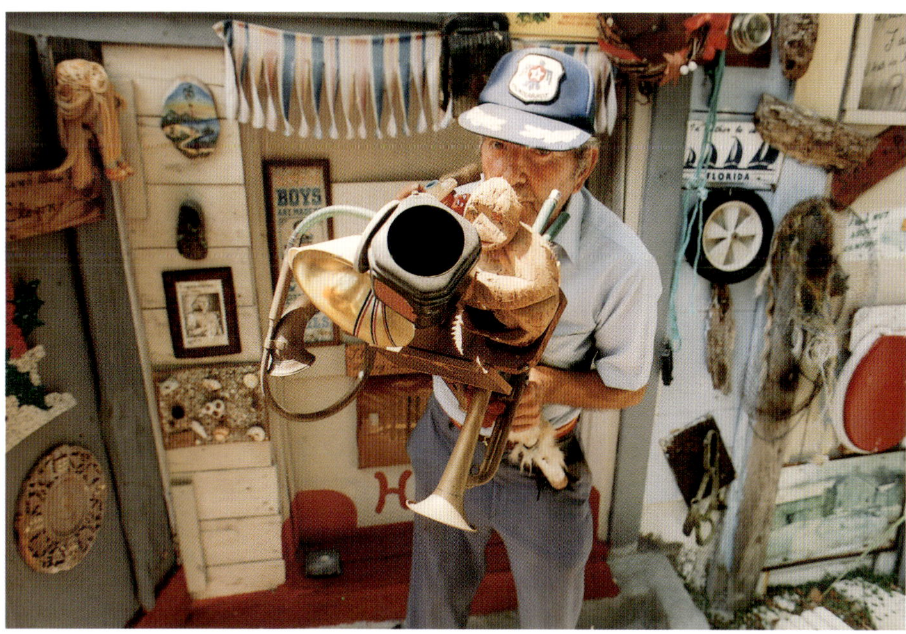

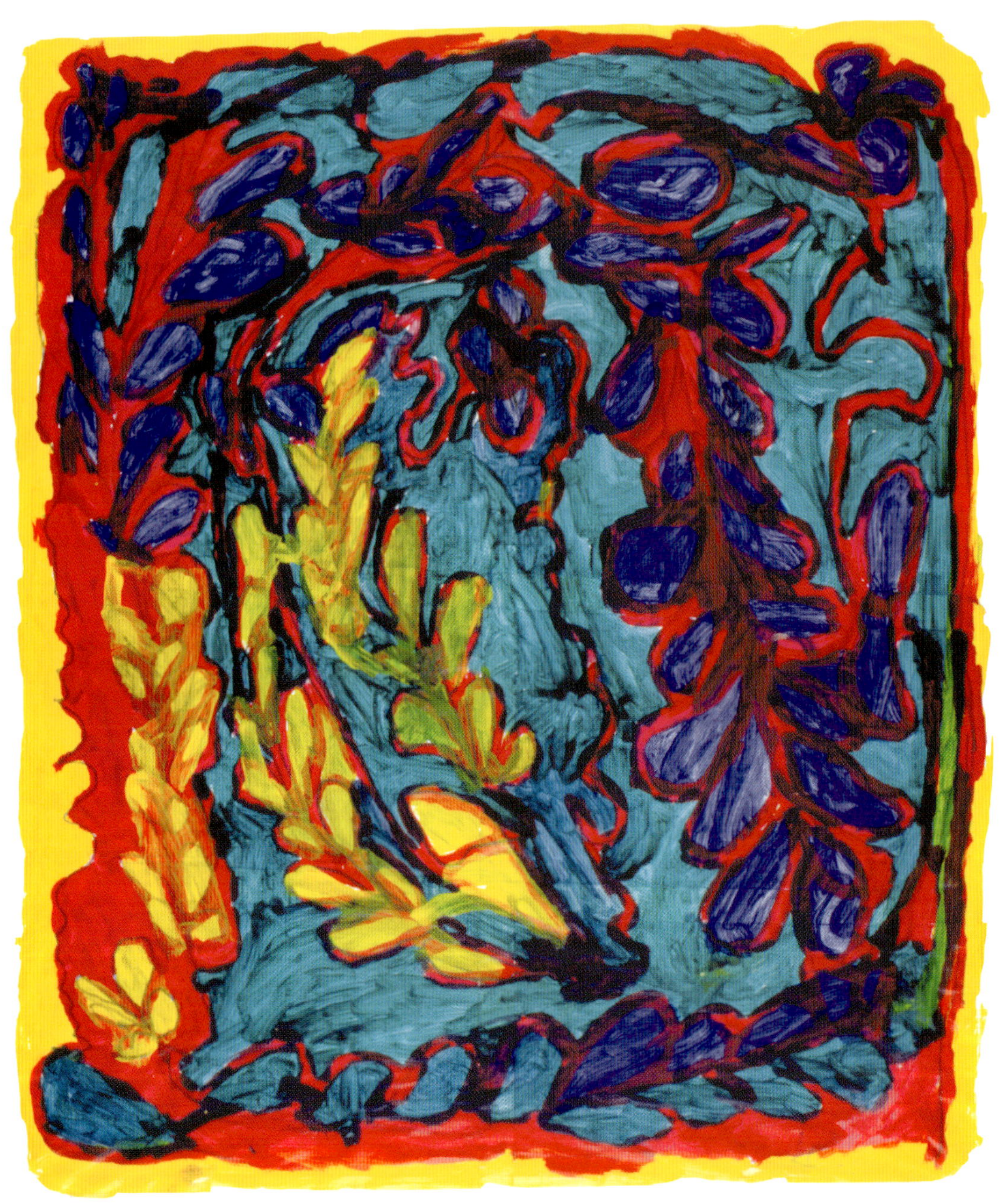

Tom Cummings. Untitled. 32.5" x 26.75". 2002.

TOM CUMMINGS

b. 1942

Tom Cummings paints pictures of flora and sometimes of houses, working off to the side of the sheltered workshop where fellow members of the Gainesville chapter of the Association for Retarded Citizens assemble packages. The association serves as a production facility for government and private industry. "It's a love of his. That's all he does," says Donald Talerico, ARC's activities coordinator. He believes painting has enhanced Cummings' limited cognitive process: "He'll do something by accident in one painting, and he'll make the most of it; he'll incorporate what he's found [in other paintings]."

"I get a lot of money. Cash money . . . two for five dollars." boasts Cummings. Numbers are meaningless to him because of his developmental disability. One of his practices is to charge by the number of floors in the houses he paints. But painting is of great emotional value to him. "He made it clear he needed paint," explains Talerico, and a constant flow of tempera followed as staff members bought the artist's works. Soon Cummings became communicative and was "always in a good mood." Although uninterested in others' art, he finds contentment as he draws and vividly paints the plant life and dwellings that inhabit his paintings.

Cummings sits behind his work table with a half-dozen of his large paintings tacked on the walls behind him and another couple of dozen stacked nearby, overseeing his world of leaves and trees and edifices as they take shape, while other ARC members perform their piece work. "All this here. I did it myself," he says. "I need a big sign." The one that says "Original Tom Cummings Paintings For Sale And Starting At Just $6" doesn't seem big enough. "Can't nobody else do that but me."

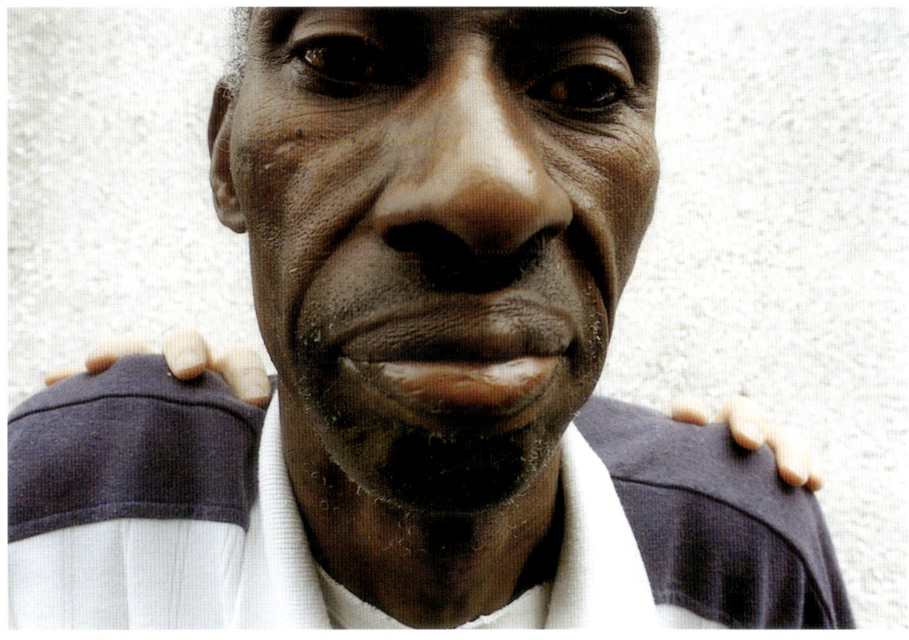

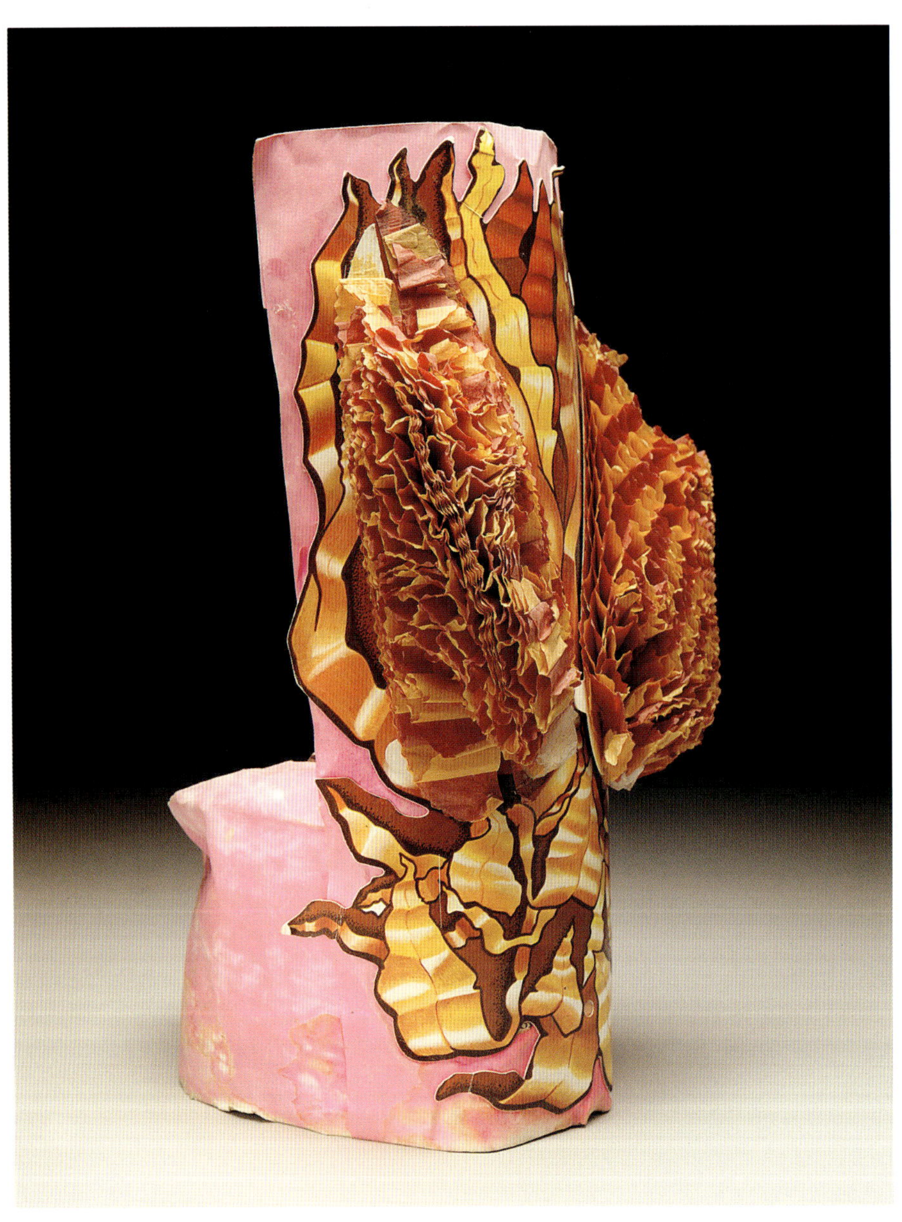

Joseph Abrams. Untitled. 14.625" x 6" x 7".

JOSEPH ABRAMS

1906–1998

At a retirement residence in Miami Beach, Joseph Abrams began making and selling hats in 1987. He continued his business venture until he passed away. Trendy Ocean Drive was his sales territory, and he kept set business hours: mornings until lunch was served at the retirement home, and afternoons between one and four o'clock.

Without a doubt, Abrams considered his work to be a commercial enterprise. His hats sold for two to five dollars each. Having spent his adult life working as a jeweler and in the family women's wear retail business in New York, Joseph Abrams knew how to make a buck. But, in retirement, tourists and locals became his customers. Sometimes vacationers took snapshots and then handed him money. "One man gave me a ten-dollar bill. I swear to God," he recalled. "He didn't even take a hat!"

Abrams began the construction of his hats by forming a skullcap out of newspaper. More paper was rolled into cones to build the sides. Each hat was uniquely decorated using ribbons or small toys. (Add-ons cost fifty cents apiece.) Some of the hats featured postcards of bikini-clad women. Abrams maintained that "Miami has the most beautiful girls in the world."

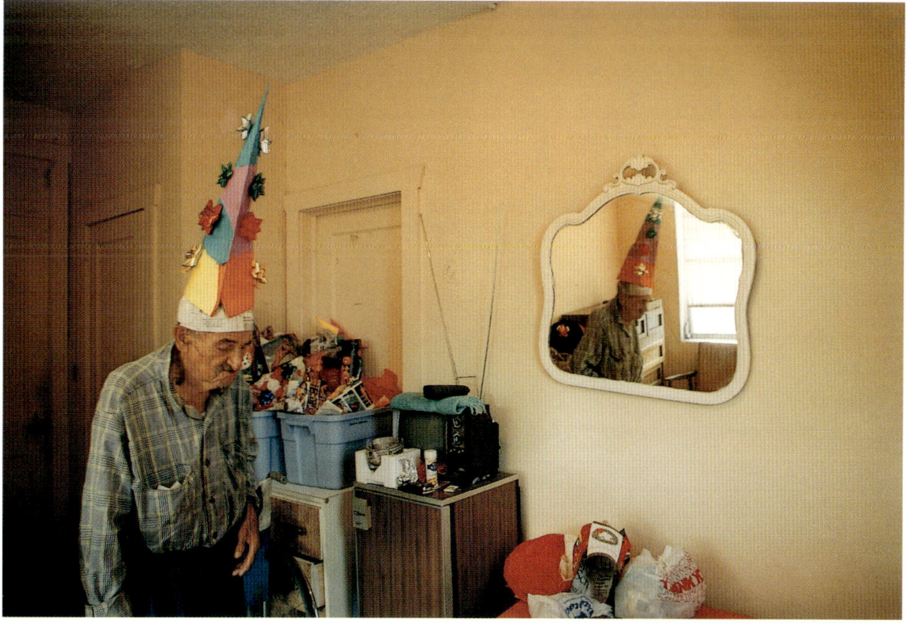

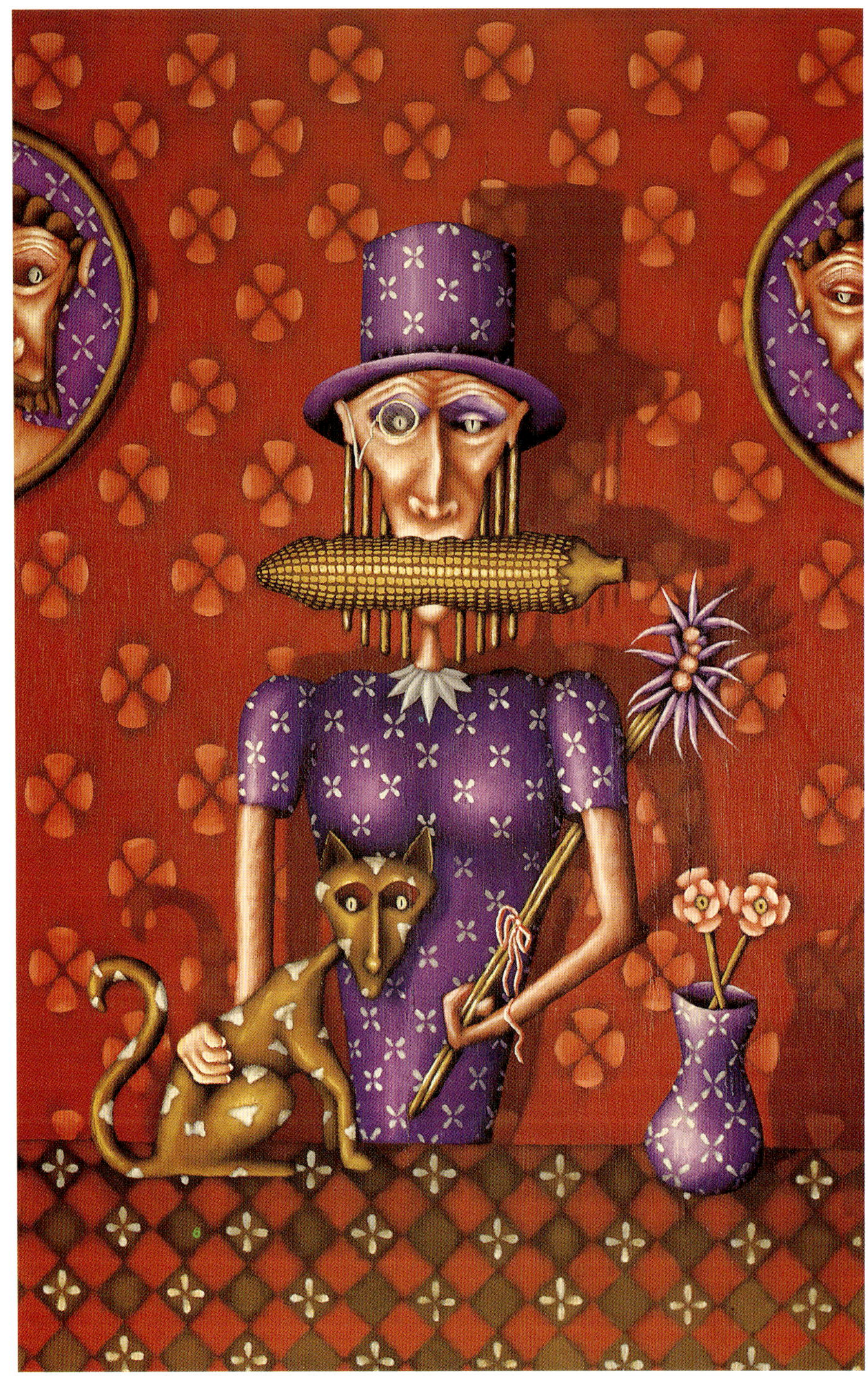

Jay Schuette. *The Impatient Silence.* 2002. 29.825" x 19.5".

JAY SCHUETTE

b. 1964

Jay Schuette, who lived on the other side of fashionable Lincoln Road near Joseph Abrams, is about three generations younger and appeared to fit right into the South Beach scene. But unlike Abrams, he didn't; he resented its decadence. He came to Miami in 1991, to find the city culturally barren. He disliked everything there except the climate and flora. He read the *New York Times* instead of the *Miami Herald,* not because he necessarily preferred the *Times* but because he loathed Miami. So he moved to San Francisco.

Schuette is best known for his "corn people" paintings. He traces this interest back to his youth in Oxford, Ohio, where the civility of formal family dining was pitted against something raw and primal about the act of ripping corn kernels off the cob. "Eating corn-on-the-cob gave me the creeps," he recalls with a shiver. This disparity became grist for more than 150 paintings, all involving people and corn-on-the-cob.

Schuette's feelings about his family, about how its members hid behind table manners, are vented by his painted people who leer through dilated eyes and whose bony arms grip the corn like both shields and flutes. The figures in his paintings are intimately strange because they express the artist's bewilderment and alienation. The scenes that Jay Schuette conjures are metaphors of his worldview and a countermeasure for his having to live in such a rude place.

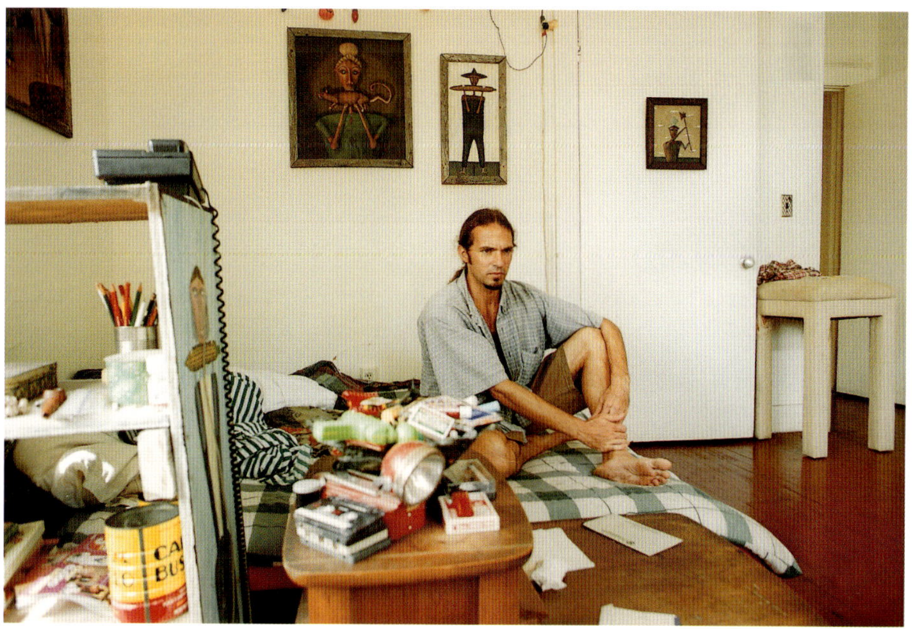

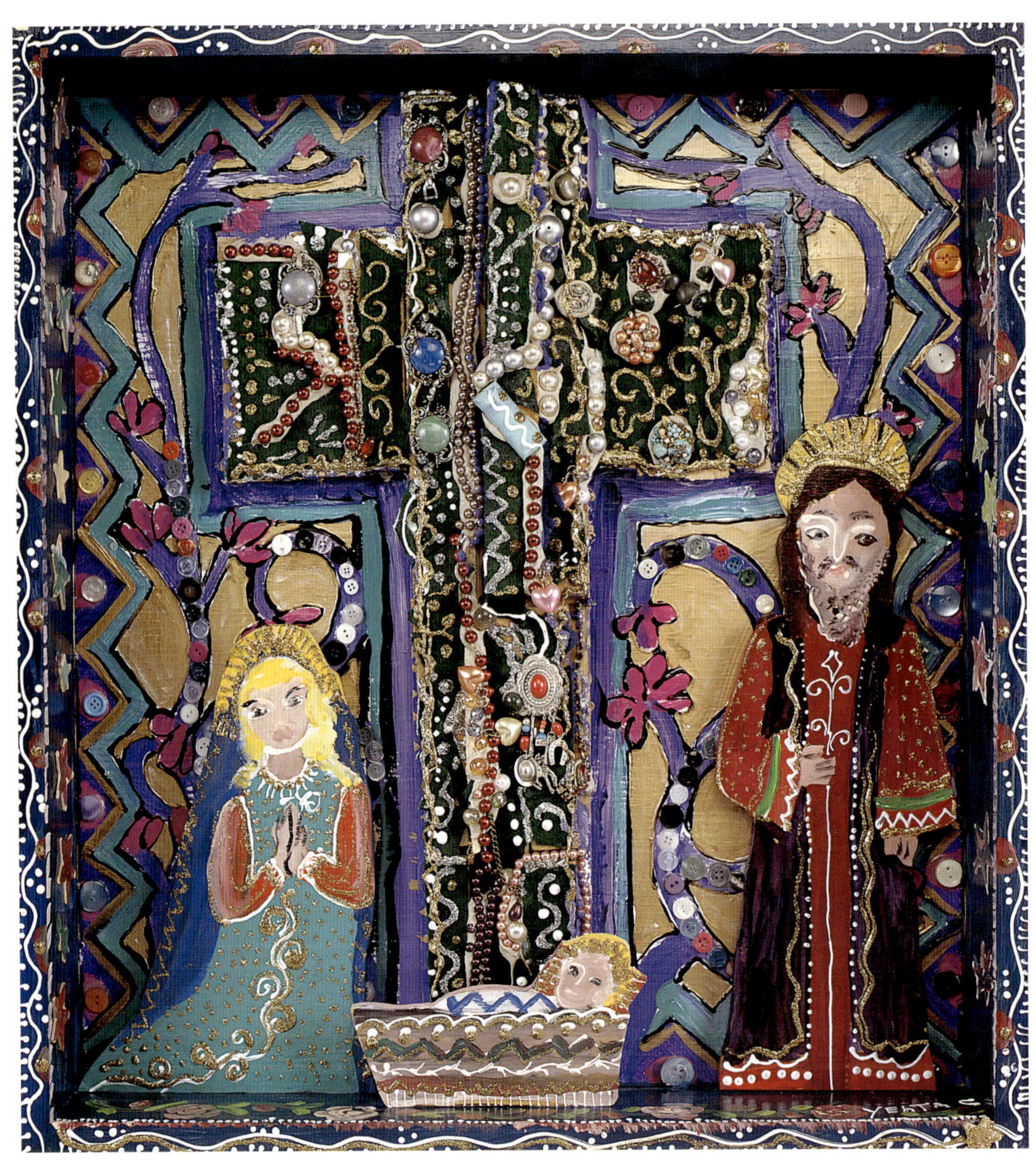

Cathey Kalista. *A Christmas Scene.* 2002. 25.25" x 23.5" x 4".

CATHEY KALISTA

b. 1934

Cathey Kalista lives in West Palm Beach and shares a small house with her daughter, son-in-law, and granddaughter. As she ages, she feels younger. "I'm going backward in life," she says. That partially explains why she signs her paintings and creations "Yehtac." She also signs her name backward to remain anonymous, not necessarily to let the work speak for itself or because she fears attention, but to avoid having people comment on her art or tell her how to paint.

Kalista has retrieved things from other people's trash for as long as she can remember. The things that she reclaims have life in them. She considers herself less an artist than an environmentalist, helping by "repairing" the world. Wood gets a new life as a landscape, often depicting row houses from her native Paterson, New Jersey, or it may become an audience of deranged children or maybe a nude. She revives broken bowls as ornate and colorful urns and enjoys arranging scrap material into monolithic sculptures.

Referring to her wide-ranging tastes, she comments, "It's like psycho." Kalista's unassuming, nonconformist attitude is refreshingly expressive of the nature of self-taught art. "I try to use as many colors as will be friendly with each other." As she says, "There's room for everything."

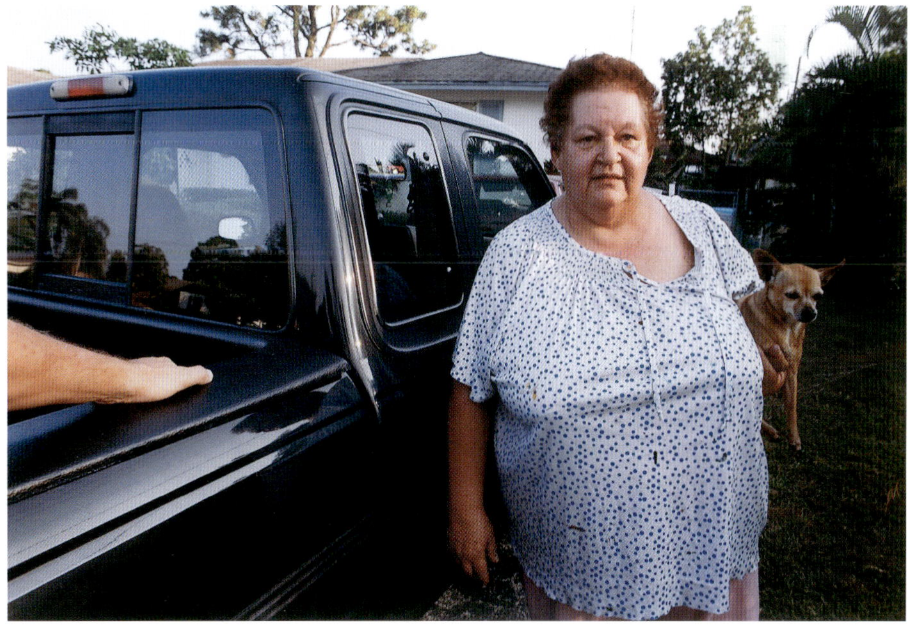

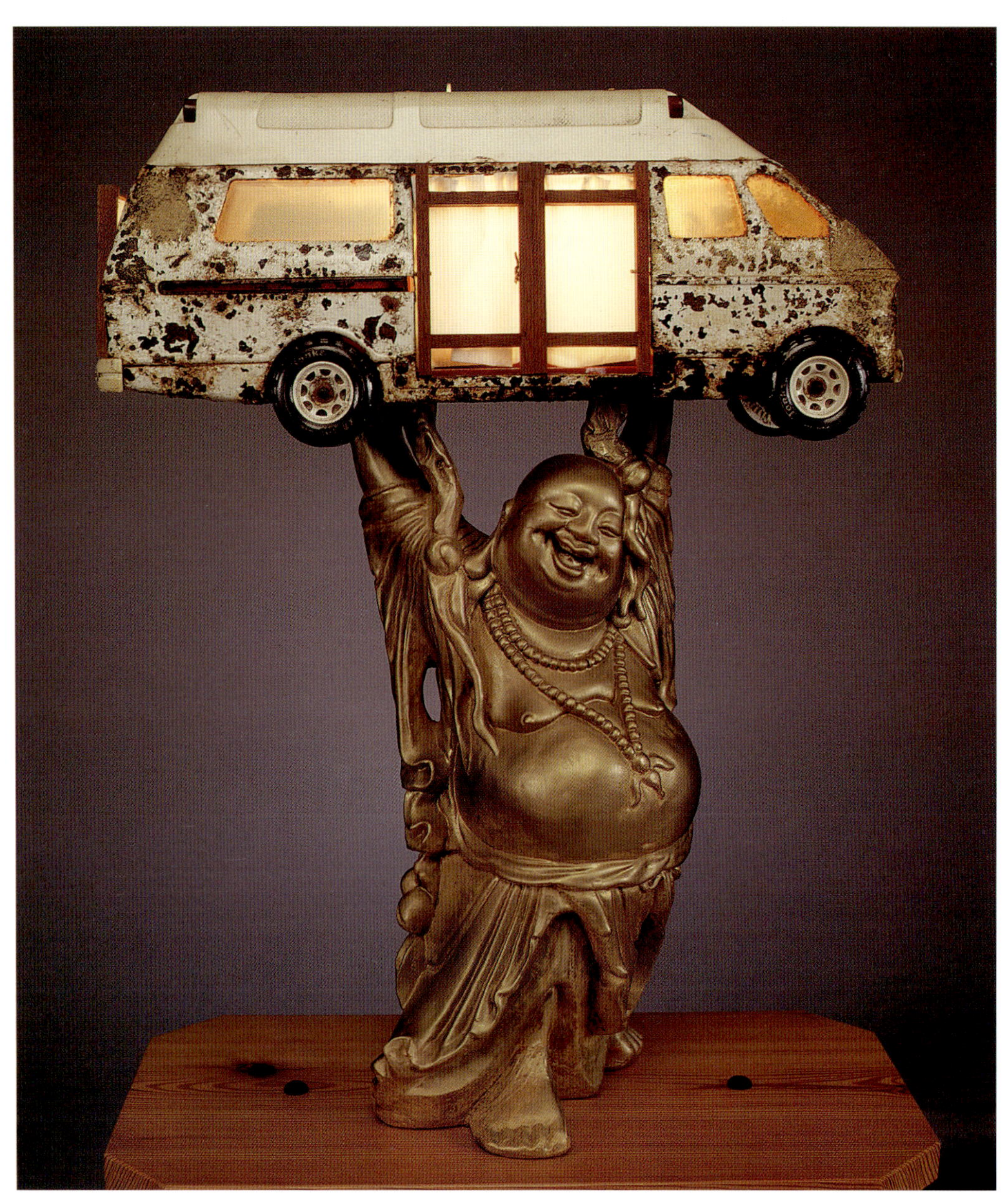

George Ferreira. *Junkyard Hotel*. 2001. 25.75" x 20.5" x 11".

GEORGE FERREIRA

b. 1946

After choosing a life in the woods near McIntosh and feeling "caught between two worlds," George Ferreira wanted to be recognized not as an "outsider" but as a vital sculptor. He makes one-of-a-kind pieces of furniture for a living. Like other craftsmen, his prized works adorn professional offices and stately homes, but he stops just shy of being "funky" for these commissions. He can get away with incorporating a long bamboo timber into the back of a bench, but his more personal style involves what he refers to as "play."

Aesthetically sophisticated but removed from the concerns of academic and professional artists, Ferreira's play yields pieces that don't quite fit into the fine art rubric. A cow bone becomes the extension for a too-short stool; a Buddha raises a model of a VW van to become a table lamp; newel posts return as lovers, embracing with their orange-tree twig limbs. Ferreira revels in how the found materials he incorporates into his whimsical artworks suggest the objects. He sees his role as an "articulator," encouraging "the natural shapes to speak for themselves" while in fact creating something new.

Nature inspires Ferreira to create "from the heart." He and his friend, naturalist and folk art aficionado Ty Tyson, made furniture together by using palm fronds as an expression of "nature's purity." (Tyson discovered the prototype, made in the 1930s, on the porch of an old black man's home in Micanopy.) For them, putting indigenous materials to functional ends was neither a lark nor a marketing scheme but was rather an ethical decision, a way of coming to terms with nature, art, and life in Florida.

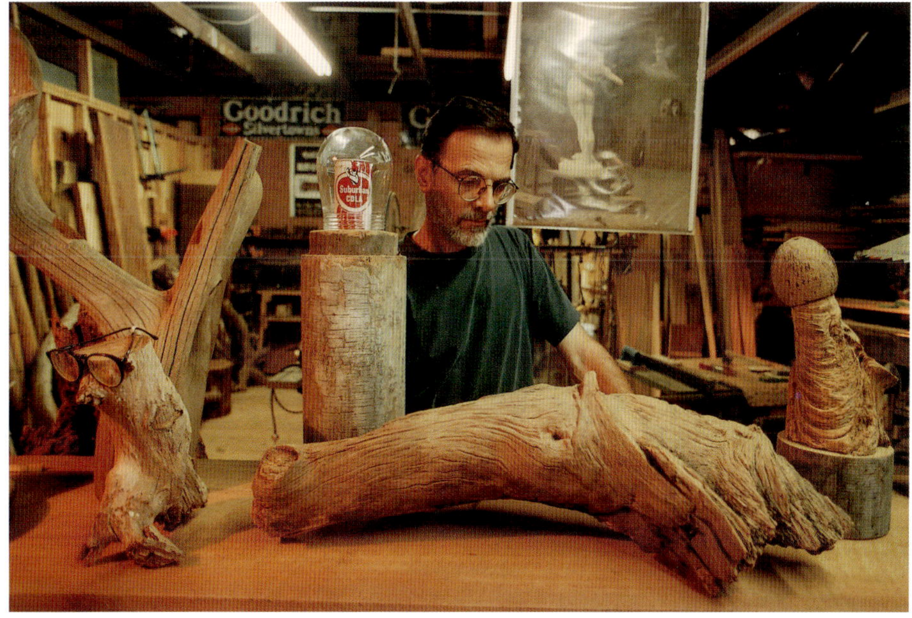

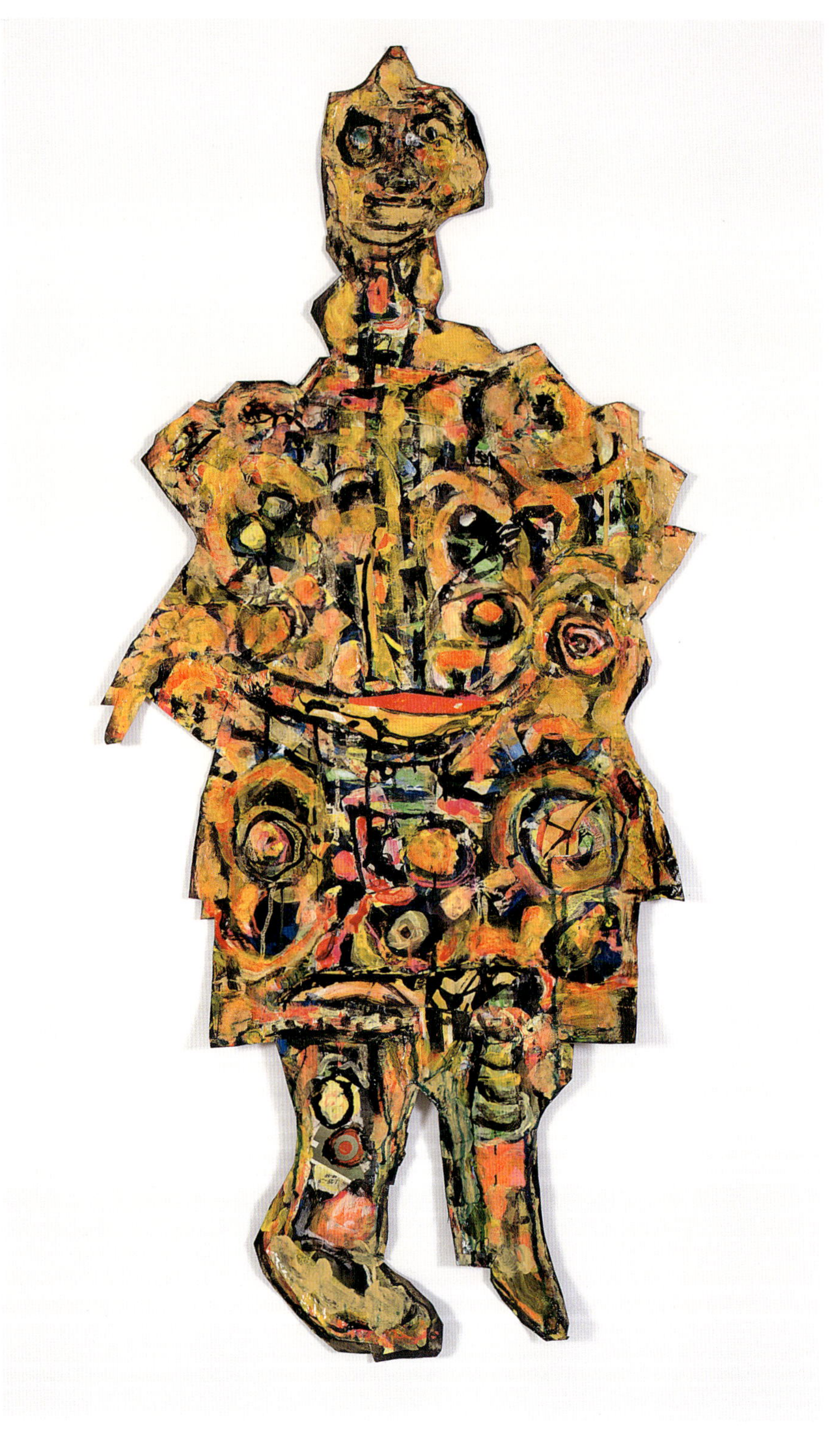

Reva Freedman. Untitled. 50.5" x 23.25".

REVA FREEDMAN

b. 1919

When Reva Freedman says, "I don't paint for fun, I paint for real," she likely means that the process of painting engenders an intuitive "dialogue" that guides her mark making. Her creativity would be stifled should another person approach her while she's working; painting would become a "thinking thing." Thought inhibits her freewheeling visual associations.

She preferred the informality of painting to the rigors of music, so decades ago she gave up practicing the violin in her search of "a better way." Her quest took her to New York City, where in 1940 she painted a rural scene in which a barn looked like a river. A country road became a mountain, and Reva Freedman was on her way to becoming an artist. It wasn't that the objects she painted looked like something else, but that they didn't look exactly like *anything* that gave her strength.

"I paint every night. I can paint all night." In a dynamic similar to that of call-and-response field hollers, she and the paintings define themselves through a give-and-take process. As she brushes and sponges fluorescent colors across large sheets of paper that are tacked on her dining room walls, her labor finds cohesive and resonant forms: "Shmeer it a little here, I shmeer it a little there." And she will return to her works, both in progress and long ago "completed," to change them again and again.

Reva Freedman is surrounded by a thousand of her paintings. Many are rolled up and stored in closets, ready to cascade down whenever a door is opened. They are scattered throughout the three bedrooms of her Aventura apartment in North Miami, where other senior citizens play golf and lounge by the pool and gossip at social luncheons. "I had a very exciting life through painting," she concludes.

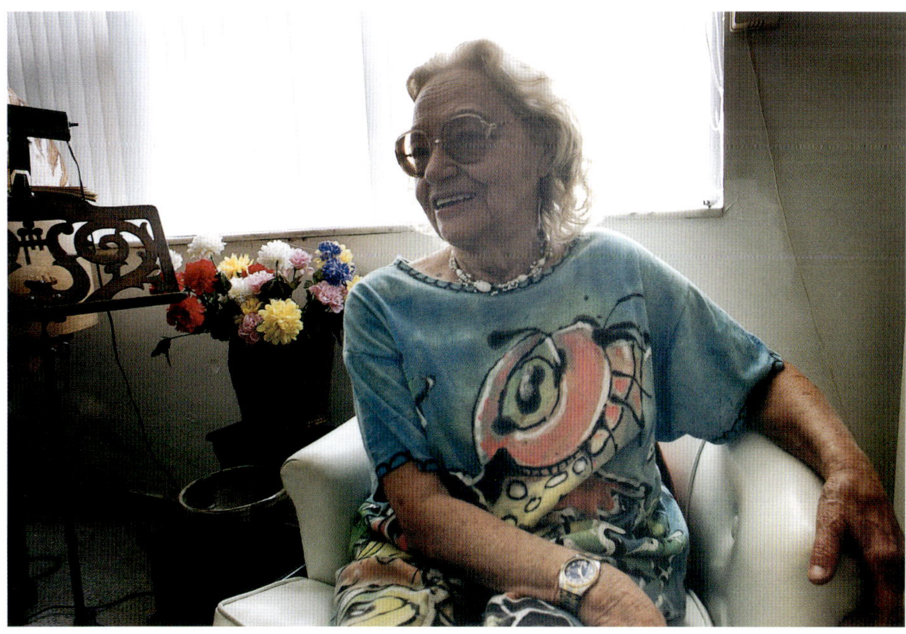

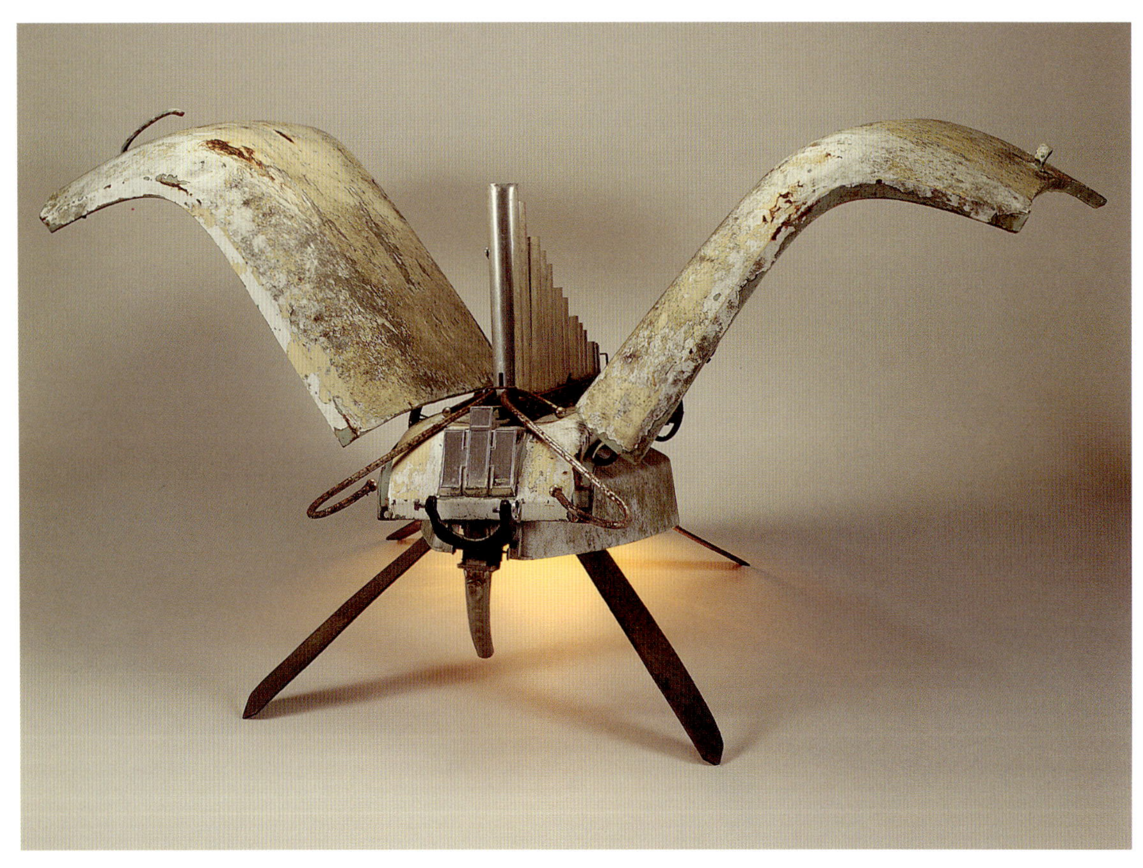

Celino Dimitroff. *Aphid Gigantus.* 2001. 29" x 77" x 45.75".

CELINO DIMITROFF

b. 1958

Born in France, the son of a military man who also was an artist, Celino Dimitroff grew up in Europe. Schools there made regular excursions to museums. Art and more surrounded him; one night he awoke to find his father working on a painting of a nude model in the living room. "Art was everywhere!" But he found "the inaccessibility of high art to people in low places" troubling.

Dimitroff didn't think in terms of his own artistic sensibilities until his son, Nicholas, was born in 1986. As a single father of a son born premature with serious health problems, Dimitroff wasn't able to leave his Gainesville home. With a lot of time on his hands, his ideas coalesced, and he began gathering things—"anything, scraps of paper; it didn't matter"—with the intention of "turning funk into function."

Perhaps Dimitroff's deep-seated fear of the dark was just as responsible as his hard times in adulthood for his creations of "light as sculpture made from found objects." In his *Life Forms* series, the artist assembles animals, humans, and plants. His *Aphid Gigantus* was gleaned from the shell of a streetlight (body), the furrowers of a field plow (legs), and a pair of Volkswagen side windows (wings). *Swan Resting* was reconfigured with lamp parts, while the wings were fashioned from cut tin. *As the World Turns*—which combines a 1940s radio on which a metal globe spins alongside a steel spiral strip, over all of which a purple light bulb hovers—transforms popular culture elements into a curious sculpture.

Dimitroff's lamps are not to be used to light a room or even illuminate the pages of a book, but it would be demeaning to describe the light his pieces cast as mood lighting. Although his work is primarily aesthetic, many of his pieces contain compartments "for stash," and there are some house clocks. But each of Dimitroff's sculptures, when connected by "a life line" (extension cord), casts unexpected patterns of light against otherwise plain and predictable surfaces.

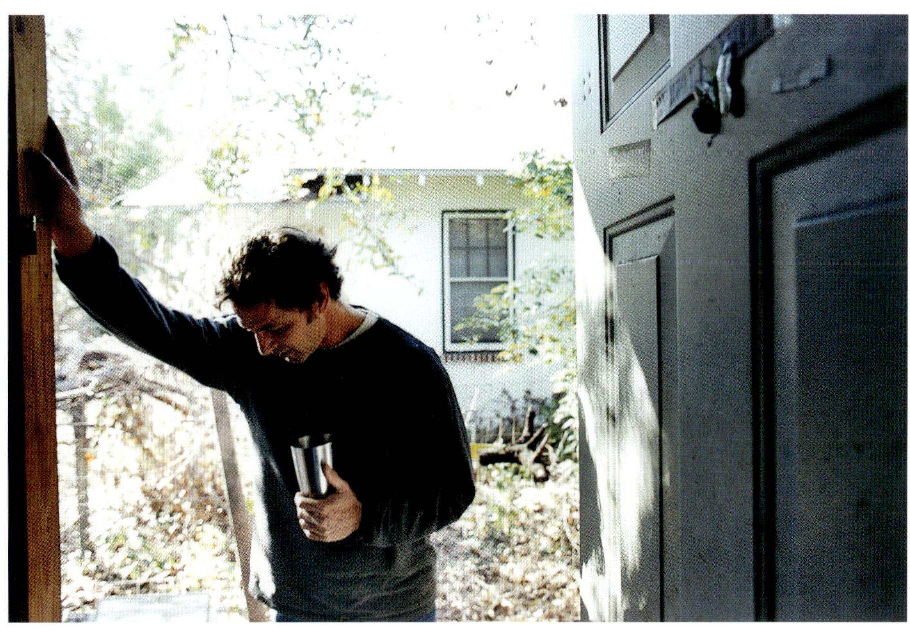

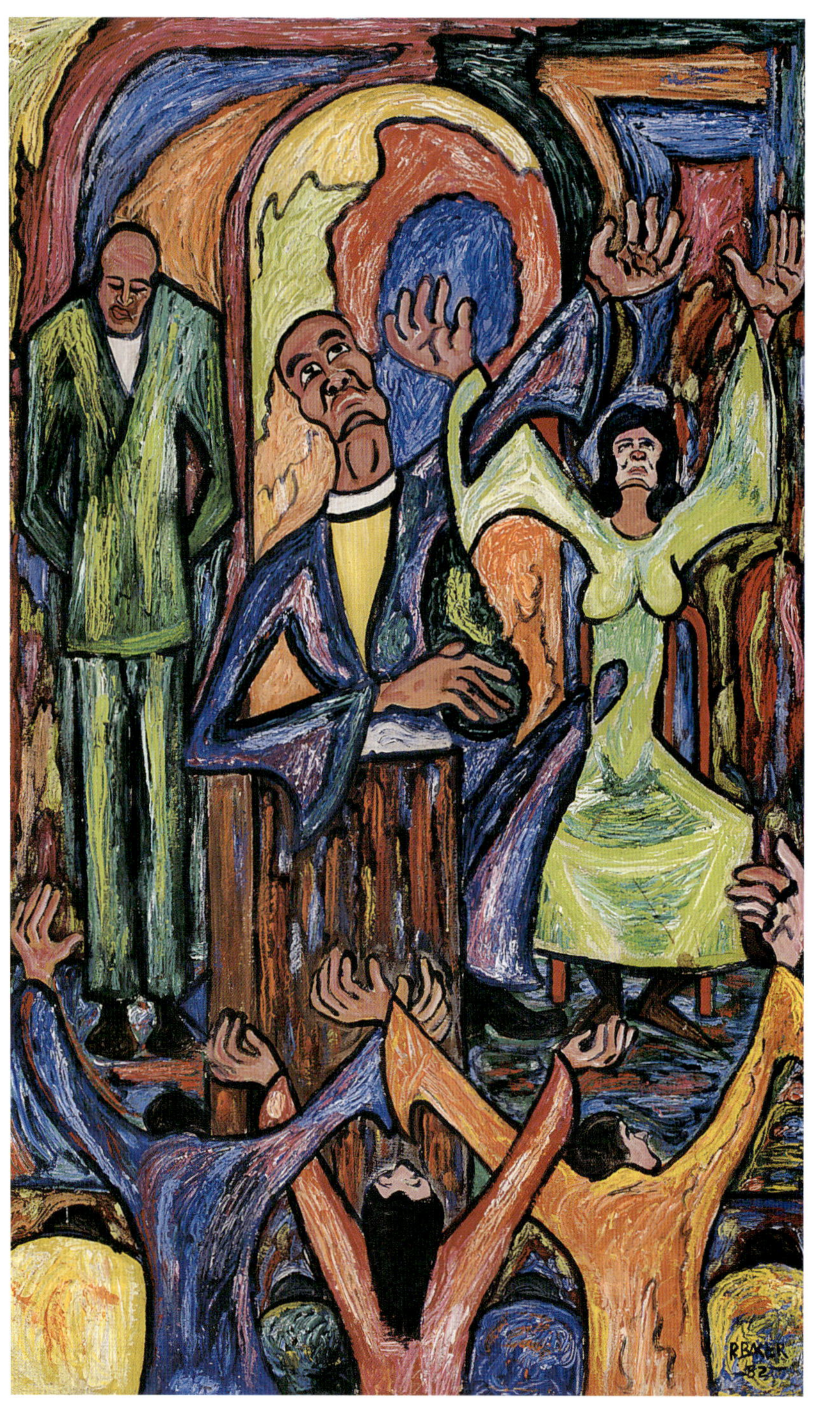

Pharaoh Baker. Untitled. 39.5" x 24".

PHARAOH BAKER

1925–2002

Pharaoh Baker linked two events as the precursors for his becoming an artist: First, his father took him to Marianna, where a black man with a rope around his neck hung from a tree in front of the county courthouse. Then only nine years old, Baker was petrified. A few years later, a preacher told him to draw the pastoral scene depicted on the hand fan upon which he was gazing instead of paying attention to the sermon. The minister gave him five dollars for the rendering!

Baker studied art at Florida A&M University, where his teachers wisely convinced him that his goal of learning to draw realistically was unnecessary. Instead, they encouraged him to develop his own style. Baker went on to work as a professional sign painter in Lake City, but on the side he painted images that projected all the anguish he felt. Looking at Baker's work was "like seeing the blues on canvas," said Blanton Owen, a Florida Folklife Program coordinator. The Florida Folklife Program, a component of the Florida Department of State's Division of Historical Resources, documents and presents the folklife, folklore, and folk arts of the state.

Baker believed in the Bible, and his paintings illustrate chapter and verse and testimony. Long lines, like woodcuts, and colors that vivify the artist's suffering distinguish the paintings. His images narrate Christian themes within a southern black cultural ethos: Peter is crucified upside down; Christ sips wine during his last earthly night in the Garden of Gethsemane; Judas bestows the "kiss of death" on Jesus' cheek.

Any angst that disturbs the viewer is but a shadow of Pharaoh Baker's burden.

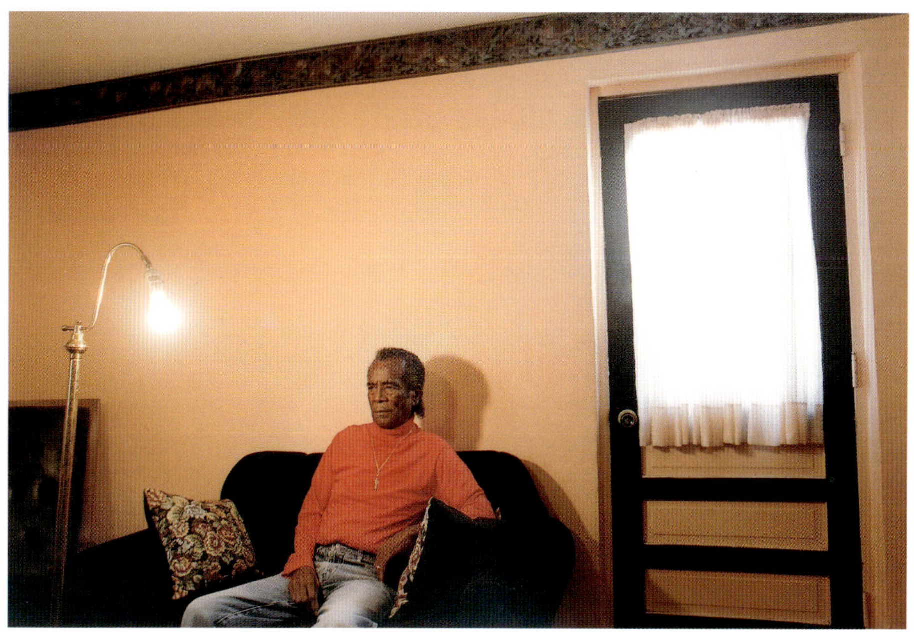

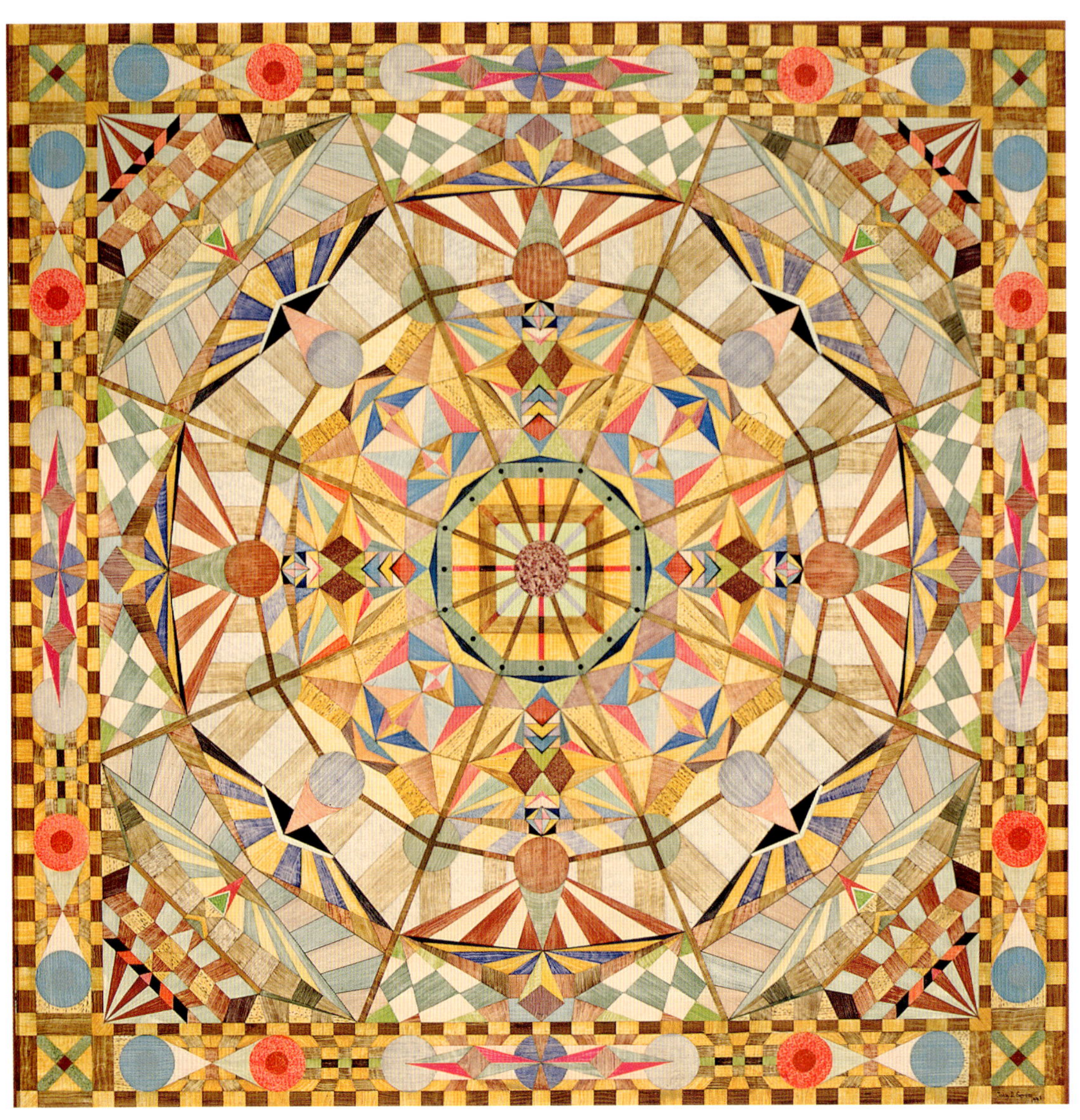

John Gerdes. *Kaleidoscope IV.* 1986. 48" x 48".

JOHN GERDES

1913–2001

John Gerdes made "inlaid paintings" that mimic different types of wood. His father, a cabinetmaker and watercolorist, was his role model. By age ten, Gerdes was making chessboards, painting the squares to look like wood rather than inlaying the real thing. By the mid 1930s, he was using his talent to make paintings of wood that evidenced a keen sense of perspective and daring design. Over the years, he developed an expert's familiarity with wood and honed his techniques to paint its color, texture, and grain with an uncanny sense of reality. Employing deft drafting skill and a fantastic ability to go beyond any presupposed limitations of pattern, Gerdes admitted to being surprised by each piece in spite of the processes' technical and mathematical determinants.

Gerdes also made sculptures that are essentially three-dimensional versions of his faux-wood abstractions. Using discarded computer circuit boards, he constructed elaborate edifices—casinos, churches, skyscrapers—that are right out of Fritz Lang's film *Metropolis.* In his "industrial works," exposed circuit boards lose their dehumanizing edge as the computer pieces are bound into squares and interspersed with tiny bulbs that blink and chirp in a pulsating harmony.

Gerdes retired to Orlando in 1970. After his wife died, he remained in the family's ranch-style home, where he maintained files detailing the phase-by-phase process he used to develop his 246 "inlaid paintings." His conceptions offer an homage to wood. Although he thought of his art in formal terms, its impact reaches far beyond the amazing surfaces. Although a first glance takes in the highly decorative aspect of his work, closer scrutiny reveals that Gerdes has addressed the theme of alienation. His trompe l'oeil masterpieces appeal to those who understand the dehumanizing effects of contemporary culture, while they placate others who prefer to be teased and delighted by the formality of abstract art.

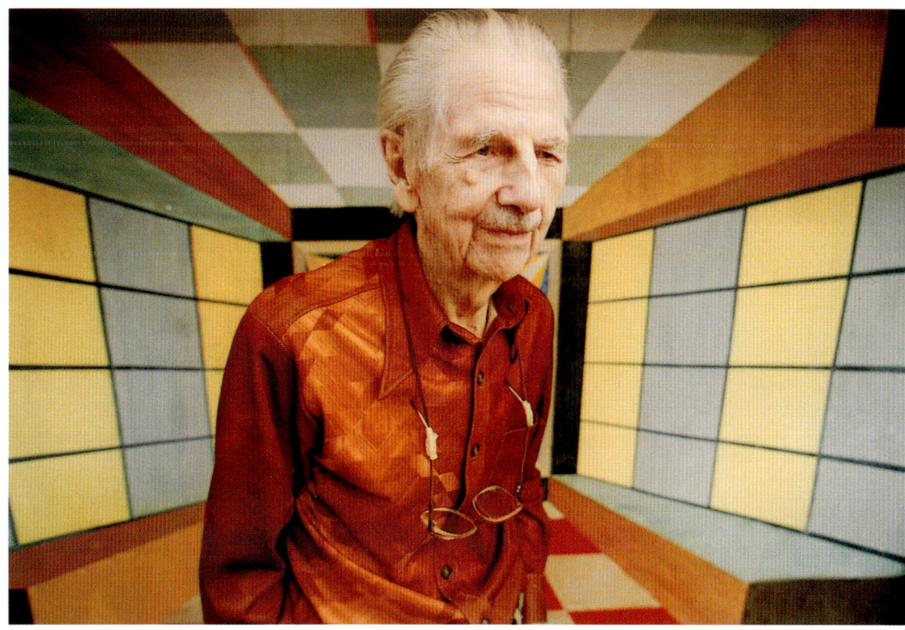

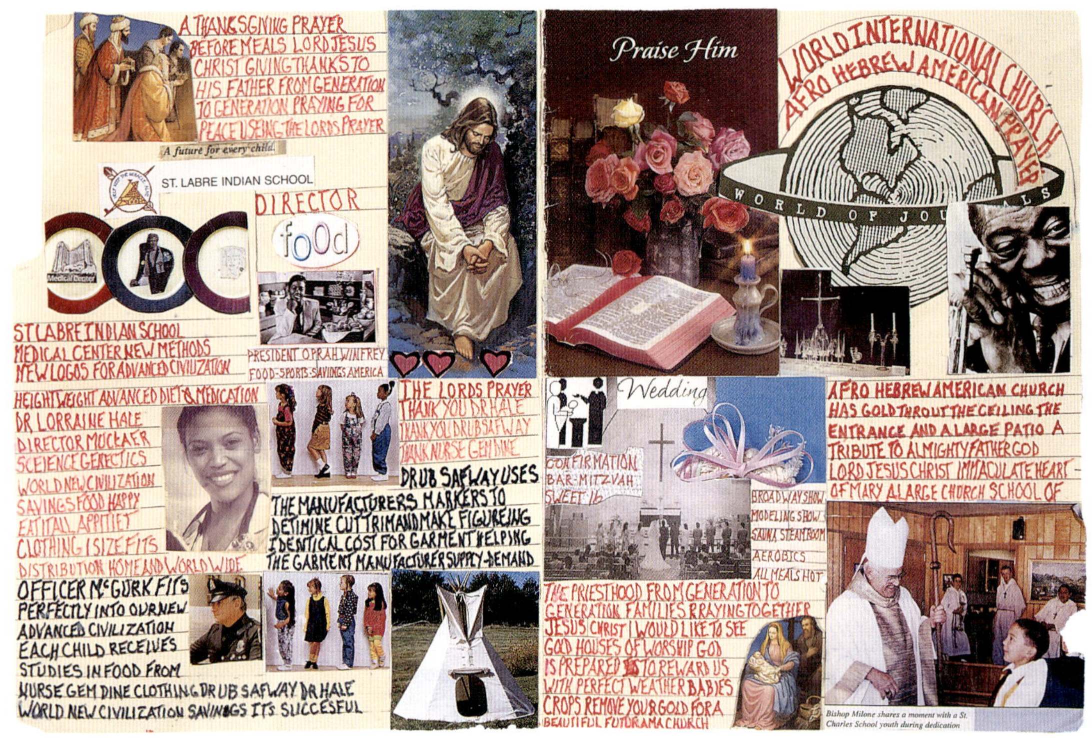

Milton Schwartz. Untitled. 11.75" x 17.75".

MILTON SCHWARTZ

1930–2003

Imagine being told that you are "mentally ill," but you don't know what that means. Your world has collapsed, and you are alone, or nearly alone—you share an old room with a stranger named Victor. This described Milton Schwartz's life in the Delta House, a Miami Beach retirement residence. The wayward souls at Delta House exist in a reality that is seemingly invisible and antithetical to the nearby art deco hotels and the beautiful people in them, who come to Miami Beach to enjoy the high life.

In 1992, Schwartz began making collages that he characterized as "the history of myself in Florida." Because history is narrative, he used 9 in. by 12 in. manila file folders to form four panels—and hence a booklet—which facilitated his telling stories in his own words and with pictures cut out of magazines.

Schwartz came to Jesus some twenty years ago, upon arriving in Florida. "I found Jesus in a church for meetings I used to go to for Overeaters Anonymous. I lost a lot of weight with Jesus. I went from 323 to 164." His faith in Jesus, whom he called "the leader of the band," was a moral underpinning of his work. Finding Jesus proved significant in his attempt to achieve a semblance of order in his life.

Although the theme of his collages is "living with Jesus Christ," he said, "most of my collages are about exercise and food." Schwartz was concerned about his diet, and he regularly worked out until his recent death. His exercises appeared to have been ritualistic exercises that were more ritual than exercise.

Schwartz freely united Hebrews and African Americans in one piece, while in another he related the U.S. Constitution to the Torah. Although he admitted, "I don't know anything about the Koran," he was quick to juxtapose a picture of George W. Bush posed by "the star-spangled banner" against a sentimental photo of an Afghan family. In this way, Schwartz created a peaceable kingdom, a sensible world where there will be "no more conflict. They'll all be friends from now on." Schwartz wished the world would follow his prescriptions, so that "there won't be any sickness or loneliness. . . . The world will be a world full of laughter."

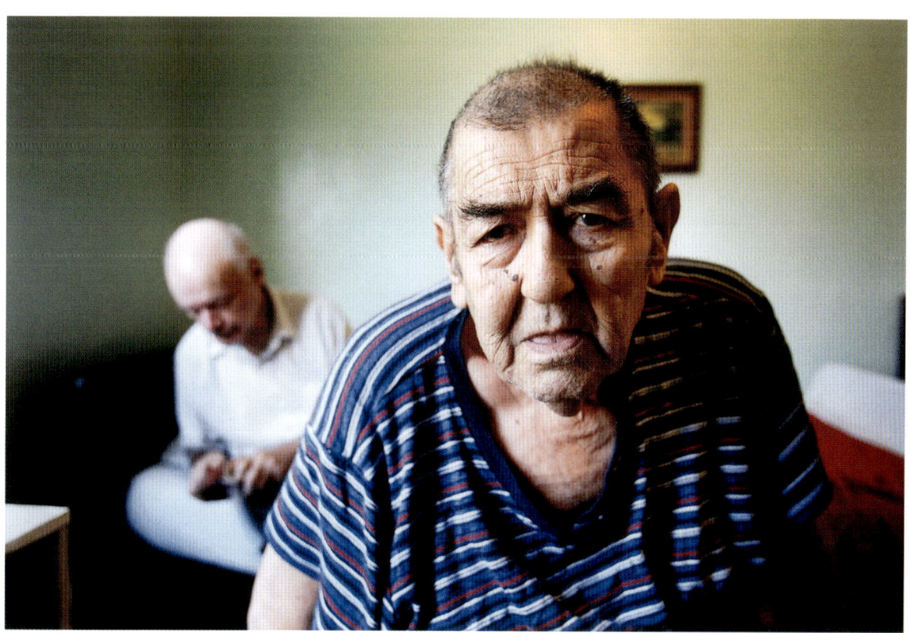

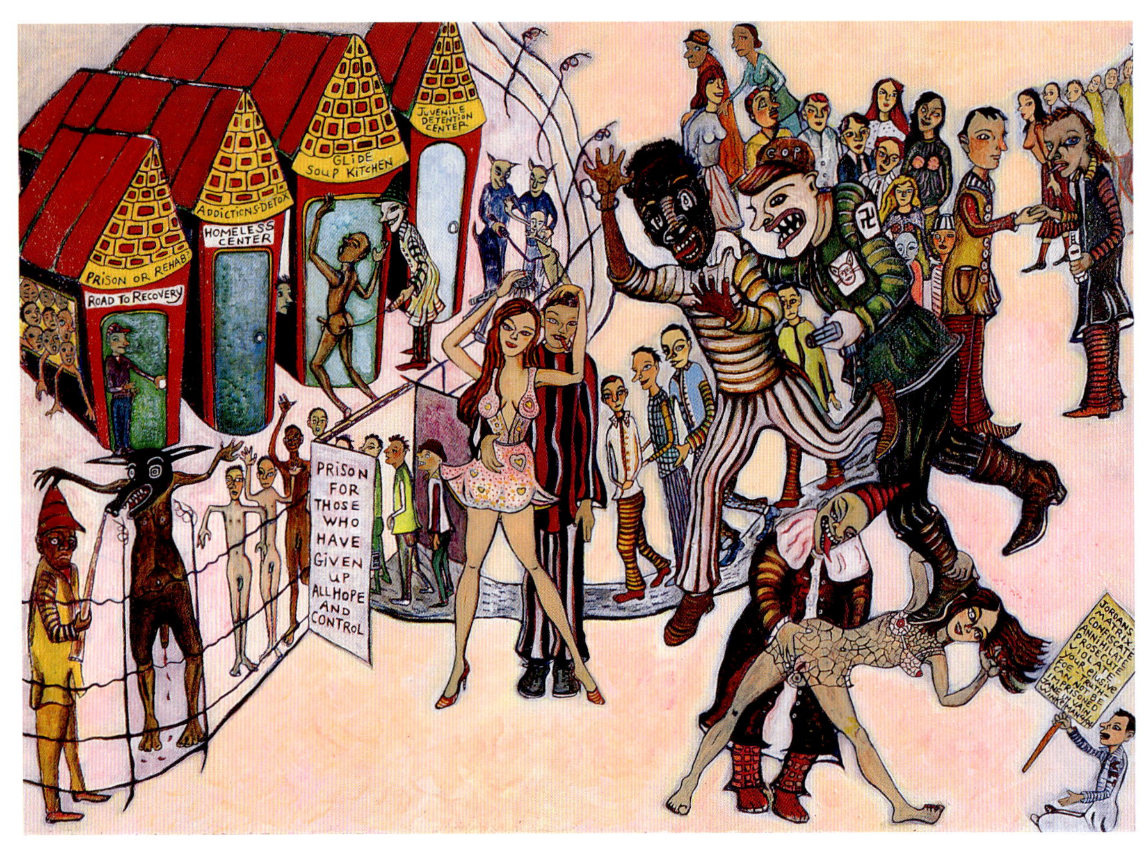

Jane Winkelman. *Out of Control . . . Confiscate, Annihilate, Prosecute, Violate . . . Your Elusive Foe—"Truth"—Cannot be Imprisoned.* 1994. 25" x 36".

JANE WINKELMAN

b. 1949

Jane Winkelman's detailed and colorful paintings are in-your-face. She rages against the machine whenever she paints. Her social consciousness is rooted in her childhood. "When I was a kid I never had toys; these [her paintings] are my toys." She adds: "Life changes, but I didn't change with it. Things didn't work out. I was supposed to settle down with someone, a lost love. Somewhere along the line I went off into the Twilight Zone."

She lives near her family's "mansion on Venetian Causeway" in Miami Beach where she grew up. However, the art deco hotel in which she now resides is the antithesis of her privileged past, as the hotel has fallen into disrepair—suspicious people come and go throughout the night. In her room there—with black visquine covering the windows—Winkelman takes her time with her paintings. "My pictures keep me company," she says. They also express her deep-seated hostilities.

Winkelman's fanciful images are often violent, never the stuff for polite society. They are edgy images made by an angry artist, one who sees herself as having fallen through the cracks and who can speak first-hand about "civilization and society." And her concerns are global: "We're making bombs. How's that going to cure disease? You can't bomb away problems." Her angst informs her imagery.

Beyond her paintings' decorative façades is a social philosophy that she expresses without reserve: "Everything is automated. Fewer and fewer people are needed. Computers will think for themselves. The rich, the powerful will squeeze us. They want to turn us into sausage. They want more and more. They never leave you alone; sleep deprive you. They are wrong. I want to free those of us who are in chains—that's 98 percent of the population. I want to see who will be left after the apocalypse. Who's going to be left when the world ends?"

Winkelman signs her paintings "Jane In Vain" because for her art making is a very lonely pursuit that forces her to live without security: "All of my life I've never been able to please the people I wanted to please the most." She amends her thought by adding that it's also about "pleasing me. I've never been able to be who I wanted to be." But in the end, Jane Winkelman has given voice to the marginalized, to those she describes as "millions of people like me."

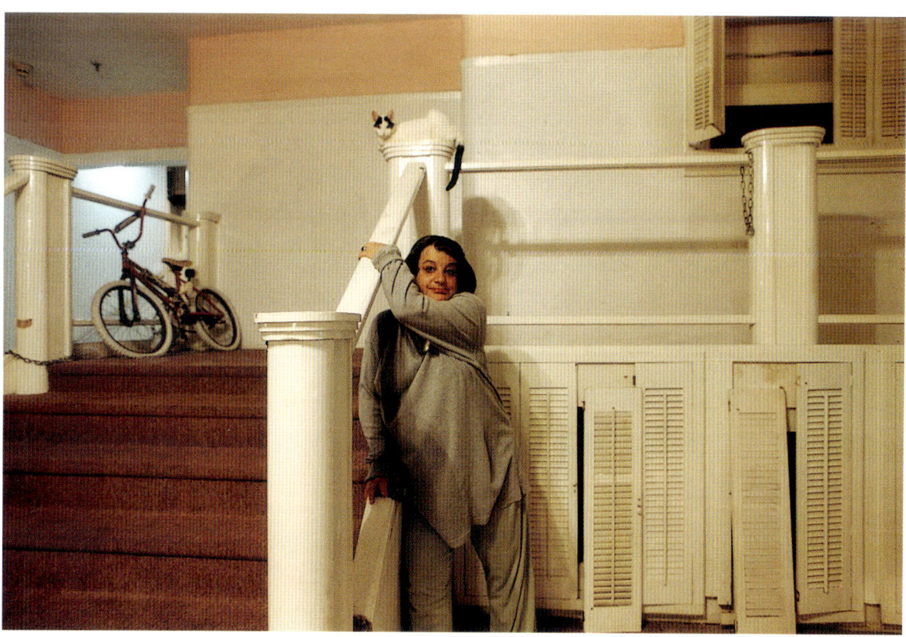

This is the Chicken Coop that
General Custer used at the
Battle of "Little Big Horn! the
Chickens were sent out as spys
against the Indians. Because of the
Hot sun most of them came back
Completly Baked But some only
traveled when there was cloud cover
or at Night so they came back
only Half Baked. This is where we
Got this term from!

DON'T GO AWAY
Halfed Baked!!

Ralph Foley. Untitled. 8.5" x 11".

RALPH FOLEY

b. 1947

"I should have been a minister," laments Ralph Foley. "Helping people through their trials or journeys is my way of getting satisfaction from life." Foley's "help" takes the form of short messages or tales that he attaches to the products that he sells at his DeLand feed store and garden center.

"How can I take your money, sir?" he quips to one customer, and to another, "If the competition's higher, I'll match their price." His often self-effacing one-liners and made-up little lies are scribbled on pieces of 8 1/2 by 11 in. paper and taped onto stacks of oats, hay, posts, pet supplies, fertilizers, and scarecrows. "Signs are a natural manifestation of my inward feelings," Foley explains, "of wanting to make other people laugh or be happy even though I'm hurting." The people who overlook the seemingly innocuous signs miss Foley's offerings of redemption, salvation from the things that have twisted people since Adam bit into the apple.

Foley's quiet humor conceals an emotional pain so deeply buried that his life has become a Beckettesque drama; the "signs" are his way of overcoming lifelong bouts of "silent killer" depressions. There's nothing ceremonial about any of it, yet the signs are encryptions, a sublime form of bearing witness. They usually go unnoticed, but if one personalizes the messages and lets the perplexing stories unfold, his riddlelike fables allow each individual his or her own interpretation.

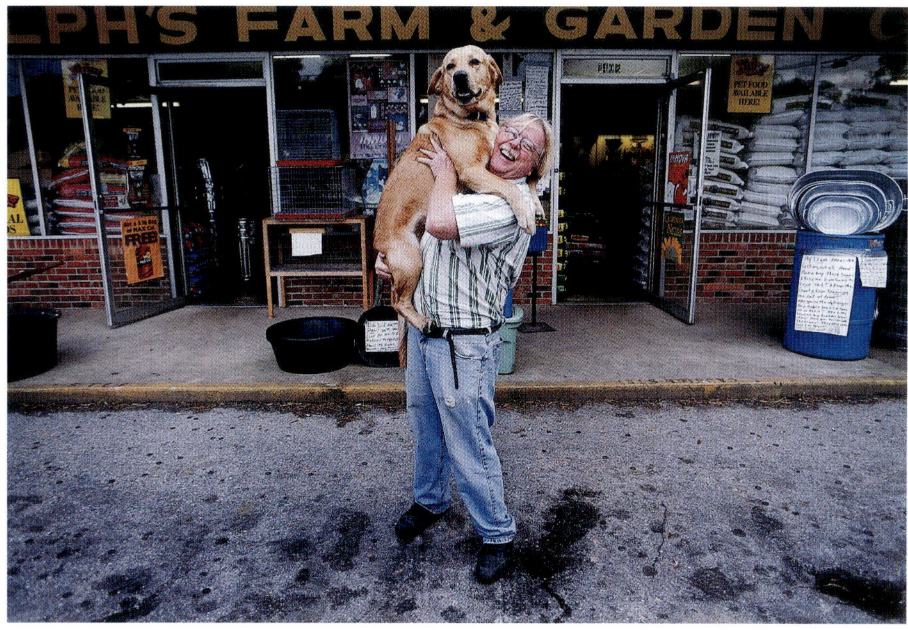

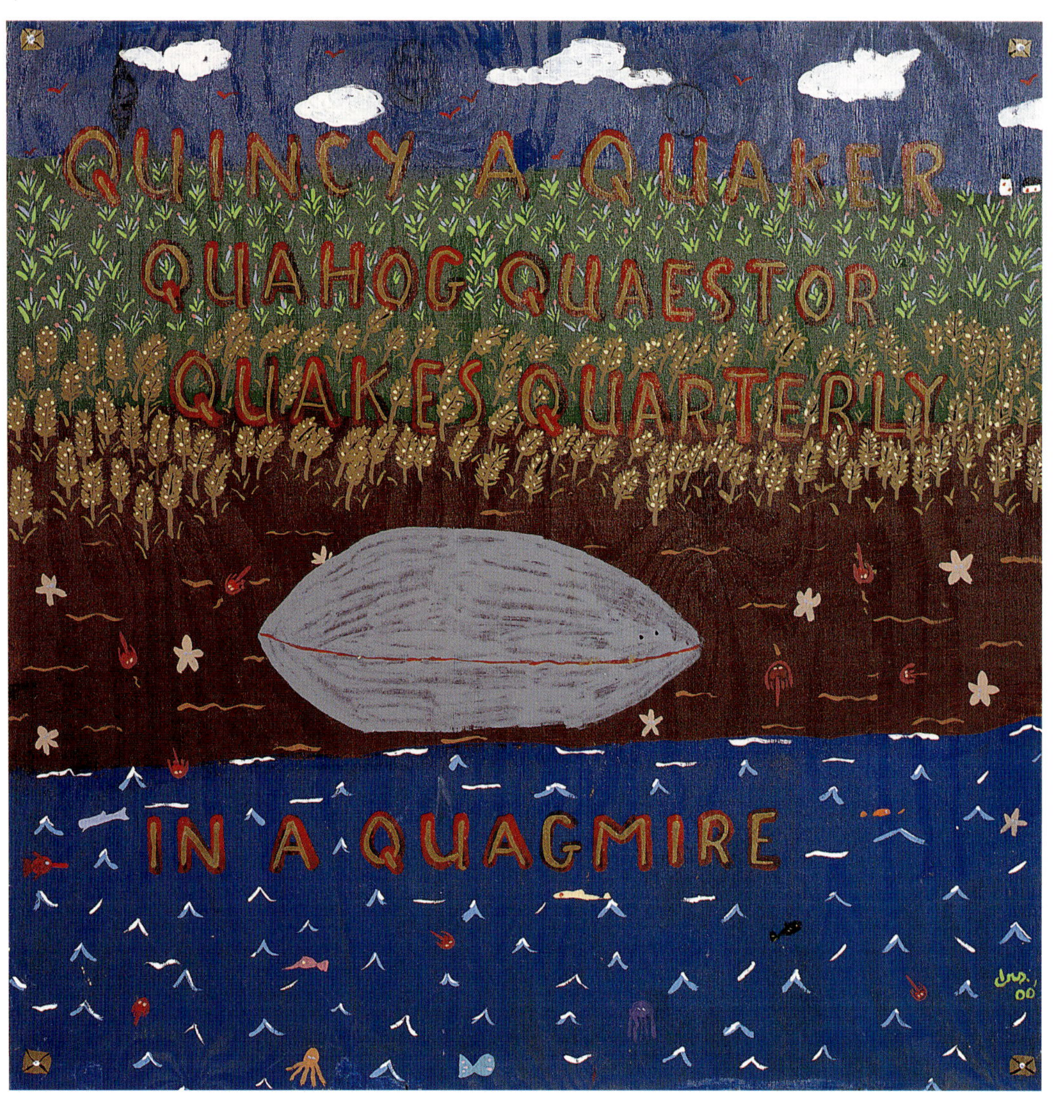

Don Stone. Untitled. 2000. 24" x 24".

DON STONE

b. 1955

When Don Stone moved back into his family's Winter Haven home, he was steeped in his family's heritage; the house had become a cornucopia of their history. His low-key lifestyle was transformed into that of a museum curator's, with object upon object begging for reflection. The artifacts offered an account of the European colonization of America, as his seafaring ancestors were among its earliest settlers and New England's finest citizens.

Don Stone's paintings pull from the treasure trove of his past; some are pure whimsy, while others reflect his intellectual curiosity. Asked about his sources, he replies, "I read." He reads incessantly, often consulting the dictionary for inspiration, a pursuit that has led to the creation of twenty-six paintings, one for each letter of the alphabet. In each piece, the words begin with the same letter to make a "cohesive" observation. They achieve poetry by chance; for example: "Aeneas, an Adorable Affable Ahimsaist Algonquin Alligator Adorns the Abbey with Algerian Apples."

That Stone explores the arcane and abstract and knows that the Trojan hero Aeneas escaped after Troy fell to spend seven years traveling before settling near the site of Rome, or that the Algonquin are aboriginal peoples living along the Ottawa and St. Lawrence rivers in southern Canada, is a result of his blending history, memory, and imagination.

His days are less adventuresome than were those of his Mayflower Compact–signing and Pilgrims' Monument–building and Women's Rights–pioneering ancestors. But his paintings of towns' buildings panned across long boards are likely surrogates for a captain's view of land from afar, and his blithe and curious circus images point subtly back to their maker's fantastic private world.

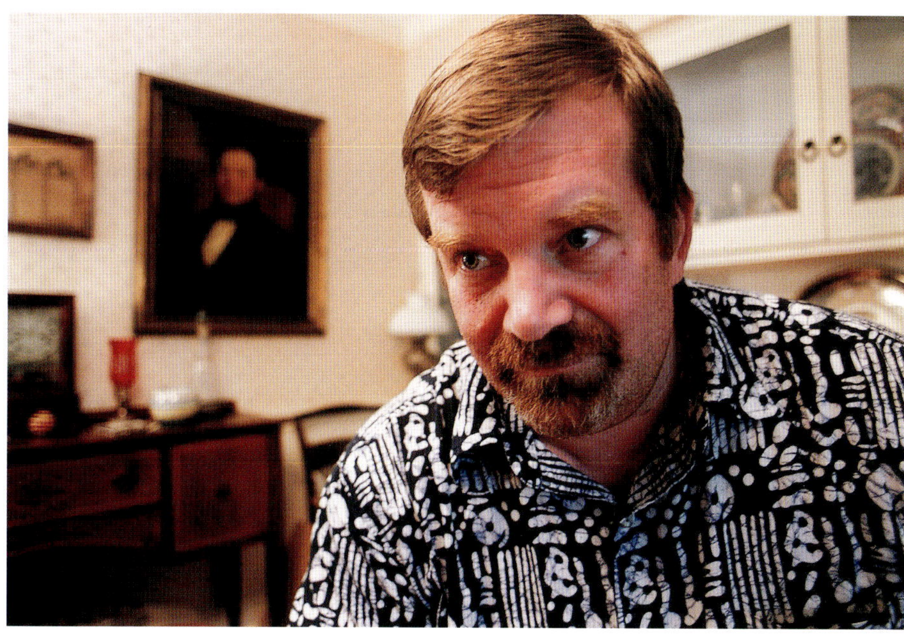

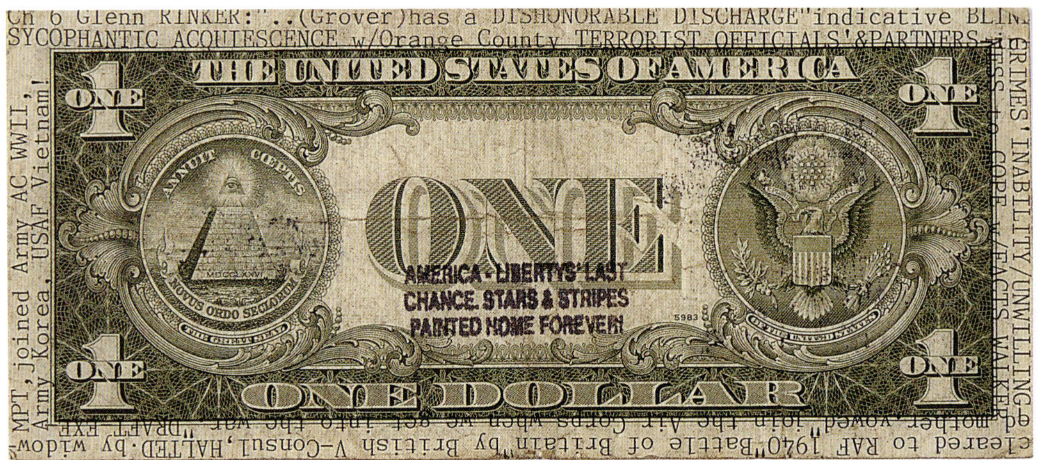

Grover Walker. Untitled. 2.125" x 6.125".

GROVER WALKER

b. 1921

To Grover Walker, words are weapons, a last line of defense. Stamping messages on paper money of various denominations was the Walker family's most inventive form of protest. Walker wrote poignant slogans against his perceived oppressor, the United States government. He had rubber stamps made and stamped his outrage to the backs of U.S. currency. Some of the early bills even had messages typed around the borders. Family members would cash hundred-dollar bills and then stamp one hundred one-dollar bills, which they would take to the bank and exchange for twenty five-dollar bills. By doing this over and over, from 1985 to 2000, the Walkers estimate that they put more than one million dollars of "Walker Notes" into circulation.

Their goal was to reveal a clandestine plot of "spiritual murder" that resulted in the U.S. government labeling Major and Mrs. Walker mentally ill—paranoid and schizophrenic—and unfit to fulfill their military duty. Sometimes they spent the stamped bills at tourist attractions, taking their story far and wide. Aware that each bill typically passes through four hundred hands, the Walkers' offspring chuckle knowing that potentially every person on Earth could have learned of their parents' dreadful plight and lifelong struggle to clear their names.

Decades ago, the family planted an 82-foot flagpole among handmade protest signs that were placed throughout the yard of their home in a working-class neighborhood in the otherwise upscale town of Winter Park. Then they raised Old Glory upside down. Although an upside down flag is a recognized distress signal, citizens of Winter Park took Walker's statement to be a contentious act. This 20 ft. by 30 ft. flag irritated citizens, angered police, and excited the media. For decades, no one could get Walker to fly the flag properly. But on September 11, 2001, the day of the attacks on the World Trade Center, Grover Walker walked across his yard past a sign titled "CHARACTER ASSASSINATION" to what he called his "Liberty Pole." He then lowered the flag, turned it right side up, and raised it proudly. To Walker, his wife, and their nine children, the issues were and are about defending America, and Walker is, above all, a patriot.

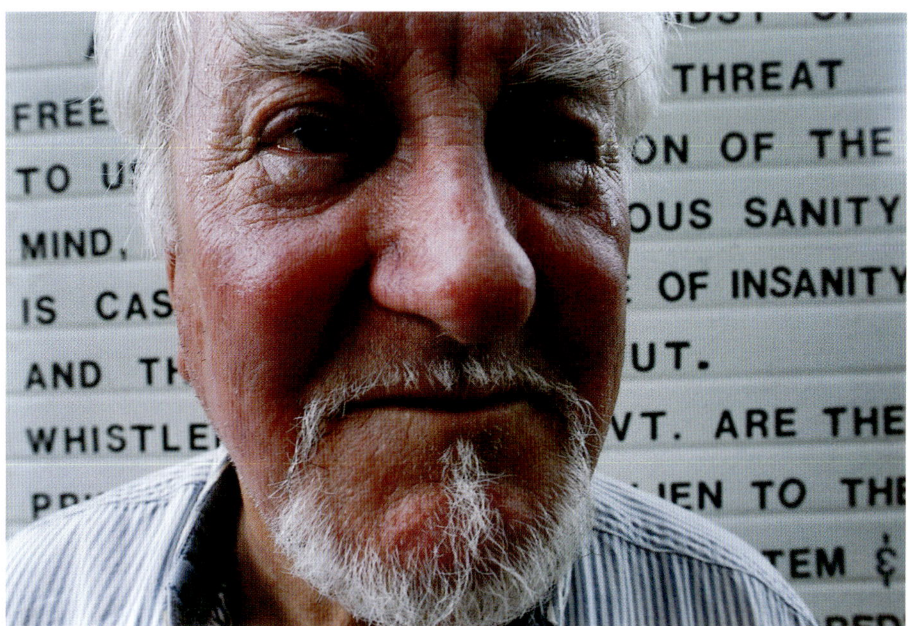

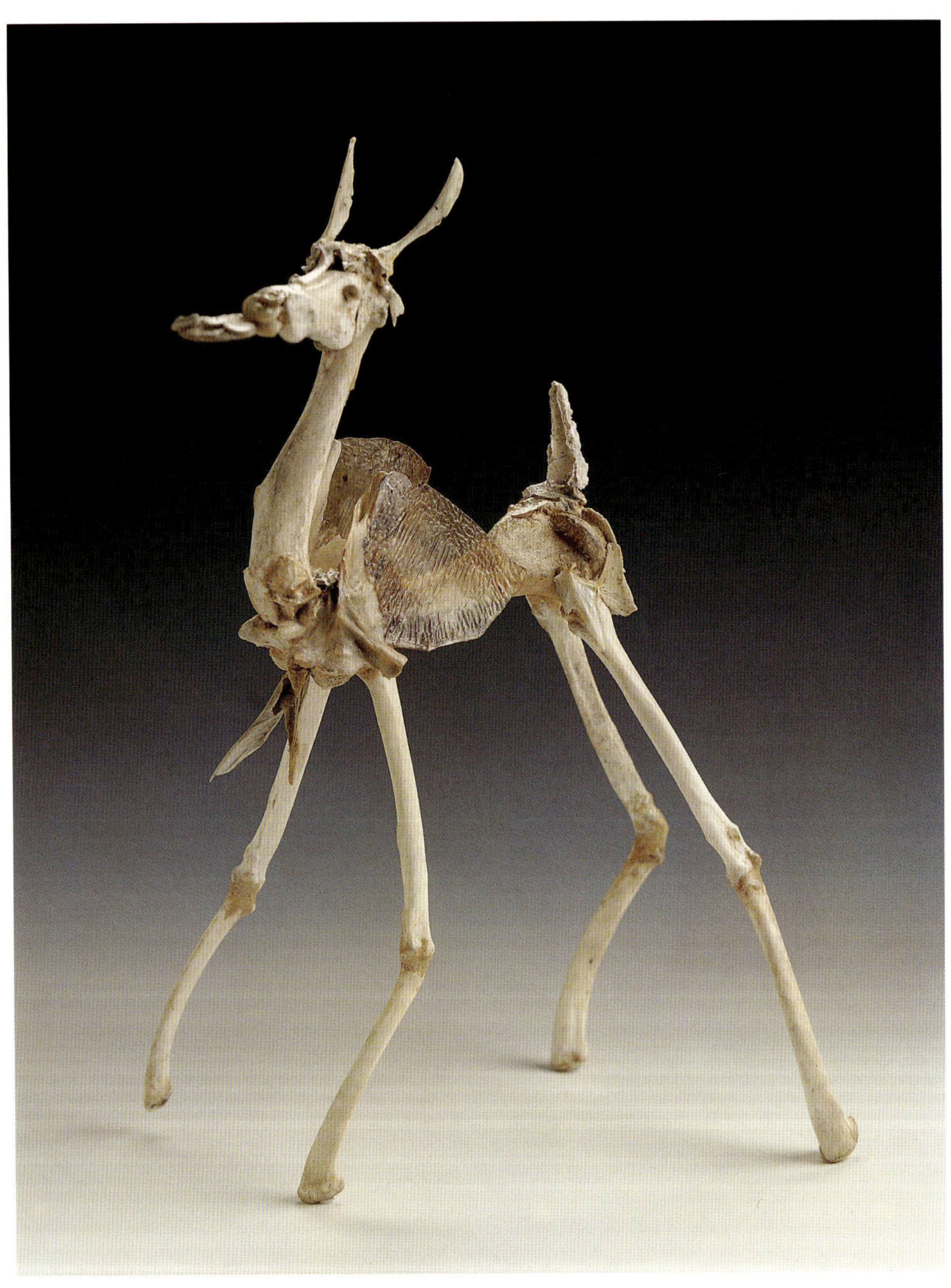

Taft Richardson. *Hope.* 18" x 14" x 6".

TAFT RICHARDSON

b. 1943

Thirty years ago, Taft Richardson was eating barbecued ribs. As he chewed the meat from the bones, he put them aside. Then he noticed that the pile of bones resembled a giraffe. "That stopped me," he says; it made him pause to consider God. At that moment he became a vegetarian.

Today, Richardson is still involved with bones, but now he finds them and uses them to create sculptures that he calls "Beauty after Death." Using dried bones and teeth, he constructs images of animals. He treats the bones with respect and communes with them before beginning his sculptures. In order to keep the process "natural," he even makes his own epoxy.

To Richardson, art is spiritual—more a means than an end. God, he claims, uses him: "I don't do it; it does me," he says. In keeping with his pantheistic views, he established the Moses House in Tampa to serve at-risk youths by offering them a safe place to direct their energy. Richardson feels that kids today are denied a magical childhood and have a need to be reached spiritually. Hidden by thick foliage, the Moses House became a refuge where children could begin to realize their potential by developing artistic talents. By instilling pride in their heritage and bringing out hidden talent through artistic activities, "the children can find inner peace and will live in a more peaceful world."

"The real world is as a fantasy that love can reinvent," says Richardson. "Everything started as a thought; everything around us is an illusion."

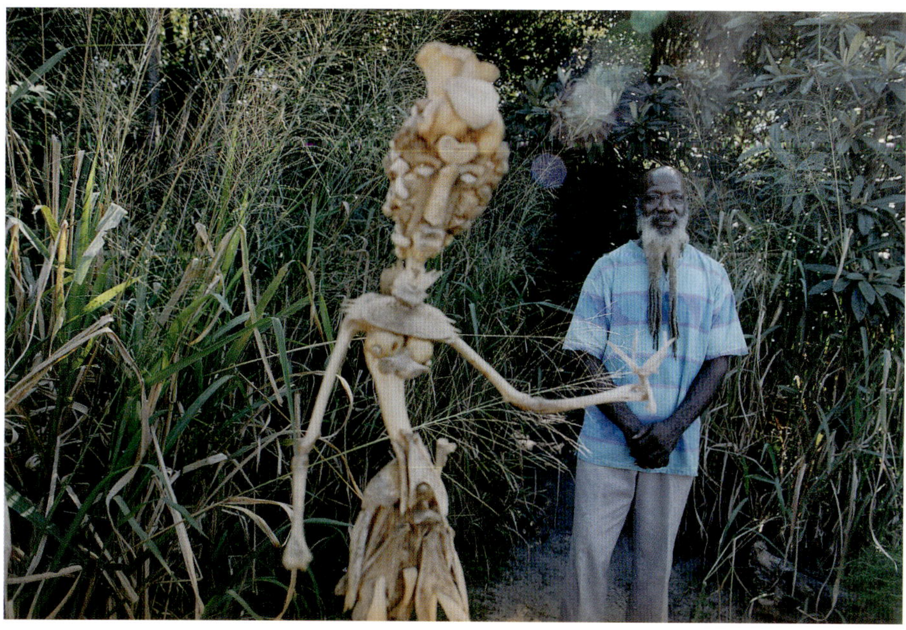

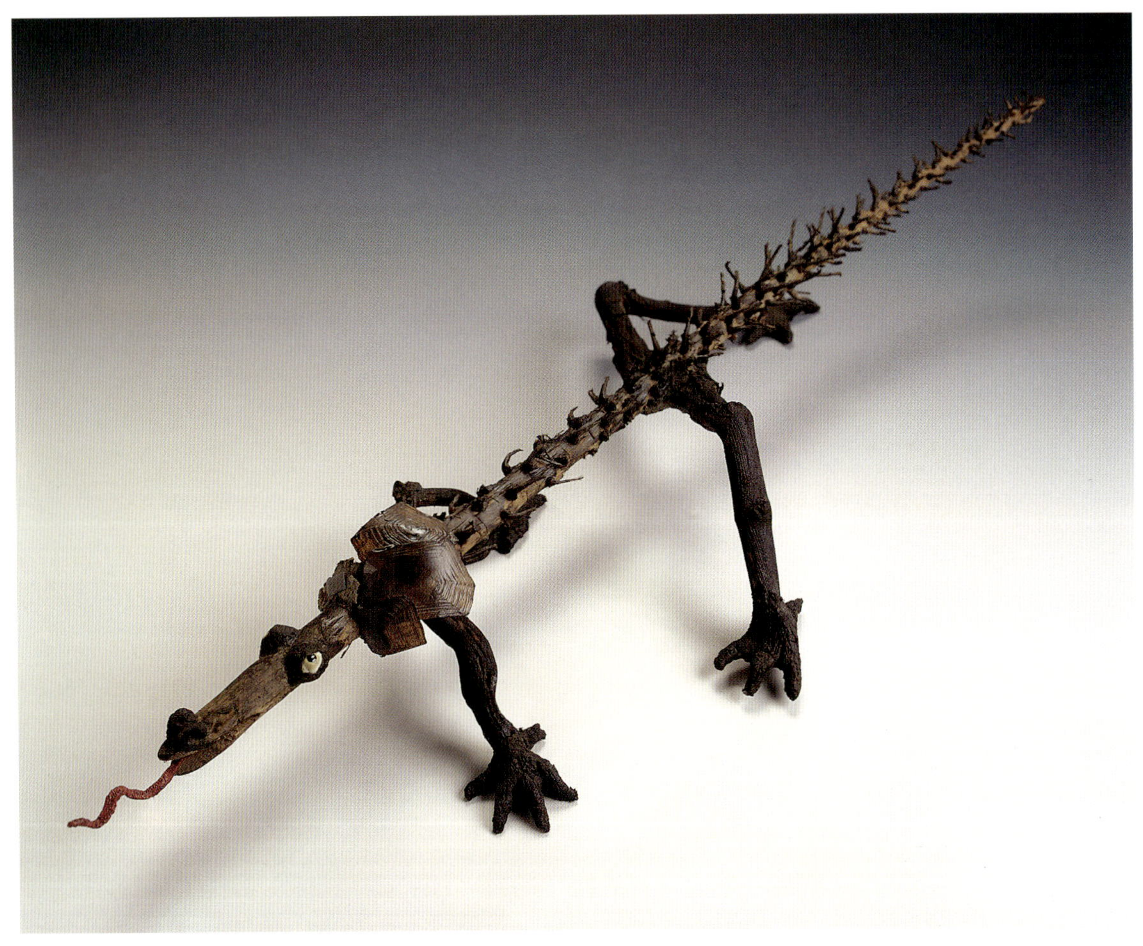

Kenny Dickerson. *Lizard*. 1997. 8" x 45" x 16".

KENNY DICKERSON

b. 1955

Kenny Dickerson's friends affectionately call him "The Mad Hatter." Since childhood, he has loved creating things, and his parents encouraged his creativity. An alumnus of Taft Richardson's Moses House, Dickerson remains in Tampa and lives in a warehouse bay unit that also serves as his studio.

The lightheartedness of his walking sticks, paintings, and sculptures suggests a spirit less concerned with salvation than with survival and enjoyment in *this* world. His creations are made out of sticks, fabric, parts of furniture, and anything else he can find. On top of a bamboo shaft—a walking stick—is the head of a rabbit with dreadlocks similar to Dickerson's own. The face of a timepiece is below a top hat surrounded by bunny ears—an astute interpretation of *Alice in Wonderland.* "I like chaos for some reason," Kenny Dickerson remarks with a grin.

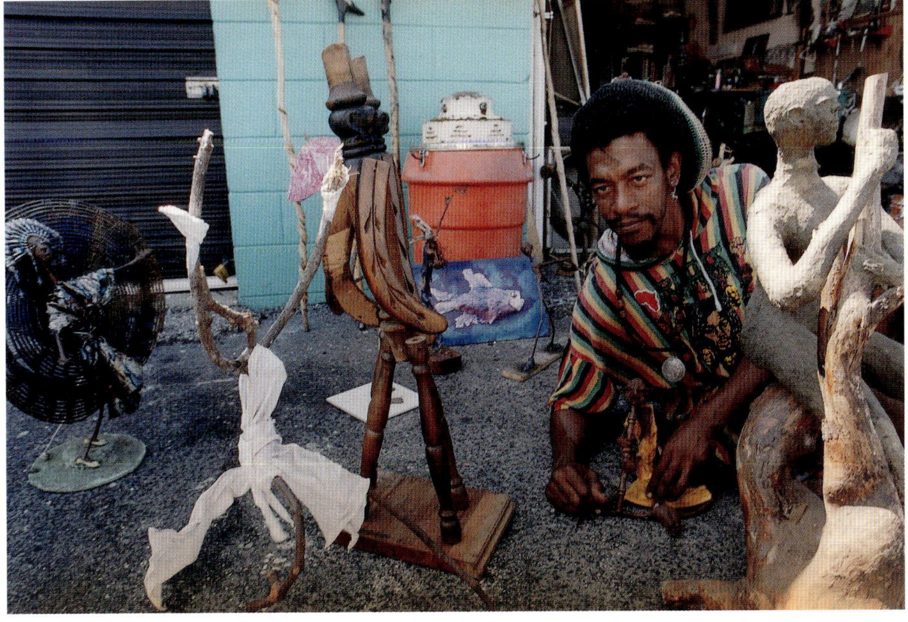

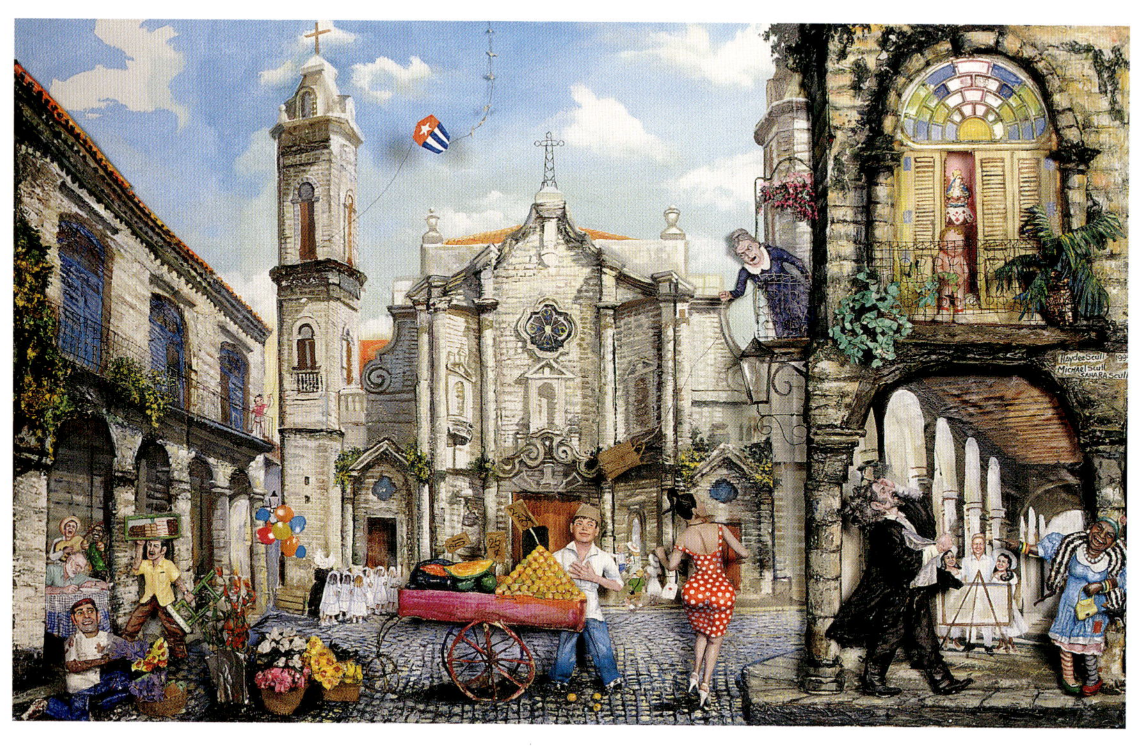

Sahara and Haydee Scull. *Gente de la Plaza de la Catedral de la Habana Vieja, 1953*. 1999. 43" x 72" x 5".

SAHARA AND HAYDEE SCULL

"timeless and ageless"

The Scull sisters are synonymous with Miami—a status they acquired soon after emigrating there on a Freedom Flight from Cuba in 1969. The sisters—Sahara and Haydee—are the embodiment of art and life united. They dress voluptuously alike, designing the matching glamorous 1950s promlike gowns that they wear every day. They move like dancers on a stage, literally rumba-ing their way about. Haydee's son, Michael, whom they trained to work with them, is flamboyant too. They fashion ties for him with the leftover fabric from their outlandish dresses. "Instead of taking his milk bottle he'd go for the oil tube and paintbrush. Michael is a natural born artist," his mother reports.

The Sculls' three-dimensional murals celebrate the colorful streets of their adopted city as well as of Havana, where they first practiced their art. They attended the Academia Nacional de Bellas Artes de San Alejandro there. However, they found the classical training at the school confining, and as soon as they graduated in 1952, they began creating their collaborative imagery. Although they practice a narrative art, vitality is their stock-in-trade.

The ideas are usually Haydee's, but the team discusses the development of each piece and shares in the sculpting and painting. The patron is consulted as well, but the outcome reflects the artists' passionate cultural observations. Six to eight weeks are required for the sisters to complete one of their revealing-as-they-are-detailed, busy, and elaborate (and increasingly commissioned) murals. No gratuitous faces show up in a Scull piece—each is a portrait, and everyone is depicted as they would like to be remembered, as long as he or she has a sense of humor. The imagery is full of zany surprises (including cheating husbands).

As viewers reminisce about or imagine themselves in the world that the Sculls conjure and describe, the lyricism of their art coalesces with a sense of pathos. The spectator becomes a witness becomes a participant in the Sculls' seductive murals, and one leaves their work with the sense that Carmen Miranda lives.

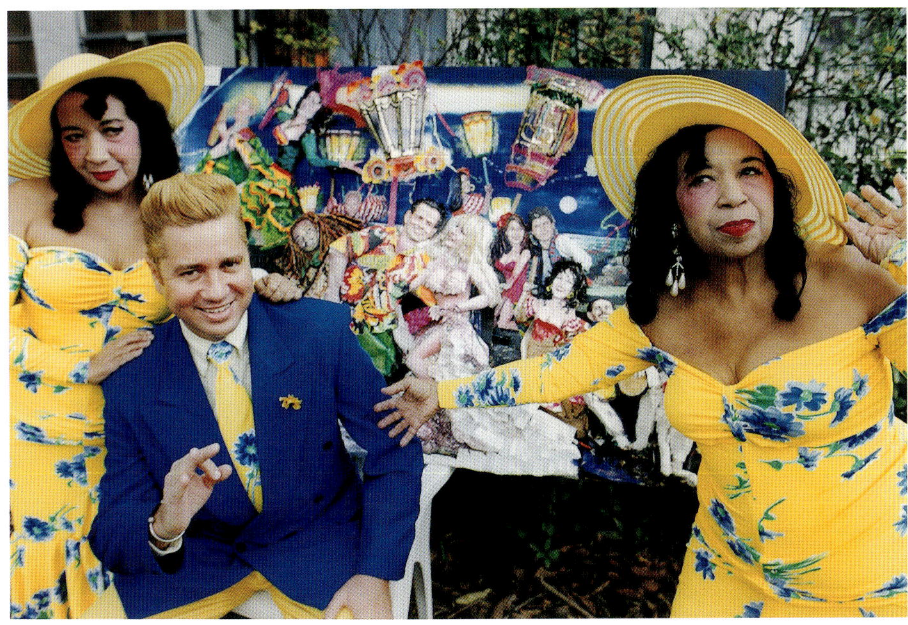

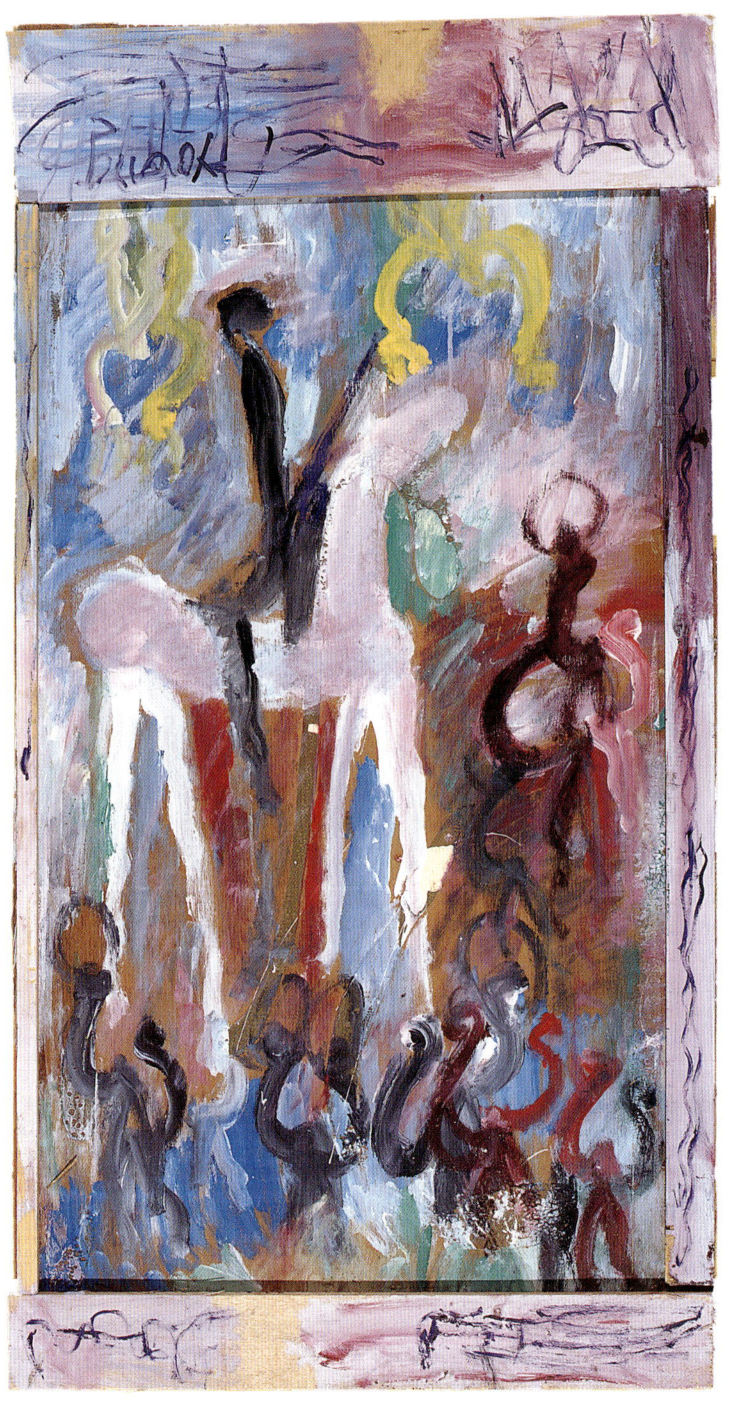

Purvis Young. Untitled. 43" x 22.5".

PURVIS YOUNG

b. 1943

Purvis Young's paintings should not be mistaken for mere commentaries. They are, rather, descriptions and clarifications of the artist's understandings—revelations of a moral vision. His mural-scrawlings on boarded storefronts and wooden barricades have been common sights in Miami's Overtown ghetto since the late 1960s. Young continues to paint his heartfelt figures on scrap wood, each piece being the idea of a dream encapsulating his time and place. The viewer is challenged to decipher Young's portrayal of life on the mean streets, to determine just how something so abstract can seem so real; how something so tenuous can ring so true; how something so anti-aesthetic can be so beautiful.

Young's painted swiggles approximate the human form, often repeating themselves while in the process of metamorphosis, as if struggling to discover their own identities. Many paintings show horses with noble riders—what he calls his "freedom fighters." Stacked cubes about to topple represent downtown. His portraits of anonymous people often sport halos. In the turbulent past they donned helmets. He paints funeral marches and pregnant women with locks on their heads—"locking out knowledge." If pressed to explain a theme, Young speaks of "struggling people," people engaged in trying to "unloosen themselves."

Young also makes books by gluing his sketches and small paintings onto the pages of discarded volumes. He has spent countless hours among the stacks of art books in the downtown Miami-Dade Public Library. He identifies with more established artists this way—those who have painted their way into another world. But Young's redefined books serve to solidify the estrangement that his paintings reflect—page after page expressing the alienation that he grew up with and into.

With less interest in realizing a masterpiece than conjuring a vision, Purvis Young's paintings creep up like a Trojan horse to take the viewer by surprise.

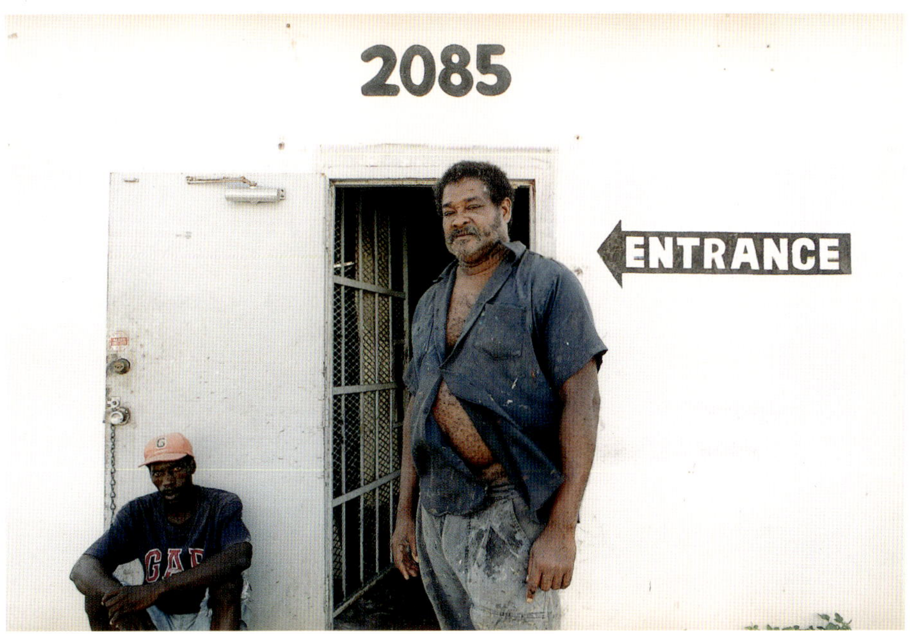

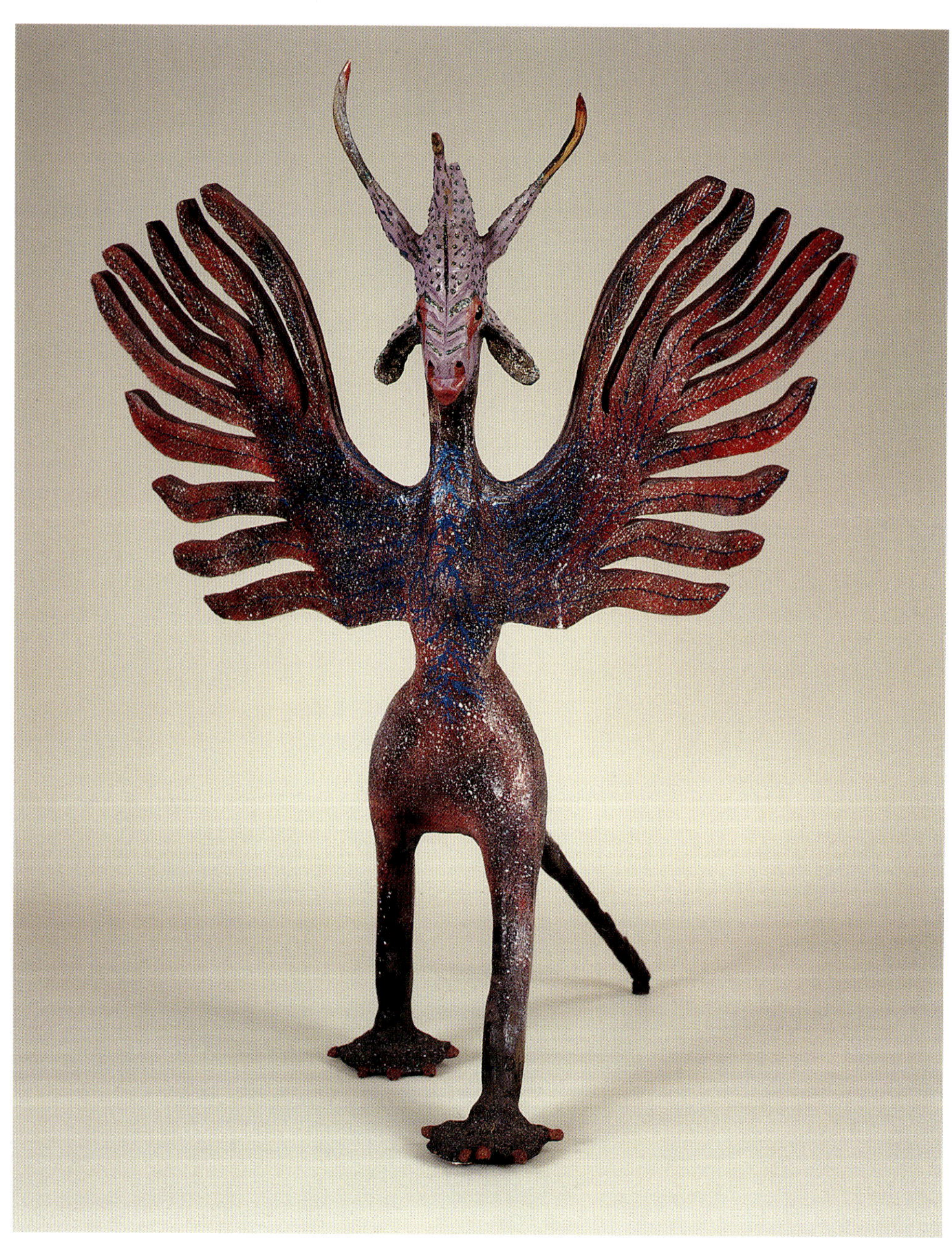

O. L. Samuels. *Lucifer.* 36.25" x 32" x 30".

O. L. SAMUELS

b. 1931

Ozzie Lee Samuels's sculptures are imposing, a quality resulting not just from their sheer mass but from the spiritual realm from which the artist draws inspiration. The scale of the pieces is consistent with Samuels's stature. Smooth-skinned, large, and strong, Samuels lives in a beat-up trailer in Tallahassee. It is easy to envision him at work during his youth, climbing trees to trim their branches or boxing in the ring in New York City. He claims that he can still jump over a car. His sensitivity is less obvious; it's even hard to glean from his sculptures. He was kept from attending school and "brought up tough" by an aunt who beat him. Yet Samuels strives intensely to be a good person, and this lends a surreal, sometimes frightful, edge to his sculptures.

His grandmother told him that he should carve when he was sad, for he was a forlorn youngster. She suggested that he relieve his anxiety by using a thread spool and a knife to fashion little animals. Instead, he learned to create beasts from trunks of trees and their heavy roots. Soon thereafter he built "skeletons" and creatures' extremities from knots of wood. By mixing sawdust, paint, and glue, he concocted a substance to use as "skin" for his figures, whose basic forms he constructs with two-by-fours. His sculptures define themselves: "The wood talks to you, like when you're cooking." He blows his breath into his cupped hands and rubs them over the sculptures, infusing his life into his creations. "The state you're in always comes through in the piece itself," he says.

Samuels realized the transformative power of the materials and sensed something less tangible about the process, how it changes him: "The scary part is not knowing who you are . . . and you're going to make your way in the world anyway." He has been down to the point of being suicidal. From "having never thought I'd see the next day" to "wanting to see how my pieces are going to look," Samuels came to believe that "God is in Art." He explains: "A spirit over me used to scare me. It was like a shadow." But through creating he realized that it was a good spirit. "I can run demon spirits away. I got the power."

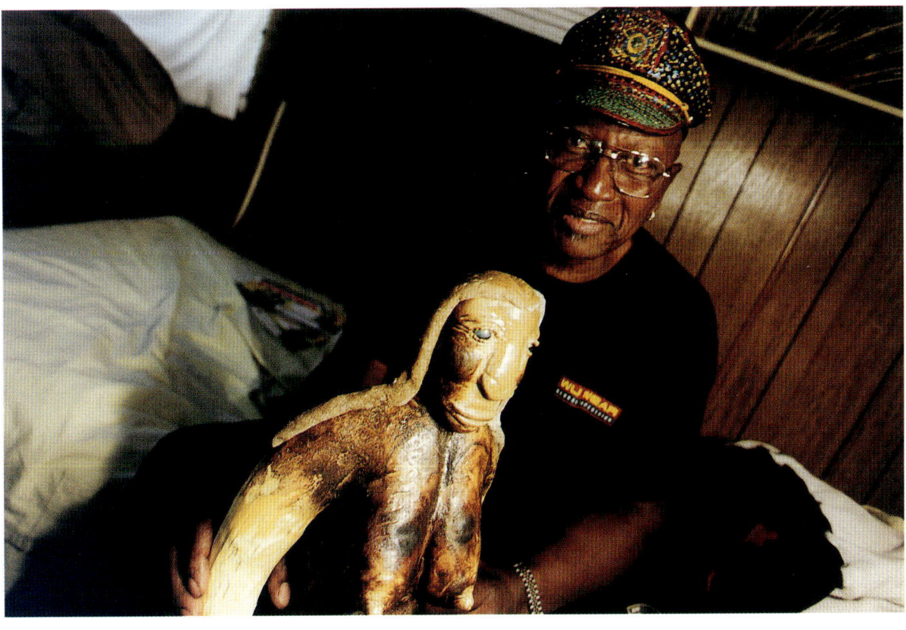

Gary Monroe, professor of visual art at Daytona Beach Community College, is a documentary photographer with a long-time interest in "outsider" and vernacular art. His work has been recognized with numerous exhibitions and awards, including grants from the National Endowment for the Arts and the Fulbright Foundation, and he has been a popular lecturer for the Florida Humanities Council's Speakers Bureau. His photographs have been published in *Cassadaga: The South's Oldest Spiritualist Community* (UPF, 2000), which he coedited; *Life in South Beach* (1989); and *Florida Dreams* (1993). His book *The Highwaymen: Florida's African-American Landscape Painters* (UPF, 2001) is now in its fourth printing. He lives in DeLand, Florida.